D1826497

Contents

The Entrepreneur's Guide Series

BUILDING A WINNING SALES TEAM

How To Recruit, Train And Motivate The Best

Gini Graham Scott, Ph.D.

ASJA Press
New York   Lincoln   Shanghai

BUILDING A WINNING SALES TEAM
How To Recruit, Train, And Motivate The Best

Copyright © 1991, 2007 by Gini Graham Scott

All rights reserved. No part of this book may be used or reproduced by any means, graphic, electronic, or mechanical, including photocopying, recording, taping or by any information storage retrieval system without the written permission of the publisher except in the case of brief quotations embodied in critical articles and reviews.

ASJA Press
an imprint of iUniverse, Inc.

iUniverse books may be ordered through booksellers or by contacting:

iUniverse
2021 Pine Lake Road, Suite 100
Lincoln, NE 68512
www.iuniverse.com
1-800-Authors (1-800-288-4677)

Because of the dynamic nature of the Internet, any Web addresses or links contained in this book may have changed since publication and may no longer be valid.

The views expressed in this work are solely those of the author and do not necessarily reflect the views of the publisher, and the publisher hereby disclaims any responsibility for them.

Originally published by Probus Publishing

ISBN: 978-0-595-46772-3

Printed in the United States of America

Preface

Although I never set out to get involved in sales, since I was most interested in developing and designing various creative projects, I soon found sales to be the key to success in all of these ventures. I had to learn how to sell my game and toy designs to both manufacturers and the general public; I had to find publishers for my books as well as learn how to market and distribute them; and besides selling myself, I began working with various sales reps who were marketing my products. In addition, in the early 1980s, I found myself involved in a number of direct sales and multi-level marketing organizations, primarily in the health, food, and consumer savings fields, where I sold direct to customers, recruited and trained salespeople, and developed programs and sales materials to support them. Eventually, this led to several books on direct selling and multi-level marketing techniques: *Strike It Rich in Personal Selling* (Avon, 1985); *Get Rich Through Multi-Level Marketing* (Self-Counsel Press, 1990); and *Success in Multi-Level Marketing* (Prentice-Hall, 1991). Additionally, it led me to develop a sales organization for marketing travel programs.

Along the way, I also worked closely with the sales organizations in companies marketing my own products, doing such things as supplying them with leads, advertising suggestions, and promotional ideas. Further, I have informally interviewed hundreds of others in the course of attending business meetings, luncheons, dinners, and conferences given by various groups, including the Association of Sales and Marketing Executives, National Association of Professional Saleswomen (of which I was a member for a time), and the National Speakers Association (of which I have been a member for about eight years). Most currently, I have been helping to find additional distribution channels, provide promotional support, and coordinate licensing arrangements for manufacturers and publishers involved with some Soviet-American projects I have developed (including a game: *Glasnost: The Game of Soviet-American Diplomacy*, published originally in the United States, and now available in German, French, and Russian; a *Glasnost* Calendar; a book: *The Open Door—Traveling in the U.S.S.R.*; a travel program to take Americans to the Soviet Union and meet with Soviets in various day-to-day activities: *Soviet Life Today;* and a film on citizen diplomacy, based on these trips). These projects have taken me across the globe to assist in building sales organizations and to promote these programs.

This book has developed out of these efforts. It is designed to be like a road map that will help you plot out when to set up your own sales organization and how to do it. Also, it is designed to help you overcome what I have noticed are some of the main problems people have in setting up and working with a sales group:

1. Many creative or technical people running their own company don't know how to sell their own products or services and don't know how to motivate others to do it. Or, if they do set up a sales organization, they tend to interfere too much in ways that are unhelpful, rather than providing their support and input where useful, and then leaving it up to the real sales pros to know what to do from there.

2. Many people with good sales skills don't know how to teach others to sell, so they have trouble getting other salespeople to be effective.

3. Some people can manage the initial stages of building a sales group, but then have trouble coordinating group activities and maintaining group enthusiasm and commitment, or avoiding internal conflict and unproductive competition.

4. Some people don't know how best to work with already organized networks of sales representatives and distributors in their field, so they lose sales that could easily be theirs with better organization and liaison.

5. Many companies and distributors lack good sales and training materials, or don't do enough to adapt their material as they go along to make it more effective.

And perhaps you have run into other problems in your own organization; this book is designed to help you solve these as well.

In short, drawing on my own experience and that of others, I have written this book to help you move in a step-by-step way from deciding it is time to create your own sales network or work with an outside sales network, to implementing this sales program in your company. It is designed for both the owner of the growing company and for the sales department manager.

Gini Graham Scott

Introduction

In today's competitive marketplace, sales and marketing are the key to success. Your product or service can be great, but if you don't have the sales force or distribution network to get it out there, few people will know about it. You've just got to have that marketing program and the sales organization and savvy to make things work.

And this doesn't necessarily mean having your own sales group, because you can plug into already organized distribution networks. But even if you do use a distribution network, you still have to know how to work with these outside sales individuals or organizations effectively to coordinate their efforts and provide support. On the other hand, there are times when it may make more sense to have your own internal sales force, or alternatively to have a combination of inside and outside people. Then, too, you need to decide if you want to set up such a sales program yourself, or hire an overall sales manager to do this. But even if you do hire someone else, you still need to be aware of and able to evaluate what that person is doing to decide if your sales program is working.

So, there are many considerations and approaches you might use; but, the bottom line is that if you want to grow and expand successfully, you need an effective sales organization, however it is organized and whoever organizes it.

Unfortunately, many entrepreneurs and growing or established businesses lose out, because they don't know how to create and mobilize a good sales force. For example, when Andrea T. tried to launch a small catering service, she tried to do most of the marketing herself. But she hated it, wasn't particularly good at sales, and preferred to spend her time making creative hors d'ouevres. She would have done better to recruit a salesperson (or maybe several) to sell her services, and then, as she expanded, she could simply have turned the whole thing over to an experienced sales manager who could coordinate her growing sales organization for her.

Tom G. had the opposite problem. He liked sales and was himself very aggres-
sive. But when he became a sales manager in a medium-sized specialty gifts
company, he found it hard to coordinate and motivate his salespeople. He knew
what to do himself, but he didn't know how to convey that knowledge to others
through proper training and support. As a result, the company was perennially
suffering from lower than expected sales volume, along with high turnover when
the salespeople quit out of frustration.

As for George L., he had the basic people skills and enthusiasm to make a go of
building a distributor organization to sell a new speciality food product through
direct sales. But he wasn't sure exactly how to do it, and he didn't get much
assistance from the distributor who had told him about this business opportunity.
So his good ideas and intentions languished.

Thus, this book has been written to help the many millions of people today—
from entrepreneurs and small business people to managers and sales managers of
growing companies—who have a product or service to sell and want to get others
to help sell it. It is designed to be a step-by-step approach to building and managing this sales group, from a very small beginning to the creation of a large national, even international, sales force. In fact, in today's global economy, with
growing international distribution networks, it is no longer necessary even to be a
large company or corporation to have a large sales force—even a small company
with a few employees and a good product to offer can now do this.

If you already have a sales group organized, you can skip the first chapter. Or,
depending on at what stage your own organizational efforts are, you can focus on
the chapters that apply to you. You'll find the following subjects covered in these
chapters:

Chapter 1 deals with how and when to set up a sales organization. It considers
when one is needed, the differences between using in-house and outside reps, the
types of compensation plans, how many people are needed, and the costs of
setting up a sales force.

Chapter 2 covers how to recruit outside reps and sales brokers and when to do
this rather than have a sales manager.

Chapter 3 deals with how to recruit your own sales team of in-house salespeople or independent distributors. It discusses how to advertise to find the right
person, and how to evaluate the rep through interviews and other sources.

Chapter 4 discusses how to orient and motivate your salespeople to perform at
a top level.

Chapter 5 discusses the process of setting up a training program for your
salespeople.

Chapter 6 examines how to effectively coordinate a sales group through time
and territory management. This way, your salespeople won't interfere with each
others' activities and can support each other.

Chapter 7 describes various ways that sales leaders can support their people,
through such methods as organizing a leads referral system, preparing sample
scripts and sales guidelines, taping sample sales presentations, putting on sales
presentations to which salespeople can bring prospective customers, and others.

Chapter 8 focuses on the development of various types of back-up sales materials, including flyers, brochures, films, videotapes, sales training manuals, sales presentation books, and newsletters.

Chapter 9 discusses how to organize effective sales meetings and covers how to use these meetings both to instruct and motivate.

Finally, the conclusion briefly summarizes the key points made in the previous chapters and provides a summary checklist you can use to keep your sales organization on target.

CHAPTER 1

Setting Up a Sales Organization

When to Set One Up

Almost any company, no matter how small, can use some sort of sales organization to sell its products or services, even if that organization consists of just one individual working from inside the company or as an outside sales representative. Unless you are the kind of person who is not only making the product or offering the service, but is also getting on the phone or making personal visits to sell what you are offering yourself, you need someone to do this for you. And if you have been doing both but don't like it, you need someone to sell for you, too.

Thus, the first question to ask is really not *when* to set up a sales organization, but *what kind* of sales organization do you want or need to sell whatever it is you are offering. The underlying premise here, of course, is that you have some product or service that people will want or need. Obviously, if what you are offering isn't very good or is unneeded, no one will be able to sell it and you'll find that any sales organization you may set up won't last. Once salespeople find there's no market for your product or service, they won't be around very long.

Thus, you have to begin with the basic foundation of having a product or service that has some market, some reason for being wanted or needed. And then, unless you have decided to do all the selling yourself, you need to start setting up a sales organization, even if at first that's just one person. In turn, many of the things you can do to help a small or even one-person sales operation get started can be used to help this organization, and the availability of your product or service, expand—such as the sales literature you prepare, the sales talk guidelines you write, the leads system you create, and the sales strategies and tips you find most effective.

Deciding What Kind of Sales Organization to Set Up

Assuming you have decided to set up a sales organization to sell for you, the first big question is what kind of organization do you want—an in-house salesperson or sales team, an outside sales rep or group of sales reps, a network of independent distributors, or a combination of any of the above? The following sections describe the differences. Incidentally, from now on I will be using the term "product" to refer generally to both products and services, so I don't have to keep repeating both terms. So if you are marketing a service, just consider this your "product."

Using an In-House Salesperson

The in-house salesperson is the person you hire to work directly for you on a part-time or full-time basis. Accordingly, such a person becomes either your employee (which means he or she is covered by the usual Federal, state, and local laws governing employees in your area, including such things as Federal withholding tax, employee social security, and the like), or can work for you as an independent contractor, subject to your following the guidelines for working with an independent contractor as distinguished from an employee. (For example, an independent contractor gets to choose his own hours and has some independent control over the way he does his work. If you closely supervise a person who works for you and require him to work certain hours, this is an employee, not an independent contractor, and you can get in trouble with the IRS or other authorities for trying to classify someone as an independent contractor, and then not paying the usual taxes for an employee, when that person is more accurately working as an employee.)

This in-house salesperson could be hired to sell directly to potential customers, or this person might be used as a sales manager to supervise other salespeople you or that salesperson hire; still another possibility might be to use this person to coordinate setting up a sales program with outside sales reps. In turn, the arrangements depend on the type of business you are, your target market, whether a network of outside salespeople already exists to sell to your market, and the size of your organization. Then, as your organization grows, any arrangements can change to suit your changing company.

These possibilities might be appropriate as follows:

Using an In-House Salesperson to Sell Direct. This kind of approach is probably most suitable when you have a limited local market or are contacting a limited number of potential clients or customers by phone. This also might be a good first step if you have been selling your own products to customers yourself and want someone to take over this function for you. Or, this person might function as a kind of assistant to you to supplement what you are already doing, and perhaps gradually learn to do more and more until he or she takes over your sales functions. Still another possible permutation of this use of an in-house salesperson by companies in their first stage of growth is to share the use of such a person, with each company contributing a percentage of the compensation, and in return, the salesperson spends a certain number of hours working for each company, or may do some joint marketing for all of the companies sharing the service.

For example, I have recently used this approach in handling both local sales and mail order sales of my game, *Glasnost: The Game of Soviet-American Peace and Diplomacy*. The bulk of the sales are being handled through the company to which the game is licensed, the John N. Hansen Company, which has its own national network of sales reps to handle sales to retailers. However, I have been able to sell the game to other speciality markets, and I have used an in-house salesperson to take care of these sales efforts instead of doing it myself. As one example, I have had salespeople run a booth at some local fairs and events; also, I have had a person coordinate a mailing to several hundred organizations involved in working toward improved Soviet-American relations that might have an interest in using the game for premium sales. While I prepared all the copy and material that would go into the mailing and obtained the leads—the names of the prospective companies for the mailing—the sales assistant I hired took it from there, managing both the initial mailing and the responses to the replies.

Other examples of when a company might want to use an in-house salesperson include:

- A small newspaper using an in-house person to solicit ads from local companies;

- A stock-brokerage company using an in-house person to contact potential customers from a list of high-income individuals;

- A furniture company using an in-house person to make calls on offices that might be interested in its furnishings;

- A company representing artists using an in-house person to visit corporate executives who might purchase this art;

- A printer with an in-house salesperson trying to generate business for the printer in the local community.

And the list could go on. As for the combined use of an in-house salesperson, I know a group of speakers with small companies just starting out in the business who have hired a single sales representative to work for them in trying to contact corporate clients and meeting planners who might want to set up speaking engagements for them. In return for this representation, each speaker's company pays a retainer for a certain number of hours per month for her to work for that company alone; in addition, she does some mailings or calls for the companies as a group.

Generally, if you have up to a few salespeople working in this kind of capacity, you can supervise them yourself. However, as the sales group gets larger, you may want to consider having a sales manager to take over the sales management functions, unless you prefer to do this yourself.

Using an In-House Sales Manager. There are two key times to consider using an in-house sales manager: (1) after your company has grown to the point where you have added so many salespeople that you don't want to supervise this sales group yourself; and (2) when you are first setting up your sales program, and you have sufficient product and funding either to start with a substantial sales group or work with a team of outside salespeople, and don't want to be in charge yourself.

Of course, one issue in using an in-house sales manager is deciding whether you want someone else supervising the salespeople, or would rather do this yourself. To decide, take into consideration your own priorities, strengths, and weaknesses to determine if you would be better in devoting your time to this sales management function or to something else. In the early stages of a company's development, the owner or organizer may end up doing a little bit of everything to help get the company off the ground. But as the company grows, it becomes important for people to specialize and for functions performed by one individual to be separated off, and new, more specialized jobs with these functions delineated. Likewise, you need to make some decisions about what you want to do in this growing company. Do you see yourself specializing in sales or marketing, or do you see yourself shifting over into some other role in the company? To help you decide whether you want to end up supervising sales or doing something else, you might ask yourself questions such as:

- What kinds of activities or functions do I most like to perform in this company? As positions become more specialized, what position would I prefer to have (i.e., director of administration, finance, production, research and development, marketing and sales)? Unless you have selected marketing and sales as your long-term goal, you would probably do well to consider hiring a sales manager or supervisor as soon as feasible, and take this into consideration in your hiring decisions early on, so that possibly one of the people you hire in the early stages can step into this management role when there are enough salespeople and the company is large enough for this to be practical.

- What do I do best within this company? What are my key strengths? What do I do least well? What are my biggest weaknesses? Be as honest as you can in assessing and evaluating yourself. Then, if you are strong in selling and marketing skills yourself, you may want to give strong consideration to stepping into the sales management role. But if you are weak in this, then it may be best to bring in someone else. Often, there will be a match between the kinds of things you most like to do and your strengths, and the decision will be easy. However, if there is a disparity—such as you don't like to sell, but you are good at—think about what it is that the company most needs at this time, to help you reconcile what to do. Generally, in this case you may need to choose to do what you do best or what you are strongest at rather than what you like to do, until the company is larger or stronger, at which time you can take more latitude in following your preferences, while turning over the functions you like less to someone else. (A CEO of what has become a large design and production company with a mixture of products in jewelry, fashion, and crafts products is a good example of this. She was always more interested in the creative end of her business—designing the products, researching what people liked, and coming up with new products to satisfy them. And she hated selling. She hated calling prospects, going to trade shows, meeting with sales reps, and the like. However, in the early stages of her business, there was no one else to do this, and so she did it herself, setting up a network of sales reps to sell her products, as well as working with a couple of local salespeople to contact local stores. But then, once the business got big enough, she hired a sales manager to take over, and she stepped into the more creative research and development role. In the beginning she couldn't do this; now she could.)

Using an Outside Sales Rep or Group of Sales Reps

This kind of approach is probably most suitable when you are manufacturing, importing, or purchasing at wholesale some kind of product in an industry where there is already a distribution system through individual sales reps or sales rep organizations, which may range from local or regional organizations to national and international groups. In turn, the use of such reps is available to any size company, from the very small to the very large. In fact, you literally can be a one-man show with a single product and still set up a national or international sales organization through one of these repping firms, as long as you are able to make the arrangements to have enough product, along with the shipping system in place to ship these products (which in fact can be done by contracting out to have someone handle these services—although that is another story and another book).

However, while working with such reps is always possible even for the smallest company, reps in general (like the retailers they sell to) prefer to deal with companies that have at least several products in their line; otherwise, they may feel it too much trouble to handle the orders. However, if the product is popular enough and sells in high enough volume, or if it is expensive enough that selling a single item becomes worth it, this resistance may be less of a problem. Also, be aware that if you are a smaller company with a smaller product line, reps willing to handle the line may want a higher commission than they would otherwise— for example, as much as 15 to 20 percent—whereas a rep will work for a larger company with a larger product line for about 10 to 15 percent at the most.

If there is already such a network in place and a rep will handle your product or product line (or lines), this may be more efficient and cost-effective than trying to work with your own in-house salesperson. The reason for this is your in-house person is selling just for you, and the cost of making a sales call relative to the potential size of the sale will be more—paid for by you if the salesman is working on a salary, absorbed by the salesperson as part of doing business for you if working on commission, or by both of you if the salesman is getting a draw and commission. Depending on the usual size of an order, how likely one is, and the time it takes to contact or visit the customer and conclude the sale, it may turn out to be more expensive to sell your product with an in-house arrangement. By contrast, the rep may have an advantage because he is already calling on these customers in the course of selling other products in his line. Also, the rep may already have set up other sales channels, such as being an exhibitor at a trade show, whereas setting up your own sales arrangements through these channels might be prohibitive. As companies get large enough, they may be able to afford their own internal sales force of reps who call on customers with only their line and represent them at trade show booths. But they can do this because they have a large enough product line to make their own sales force effective. If you are still small you can't do this—it's just too expensive—so an outside sales rep organization might be the way to go.

Some of the industries where you will find well developed outside sales rep organizations include:

- Toys and games
- Gifts
- Stationery items
- Jewelry
- Fashion
- Food products

To learn about who these reps are or to contact them, you might start by obtaining copies of the trade publications in your particular industry (you'll find lists in your local library, as well as copies of some of these publications in collections of business publications). You'll find some reps will have a display or classified ad. Also, if you can attend any trade shows for your industry (advertised in these publications or listed locally with your local Convention and Visitor's Bureau), you can meet reps who have booths where they represent other companies' products. Still another possibility is to contact local retailers selling products in the same category as yours, and ask them who the major reps selling to them are, get their names, and contact them. Then, too, if your company is in a large city, there may be a local merchant's mart, gift center, fashion center, or other showplace for the trade where many reps will have their own display rooms. If so, you can make arrangements to go there, possibly making an advance contact with one rep or manufacturer who has a showroom there so you can get in. Then, you can look for reps selling your kind of product and discuss the possibility of them representing you.

In working with these reps, you have several options: (1) selecting different reps to represent you in different parts of the country, and working with them directly or through an in-house sales manager; (2) working with a master rep, who assists you in setting up a network of national reps in different areas, by giving you leads, and perhaps taking a percentage for doing this—although, you or your in-house sales manager still work with these reps directly; and (3) working with an exclusive national rep, who has a network of his own salespeople, and you or your sales manager work only with this single rep.

All of these options are possible regardless of the size of your company although the exclusive national rep arrangement might be especially helpful if you are still quite small and would prefer to let someone else take over the sales function as much as possible. However, in this case, because all of your sales efforts will be concentrated in one place, it is very important to make sure that you have chosen your exclusive repping agent carefully. It should be someone with a track record in your type of product, someone who will be selling actively to your target market, and someone who indicates a true commitment to your product line. It's also important with an exclusive to include an out clause in any agreement, so that you are able to withdraw from the exclusive representation if after a certain period of time the rep doesn't show a certain level of performance, and you should continue to have such an option if performance slacks off (i.e., a mutually cancellable agreement with 30 days' notice if sales are below a certain minimum—you pick the figure). In turn, if any agreement should be cancelled, you are, of course, responsible for any commissions due during this period. Working with an exclusive rep, you can expect commissions to be about 15 to 20 percent, since the exclusive rep will have to pay out commissions to the other salespeople who work under his umbrella banner.

If you do work with different reps, perhaps with the assistance of a master rep to help you set up your network, it is important to carefully define territories, because reps will normally want an exclusive in the territories they handle, or at least in the territories of major concentration. Since some reps may handle several regions within a state or several states, and some may have their own sales network working under them in large areas, this process can get confusing. Accordingly, before you sign up a rep, it is important to look at the various territories where you want to sell your product as a whole and to consider the various arrangements that might be possible with different reps in different positions. The select process is a little like a military commander allocating the troops. You should determine which reps are strongest in which areas and note overlapping areas. You can then readily assign reps you like where there are no potential conflicts. However, where there are overlaps, one possibility might be to talk to the reps involved and see if you can work out an understanding that while they will have an exclusive in other areas, they will both sell in this area. Some reps will agree to this, particularly if the areas involved are at the edge of their territory or are areas where they have limited sales anyway. But if the reps don't agree, then decide who you feel is the strongest rep or the one covering the most important territories for you and use that rep, while finding another rep not in conflict with this one for the other territories. Very often the reps themselves can recommend reps for other territories, and this is a good source of leads for your network.

Whichever arrangement you enter into with reps—using different reps, using a master rep to help you set up a network, or using an exclusive repping arrangement—it's also important to define exactly what types of markets the rep will be reaching within the territories selected, so you can make sure all the markets you want to hit are covered. If not, you can hire other reps within these same territories to reach these other markets, using the same or a different arrangement, and using the same or different territorial breakdowns. For example, say you have a adult toy type of product. It might be sold by different reps covering each of these markets, though some reps might cover more than one market:

- Toys
- Stationery
- Gifts
- Bookstores

Another important consideration is what other products the rep is selling and how many. You want to avoid going with a rep who will be selling directly competing products, or one whose other product lines are so different from yours that there's a lack of fit. Very often, a rep you contact will eliminate himself or his sales rep network, if he feels there is a product conflict or lack of fit; but check for yourself, since you may have different views about the competition and fit. Also, weigh the pros and cons of working with a small rep or a large rep. A smaller rep with fewer lines may be able to give your product more attention, and there will be less competition from other products; but alternatively, the rep may not have as much clout in getting products placed with retailers, because he is smaller. Conversely, the large rep with many lines might be able to give you the advantage of having a bigger reputation, which makes it easier for him to open doors and place and promote products. But on the other hand, because of his very size and power, your own product line, particularly if small and not yet well known, could easily get lost in the shuffle. So it is important to check with potential reps about these concerns and see how they respond.

Finally, note the level of quality or sophistication of the other products your rep handles. Again, it is important to have a fit here, so your product isn't out of place or even tarnished by association with these other products that aren't appropriate or as good. For example, if you're a manufacturer selling high-quality wooden articles, you might not want these sold alongside the products of someone who makes inexpensive souvenir store-type junk—their lower cost and tacky image would serve to diminish the value associated with your own high-quality goods. Similarly, if you have a product aimed at a well-educated market (such as a bedstand bookrack), it would be a mistake to place it with a rep selling products appealing to a more mass market or lower-income type of market (such as a rep selling sexy greeting cards and roadside advertising signs).

Using a Sales Broker or Group of Sales Brokers

In some industries there are also independent sales brokers who can represent your service, along with related and complementary products and service. They act a little like employment agencies representing companies with a particular type of service, and generally they operate just within a specified geographic area, though some have national connections as well.

In contrast to the repping organizations just described, they generally don't require an exclusive for their area. But at the same time, you usually can't rely on them for most of your sales. However, they can supplement what you and any salespeople are already doing. Your relationship to them is that of an independent contractor; they take a percentage, from either you or the person they connect you with, of what you make. Depending on the industry, this can range from about 10 to 50 percent. While some service brokers have set fees, with others it's negotiable.

Often brokers represent just one service, such as writing, speaking, art, or performers. But there are also many general business brokers that represent people with varying business skills—word processors, bookkeepers, public relations specialists, etc. But they differ from employment agencies in that they do not hire you out as an employee; rather, you are a service business they happen to represent.

An example of how these services work is the way brokers work for speakers in the speakers' industry, where they are called "speaker's bureaus." Many speakers work with several bureaus in different parts of the country, and where there are several bureaus in an area, they may list their speaking services with more than one. The only requirement that the bureaus have is that the speakers should be consistent in the fees they charge, so that the speakers and all bureaus representing them quote the same fee.

However, while working with these bureaus, most speakers have other kinds of sales arrangements (such as using an in-house sales manager or cooperative sales arrangement with other speakers to share a manager jointly) that handle the bulk of the sales, since generally speakers only get about 10 percent of their business through these bureaus. However, this extra can be substantial, with many speakers earning more than $10,000 a year in broker sales. In addition, many of these bureaus offer product sales as well, which provides the speakers with extra royalty or product income coming in from their books, videos, and cassettes.

Similarly, in other fields, these services can market whatever you are offering in various ways.

Working with a Network of Independent Distributors

Another possibility, if you are selling a product as part of a multi-level or network marketing sales program, is to sell through a network of independent distributors, who you recruit into the program. These distributors are like independent contractors with their own independent companies, and you get a commission or override on the products they sell.

If you are the manufacturing company or the company providing your service yourself, then you have to comply with all sorts of regulations for setting up a legitimate multi-level company, which are beyond the scope of the book. (Very briefly, these include regulations by such organizations as the Securities and Exchange Commission and the Federal Trade Commission to make sure you are not illegally engaging in the sale of securities or the operations of a franchise, as well as local and state regulations, which in some industries can involve posting a security bond with the Secretary of State.)

However, if you are simply an individual or sales organization that has signed up as a distributor for one of these multi-level companies, then, subject to the guidelines and policies of the company you are representing, you can set up a sales network yourself to help promote that company's products without dealing with all of these special regulations. (Though you will still need to comply with the local and state regulations governing businesses in your area.)

If you do set up such an arrangement, there are no exclusives, and you can recruit distributors anywhere. In turn, these distributors can represent any other companies or product lines they want. The advantage of this approach is the great freedom everyone has in being independent in marketing the product line of the company represented. The downside is that there can be a lack of commitment to the program, so that there is often a high level of turnover, with people who sign up to be distributors under you often dropping out after a few months, if their sales income doesn't become high enough soon enough. Or you may find that many of the people who sign up as distributors don't put much effort into it because they are just doing this as a part-time hobby or have other multi-level companies they represent, which diffuses their efforts. It is, of course, always possible to hire salespeople to work with you on a multi-level program as inside salespeople on a commission or draw arrangement, with you fronting the usual independent distributor costs to join the program; you can also hire people to work for you in a salaried sales position (such as to provide largely administrative or clerical support). But generally, people enrolling in a multi-level program bring in other salespeople as distributors within their sales organization; then any commissions paid are those pre-established by the company itself for distributors based on their sales volume and on their place in the sales organization of other distributors who are over them in the pyramidal-type sales network created in these programs.

One other important consideration in deciding whether to set up such a sales network for an MLM or network company is the strength of the company with which you are working. Be sure to check it out very carefully first. While many MLM companies are quite legitimate and offer good products, some have encountered problems with the authorities because of dubious claims or sales recruitment scams; you don't want to put your efforts into representing a company that will go out of business or end up with legal problems.

Compensation Plans

When you set up your own in-house sales organization, there are several possible compensation arrangements: (1) commission only, (2) draw and commission (or a draw against a commission), and (3) straight salary (and perhaps a bonus).

When you work with outside reps, the usual arrangement is commission only, with the commission normally within a limited range set by common industry practice.

One consideration in the type of sales organization you set up may be whether you are paying a commission only or must pay a draw or commission, because a commission-only arrangement means you don't have any costs (apart from the sales material or logistics support you might provide) unless there are sales. However, you may find in some businesses, particularly if you are small, growing company, that you can't find an in-house salesperson to work for you on commission only, because the income prospects seem too uncertain or too small on that basis. Then, too, to obtain a more serious commitment from a salesperson, you may find you need to pay a draw, or that it may be common practice in your industry (i.e., many people in the personnel headhunter business get a draw against a commission). Thus, practices in your industry can be a good guide in determining whether to go in-house and what kind of compensation arrangement to use, or whether to use outside sales reps.

More specifically, the types of compensation arrangements, costs, and pros and cons are as follows:

Setting Up an In-House Sales Organization

Commission Only. This can be the most cost-effective arrangement if you can set it up. Usually, you should set the commission rate a little higher than you would if you were paying a draw and a commission, because the salesperson is assuming more of the risk. In turn, a good salesperson usually expects to be able to make more through commission-only sales jobs than ones with a draw, assuming a good product and a receptive market.

The advantage of the commission-only arrangement is that you have to pay it only if the salesperson sells something. Also, this can be a useful approach if you are going to be using a lot of part-time salespeople, or have a sales program that lends itself to having numerous people who are working relatively independently of each other and of you. For example, some typical situations involving commission-only sales might be:

- College students doing door-to-door sales of some product
- Real estate salespeople working out of a real estate office
- Insurance salespeople working for an insurance broker
- Distributors involved in a multi-level or network marketing sales program

However, the downside of setting up a commission-only arrangement is that you have less control over how your salespeople are selling, as well as less commitment from them to your sales effort, particularly in the beginning, because you have paid out no money up front. Thus, your salespeople will feel less beholden to you, and they can readily move on to something else if they don't find an early pay-off for what they are doing. Then, too, when you have a commission-only set-up, you may find that your salespeople may be more apt to engage in other employment—whether selling other products along with yours or having some kind of back-up fixed-income job, so they have some assurance that something is coming in. If you try to prevent anyone working for you from having something else on the side, this may cut down the number of prospective salespeople willing to work for you. Moreover, in some cases, it may not be legal to impose such restrictions on a salesperson working for you in what is essentially an independent contractor arrangement. (Since the laws vary from state to state on what you can and cannot do, check with your local city or your state on applicable laws.)

In any case, the level of commission will vary from industry to industry, within a certain range, with commissions on more expensive products being lower than on less expensive items. For example, while real estate commissions are about 6 percent, commissions in the toy and gift business are about 10 to 20 percent, and in many direct-sales health and food programs, they will be about 25 to 33 percent. Find out what is common in your industry and use that as a guideline. In some cases, these commissions may be set by law (i.e., in real estate) or by the organization whose products are represented (i.e., if you are a distributor for a multi-level marketing program who has recruited other distributors to work with you).

If you find this more independent commission-only arrangement works for you, fine. But if you find you want more control, or have trouble keeping committed salespeople, you might want to use a draw and commission (or draw against commission) plan instead.

Draw and Commission (or Draw Against a Commission). With a draw and/or a draw against commission arrangement, you have created an employer/employee relationship with the salesperson, rather than the independent contractor arrangement usually created by the commission-only set-up, so you have more control over what the person does (plus having to comply with local, state, and Federal laws governing employees). This kind of arrangement can be good if you do want that greater control and employee commitment, or if you want the person to work out of your offices or at certain times, perhaps even following certain required guidelines established by you or your sales manager (such as a specific sales presentation or telephone sales pitch).

At the same time, the draw is normally set lower than the person is expected to make if he or she does well, to give that person an incentive for selling to make more. Alternatively, the draw can set a minimum baseline, which the person must meet over a certain time period in order to continue working with the company. For example, if the person's commissions based on sales don't at least meet his draw over a two- or three-month period, especially when the person is first hired, then the person will be terminated. He will receive the minimum draw as agreed for the period he worked, but nothing else.

In many industries, the draw is a common or usual arrangement, such as for:

- Travel agents
- Personnel agency employees
- Furniture salespeople calling on offices
- Telephone solicitors
- Some real estate offices
- Industrial product sales
- Some retail stores

One downside of this arrangement is that you will have to pay out this draw even if the person doesn't perform up to par. But one compensation for this is that because you have more control, and the person is working more closely with you or your sales manager (i.e., out of the same office), you can supervise that person to learn if he or she seems to be having problems in selling your product. Then, if this is the case, you can provide more training or other assistance to help that person improve. Or if the problem seems to be a lack of sufficient work (say the person is goofing off), or a lack of experience or ability that is interfering with performance (say the person misled you in the hiring interview), then you can probably dismiss the person for good cause before a termination agreement based on not meeting the draw is up (though here check the employment termination guidelines for your own state to avoid legal problems).

What kind of draw can you expect to pay? Again, it depends on your particular industry, and it helps to check on what others in your field and in your local area are paying, which will help you stay competitive in attracting salespeople to work for you. However, in general, these draws will average about $200 to $300 a week, or about $1000 to $1500 a month. Use the weekly draw if you are hiring some salespeople to sell for you on a short-term basis (i.e., for a brief telephone sales campaign). Or, if you hope to have a long-term arrangement if the person works out, the monthly draw arrangement is probably more appropriate, though you might also consider a weekly draw as a trial arrangement if the salesperson can be expected to close sales with a short-term turnaround, thus providing a way to measure performance quickly.

The distinction between a draw and commission and a draw against commission arrangement is that in the first case, the salesperson receives a base salary and then a commission for any sales, with no deductions for that base salary, whereas in the second case, the salesperson's draw is deducted from his commission. In many fields the draw against commission arrangement is more common, with the draw being viewed as a kind of advance against what the salesperson is expected to make. But again, check your local area for what is common in your industry.

Straight Salary. A straight salary is not usual in most sales situations, because the salesperson's performance is judged by his level of sales. Therefore, he should be paid accordingly, with his pay being a percentage of sales (whether determined by a commission-only arrangement or a commission and draw). However, there are some situations where a straight salary may be most appropriate:

1. A retail store, where the salesperson is really more like a ringer-up of purchases, and has little opportunity to make much difference in whether the person buys or not;

2. A direct mail operation, where the "salesperson" is really more like an administrative assistant doing mailings, rather than someone in charge of a direct mail campaign;

3. A telephone sales operation, where the person is just reading a routine script to get leads, and then another salesperson will follow up with the direct contact;

4. A counter-person in a fast-food restaurant or snack bar.

In short, the straight salary arrangement may be most appropriate for people in low-level sales positions who have little sales skills and are really acting more in the capacity of administrative or service personnel, than really selling. In this case, the typical amount you might expect to pay would be about $4 to $8 an hour, and you might normally expect to hire unskilled, part-time, or perhaps student employees for such positions. Also, older, retired workers might be good for such sales positions. In some cases, you might consider making such positions available as entry-level positions, and then advancing such people who perform well into the more skilled, better-paying commission or draw and or draw against commission positions (for instance, if you hire college students on a part-time basis, they may be especially interested in moving up). But in other cases, just recognize these as short-term, often part-time positions, for someone who is not particularly interested in a sales career and just sees the job as a chance to make some immediate money.

Setting Up an Outside Sales Organization

Working with Sales Reps. Normally, any payment to an outside sales repping organization is set up on a commission-only basis. Industry standards vary, as with setting up an in-house sales organization, and a key factor is the size of your company and your product line. The larger it is, the more products you have, the more volume a sales rep can do for you on a single sale, the lower the commission rate might be. Then, too, as you grow, your company may be able to command a lower commission rate, because as it becomes larger and better known, the sales rep has an easier job of selling for your company, and is more sure of doing well in repping the line. Your business thus becomes more appealing than a small company, newcomer, or unknown, where any repping arrangement is more of a risk.

To take a typical example of likely commissions (though again, check ranges in your own industry), say you have a retail product you want to distribute through the usual sales-to-retailer or sales-to-wholesaler for resale to retailer channels. Generally, as a large company, your commission for sales to retailers (generally at 50 percent of the retail price plus sometimes an extra allowance for advertising) will average about 10 percent when you are working directly with individual reps, and perhaps 12 to 15 percent if you are working through a master rep or exclusive rep, who each have their own sales network. Or, if you are a smaller company, your commission will probably be more like 15 percent when working direct, and perhaps up to 20 percent if going through a master rep or exclusive repping agency. If your rep should happen to sell to a wholesaler, who buys in larger quantities for resale to retailers, the rep will normally get a smaller commission, while the wholesaler will get an extra discount. (A common arrangement is for the sales rep to get just 5 percent on these wholesaler sales, while the wholesaler gets a discount of anywhere from 10 to 25 percent on the wholesale price, depending on the quantity of goods he buys.)

Note too that when you have an exclusive arrangement with a rep in a particular territory and market category, then if anything is sold in the area where the rep has the exclusive, including by you, the commissions on those sales belong to the rep, unless you have made a special exemption for selected house accounts.

Many repping firms you contact will already have their own standard policies that they use with other firms they represent, although they may be open to some negotiation, depending on how much they want your line.

Also, note that there may be common industry practices about the timing of payment that these outside reps follow and will ask of you. For example, some will expect to be paid within a certain time of them writing and you receiving the order, with any further responsibilities for collections up to you (assuming the rep has followed your own credit guidelines in writing the sale). However, other reps may be willing to agree to wait until you have been paid, especially the smaller reps who are seeking more clients to get established. You can discuss these alternatives when you work out your representation agreement with the rep. Try to get an agreement to wait to pay the rep until you are paid if you can, though this is not always possible.

Working with Sales Brokers. With sales brokers (such as the speakers' bureaus previously described), most arrangements are commission only, which again vary from industry to industry. Typically, these larger, established brokers will already have their commission arrangements standardized, and even printed up as part of their standard contract, so that if you hire a particular broker and that broker makes a deal for you, that is what you will pay. But in many cases, especially with smaller, less established brokers, such commission arrangements may be negotiable, and the more the broker would like to represent you the better deal you may be able to make (for instance, if you or your business has established a national reputation with name recognition, you are in a better bargaining position than if you are new).

In any case, subject to these various considerations, you can expect brokers' commissions to range from about 10 percent in some fields to 25 to 40 percent in others, with an average of about 20 to 25 percent.

Working with Independent Distributors. If you are setting up a network of independent distributors within the framework of an MLM or network marketing program, you will find the commission levels set by the company guidelines (or if you are the company, you set them yourself in your marketing plan for all distributors recruited directly by your company and thereafter recruited by other distributors).

Generally, the company will designate a certain percentage of its sales price for its products that you and your distributors buy directly from the company to be paid out in commissions (commonly about 50 to 60 percent, with some going as high as 70 percent). Then, the pie is divided up in various ways for distributors and the distributors under them in their sales networks. These divisions can become extremely complicated (often necessitating the use of a computer to sort out the payment arrangements), depending on how much immediate commission goes to the person who makes the immediate sale and how much is paid out in overrides to the members of the sales network who are above the salesperson, and qualified to receive overrides on his sales. For example, say you have recruited a salesperson to work under you in your sales organization. In a representative company plan, that person working independently of you (though you may provide some back-up support, sales training, and assistance) may receive a 25 percent commission for what he sells. Then, as that person's direct supervisor (commonly called a sponsor in the MLM industry), you might receive 10 percent; the person who sponsored you into the program might receive 5 percent; the person who sponsored that person might receive 3 percent; the person the next level up might receive 2 percent; and finally, the next highest person 1 percent; with further overrides being cut off there. However, on top of these immediate commissions, there might be additional pay-out commissions based on total volume, so if an individual or a sales group passes a certain level, they would receive a bonus—perhaps up to an additional 10 percent.

In any event, since the guidelines are established by the company, you work within those guidelines, and the commissions paid to the people you recruit as well as the people they recruit are paid directly by the company, just as the company pays your own commission earnings on sales to you.

How Many Salespeople Do You Need?

The answer to how large a salesforce you need depends on the size of your product line, your volume, and how many salespeople comfortably can sell what you are offering. To some extent, the question may answer itself if you have salespeople working on a commission basis. If they can't make enough selling your product, they won't stay.

However, to help you decide, in general, consider how much you are able to produce of a product or offer of a service, how much time is needed to sell it (i.e., make a sales call or telephone contact), and what the average earnings are likely to be for the average salesperson making those contacts.

When you are working with an outside sales force, it's not as necessary to work out such projections, because you aren't going to have any major up-front costs to consider, such as a weekly draw. Your only major expense is apt to be product samples or sales sheets or catalogs for your reps. Thus, you have more flexibility, and if your reps sell more or less than you expect, you can always increase or decrease production to some extent to adapt. (Though if a rep sells much less, consider getting another rep.) Also, your reps can often give you a general idea of how much they are likely to sell of your line, given their experience with other similar products for the market they handle. Then, if additional sales personnel are needed in the particular territory or market they are covering, they and not you will usually be responsible for adding additional salespeople (because generally you will have given that rep an exclusive for that territory and market).

If you are working with either sales brokers or independent distributors, you also normally do not need to work out such detailed projections. With sales brokers this is the case, since there's no exclusive arrangement, and they usually are only going to be making up a small percentage of your sales, you can hire as many as you want, and you probably should sign on as many as you can until you find out who is really going to produce for you. Then, as long as your sales brokers don't outstrip your ability to provide your services or products, you can keep them on.

By the same token, when you work with independent distributors, the usual approach is to try to build as large an organization as possible of active distributors, subject to any limits the company itself may have in providing its product. (If you are the multi-level or network marketing company, then you may have to work out these kinds of projections to control your own growth, but as a distributor for such a company, unless you hear to the contrary, you can usually assume that the company has the ability to respond to orders, and can expand its production as necessary to accommodate additional sales.) Many distributors do attempt to project their income based on recruiting certain numbers of distributors selling an average of so much in sales volume, and then set targets for recruiting distributors accordingly, along with estimates of how much time they need to devote to obtaining these distributors (assuming a certain number of contacts necessary to gain an active distributor). But beyond that, their goal is to grow as rapidly as possible, rather than asking how many salespeople are needed. Since this approach to building a sales force is fairly specialized, I will discuss it only tangentially in the future—readers requiring more specific information on working with and building an MLM sales group may consult other works by the author dealing exactly with this: *Strike it Rich in Personal Selling* (originally published by Avon in 1985; now available from New World Books); *Get Rich Through Multi-Level Selling*

(Self-Counsel Press, 1990); and *Success in Multi-Level Marketing* (Prentice-Hall, 1991).

On the other hand, with an in-house sales force, make some initial projections about what you think the average salesperson is likely to sell, given an average day or week of making sales contacts, and figure out how many people might be necessary to handle your current volume of production in the areas where you are selling. Or, figure out how many hours might be necessary to do this, so you can split out the likely sales effort into part-time positions, if you are going to be doing this. One way to make these estimates is to do some initial selling yourself, or have the sales manager you hire do this. This way you establish a track record of what someone might be able to do, and then can divide up the work and territories accordingly. Then, when you do have salespeople out in the field, monitor their results, which will not only help you decide whether individual people are effective, but overall how much sales you can expect from each salesperson, so you can further fine-tune estimates about your needs for salespeople based on your current, possible, and desired projected levels of production. Exhibit 1 can help you in making these breakdowns and estimates and in assessing what you are likely to need. However, be ready to update this as your own levels of production or your ability to offer services changes or expands, and as you get more feedback about what your salespeople are able to do.

The Costs of Setting Up a Sales Force

The cost of setting up your sales force will depend on what type of sales system you have (i.e., outside or in-house sales reps), and on how many salespeople you will be working with.

The lowest-cost approach is using a commission-only arrangement, working with outside reps. Working with outside reps cuts your costs even more, because you don't have to provide any in-house support in the form of training, and you will normally have to spend less time in recruiting, since you will be contacting already established people in your industry who already know how to sell and are organized to sell within their own territory. However, you still can expect to have some basic costs for supporting sales material and for some field liaison, such as phone calls and faxes, and sometimes you may want to participate with your outside reps by being present in their booths at some trade shows. (Sometimes this may only involve your cost of getting and staying at the show, though some reps may ask for some contribution from the companies they rep to cover their costs of being in these shows; it is helpful to check out these policies in choosing a rep, because this will affect your costs).

To figure out your costs in working with a rep, include your estimated costs for the following, over a selected time period (i.e., one month):

- Amount of sales material requested or needed (i.e., catalog sheets or catalogs, order forms, descriptive product materials, press clippings, etc. If you are going to produce color catalog sheets or catalogs, figure on an initial run of about 1,000 or 2,000 copies. If you are using black and white copies, you can start with a smaller amount, perhaps 200 to 500 copies; then see how things go before you increase the order)

- Average number of phone calls and faxes per day to contact the rep, multiplied by the average cost per day

- Expected costs for trade show attendance or participation

The next-lowest cost arrangement is using a commission-only plan with your own in-house people. You can use the same sort of categories as above, plus add in additional categories to cover your extra costs for recruiting and training. Some of these additional categories might be the following:

- Cost of advertising for salespeople

- Cost of answering and screening calls (i.e., if you have an administrative assistant doing this, figure in the amount of time spent in doing this times the hourly wage paid)

- Cost of recruiting interviews (i.e., how much time is being spent on this, by who, and what is that person's hourly salary, if paid on a salary)

- Cost of orientation and training meetings (i.e., besides the costs for time involved, you may also need to figure in the cost of handouts used to explain the program, films to teach techniques, etc.)

- Cost for ongoing sales meetings (i.e., time and materials involved)

If you are using a draw against commission arrangement, add in the fixed costs you have to pay for the draws.

Finally, if you have someone on salary, note how much this is costing you over a specific time period.

Later, as discussed in the final chapter, you can evaluate the cost-effectiveness of your sales program by applying these costs against the sales income you receive.

Exhibit 1.   Estimating the Number of Sales People You Need

The following are some of the general categories you might take into consideration in projecting how many sales people you may need. However, beyond establishing general sales territories, it is often difficult to be quite this precise in the early stages of setting up a sales program, since there are so many uncertainties about the level of production, how much individual salespeople can sell, and how much time in general salespeople will need to make the sale. One way to help you get this kind of information might be for you or your sales people to keep sales log books showing the amount of time devoted to selling, the number of sales made, and the amount of volume sold. The categories to consider are:

- Volume of products or services currently produced or expected
  (combine individual totals or use overall projections to determine this)

- Territories where products are sold or services offered
  (list individual territories and possible regional groupings)

- Retail income from your current or expected level of sales in each territory or regional group

- Sales commission possible from this current or expected level of sales
  (commission level × total sales earnings expected)

- Estimated amount of time needed to achieve sales projections in each territory or regional group
  (i.e., from phone calls, sales calls)

- Number of full-time positions or part-time positions possible within each sales territory or regional area
  (assume 8 hours a day for each full-time position; 4 hours a day for each half-time position; 2 hours a day for each part-time position)

CHAPTER 2

Recruiting Salespeople: Outside Reps, Sales Brokers, or a Sales Manager?

Once you have considered the various options of what type of sales organization you want to set up and have made a decision, you are ready to start recruiting salespeople in that category, as well as preparing the material you need to provide them to show what you are doing. Much of this material is sales support material and will be discussed in Chapter 8, on "Developing Sales Material." However, the material you prepare specifically for the recruitment process is discussed here.

Deciding on Your Own Role in the Recruitment Process

One early consideration is whether you want to act as the sales manager yourself, hire a sales manager in the beginning, or take charge for a while, and then turn things over to a sales manager as soon there are enough salespeople on board and enough company earnings to do so.

If you decide to take charge initially or take the role on for the long term, it naturally helps if you have had some sales experience yourself, so you can draw on this in training and assisting your salespeople in the field. This sales background is particularly useful if you have a product or service that needs some explanation and skilled saleswork to sell it. However, it can still be possible to set up an effective sales organization even if your sales experience is limited, if you hire people who are already experienced in sales, thus minimizing the amount of training and personal support you need to provide (though of course you still have to provide the usual sales literature and coordination assistance). These experienced people can be hired as either in-house salespeople or outside reps and independent distributors, depending on the type of sales network you have decided to set up.

Alternatively, if you have decided to hire a sales manager, turn these sales force recruitment decisions over to the manager, though perhaps you might still provide some input. However, when you do have a manager, it's important for that manager to feel in control of the people working with him, whether he is able to select them or takes over an already hired group, before adding his own people. Thus, as long as the sales manager seems to be doing whatever he is doing responsibly and seems committed and gung-ho about your product line, it is probably best to back off from being too actively involved in day-to-day sales activities and giving too much advice and direction. Along with being in charge comes a feeling of commitment, and you want to be sure your sales manager feels this sense of being in charge so he feels this commitment to your product, too.

This chapter and the next describe how to recruit these five types of salespeople, depending on which way you decide to go in setting up your team: (1) recruiting outside reps, (2) recruiting sales brokers, (3) recruiting a sales manager, (4) recruiting in-house salespeople yourself or (5) recruiting independent distributors. The first three approaches are described in this chapter; the latter two in the next chapter.

Recruiting Outside Reps

If you are in one of those industries that has independent sales reps who can handle your product, and you have decided to work with a sales rep, you should in your recruitment efforts discuss not only what the rep can do for you but the rep's expectations about a commission payment.

If you haven't already determined what the going commission rate is in this field, do this by asking around, either before you start actively recruiting reps or as part of your recruiting process. As discussed in the Chapter 1, and just to recap, reps typically work on a 10 to 15 percent commission, and occasionally as much as 20 percent, depending on the field, how many products you have, how long you have been in business, your previous track record if any, and how much they want your item. With high-volume items like toys, the commission tends to be lower—about 10 percent; with specialty items with a higher mark-up and fewer sales per order, the commission is a little higher—about 15 percent is average. However, when you have only a few products, are new in business, or have an untested product, you may end up giving up a little more. At this point, you need the reps more than they need you, and the higher commission you may pay reflects this.

Second, as part of your recruitment efforts, you will want to figure out who can represent you where, by determining what exclusive territories reps want, and where they are willing to share overlapping territories with adjacent reps. These territories can range from very local areas to regional, state, multiple state, and national regions (i.e., the San Francisco Bay Area—Northern California; all of California; California, Nevada, and Arizona; the West Coast; West of the Mississippi; national, etc.). Find out from each rep not only what areas he covers, but how many salespeople he has working for him in these areas, so you can better evaluate the rep's depth of coverage.

Also, to help you determine who to recruit, find out about the rep's range of coverage (e.g., toy stores and toy departments; gift and stationery buyers; boutiques and clothing stores). If a rep handles one market, but not others, then you can have reps in the same territories handling these different market segments.

It's usually best to have preliminary discussions with a number of reps when you are first establishing a network, so you can decide what might be the best approach for you—a single national rep handling your whole line, a master rep who helps you set up arrangements with other reps, or a number of independent reps in different areas coordinated by you (or your in-house sales manager). As you get information, weigh the pros and cons for each arrangement, as discussed in Chapter 1.

If you are considering a single national rep, be especially careful that this is the right fit for you. Look at the other product lines the rep is handling, and, assuming the rep does want to handle your line, consider whether this line will fit well with the rep's other products. Make sure there is nothing directly competitive that would detract from your own sales. Your goal should be to find a rep with complementary products to yours that have the same sort of appeal to the rep's major markets.

Also, ask questions to learn how many salespeople this rep has; how good his coverage is in different areas; and what he thinks likely sales targets for your product nationally might be. Consider if the rep appears to be able to sell enough (based on both his estimates and the number of salespeople he has in the field) to justify committing yourself to a single national rep in that market segment (or segments) he handles.

Then, too, make sure you have an understanding with the rep about levels of performance, and an have option to end the agreement if the level of performance doesn't meet this minimum. Very often, the rep may not want to handle your product line any longer if he finds he can't sell enough. However, you want to be sure you have your own out in case you decide the rep isn't doing enough, but the rep claims he is. Negotiate some kind of termination as part of your agreement to hire this rep in case there is such a problem before the agreement's regular termination date. Commonly, this regular termination date will be for a year or for a particular selling season, with some kind of option to renew by mutual agreement or if the rep has achieved a certain target level of performance. When the agreement is made for a selling season, this normally begins in January, or whenever you hire the rep, and runs through December. Also, aside from any special termination arrangement you may negotiate, many of these agreements have a mutual cancellation clause allowing either you or the rep to end the arrangement with a 30-day written notice of termination (but then the rep gets the credit and the commission for any sales made prior to this termination).

If you are considering working through a master rep, who will supervise your sales rep network, ask questions to determine whether this person is the right rep to do this. Find out exactly what this rep will do on an ongoing basis, apart from just giving you referrals to other reps. Some reps will give you these referrals for no charge, whereas others will ask for some kind of percentage; if they do seek a percentage, they should also be willing to do a little bit more to help you with planning and organizing your network. For example, you might expect a master rep to give you some input on the kinds of catalog sheets you need, the way you should price your merchandise, the kinds of trade discounts you might offer for quantity purchases, and the like. If the rep you are considering as a master rep seems reluctant to do these little extras, you might want to reconsider if you really want this person to be in a central position in your network and earning a percentage off your other reps. There are other ways to find these reps yourself, without using a master rep for referrals, if he is only going to give you referrals and not do much else.

If you do work with a master rep, your agreement about what the sales rep will do, the commission, and any termination clause will be much the same as described above, except that you will have separate agreements with the reps to whom the master rep has referred you. If the master rep is getting a percentage for overseeing the network, that should be spelled out in the contract with him, indicating what you expect him to do for this percentage and how much of a percentage override he will receive from the sales made by those to whom he has referred you.

In any event, before you do decide to make a commitment to work with a master rep or an exclusive national sales repping organization, it helps to talk first to some independent reps to see what they might do for you individually, or to whom they might refer you. This way you can better compare your options. For instance, you may find you may be able to put together a national network of independent reps just by using an informal referral system, since once you hire a rep in one territory, he or she can frequently recommend reps in other territories, and they may have their own referrals. So in short order, you may have a national sales network. Or, just going through the process of interviewing potential independent reps can help you better determine what is best for you in your industry, by comparing the experience and strengths of the reps who are allied with a master rep or an exclusive national distributor, versus going the independent route. Then, you may be better able to weigh objectively what's best for you. Moreover, by shopping around, you may find that the reps you speak to are willing to give you a better percentage, because now they know they have competition.

Also, as part of your evaluation efforts, check on what kind of costs to expect, besides the commission on sales, and discuss when the rep expects to be paid—within a certain time of sending you the order, or when you are paid. It's important to check on extra costs, because you may find that some reps will ask you to share a percentage of their booth fees for participating in shows (generally the smaller, less established reps, who need the money to be in these shows may do so, while others will not). While some of the smaller reps may work harder for you, since they have fewer products, often you will be better off with the larger independents, who will have their own booths at shows, and even established showrooms. Also, it's better if you can work out arrangements so that the rep is paid only after you are, because if it turns out the customer doesn't pay you, why should the rep make a commission? On the other hand, some reps will say that if they follow your guidelines for checking credit and you accept the order, then it's your responsibility to pay them and your responsibility to handle any collections if you aren't paid. Check out the possibilities before deciding what you want to do.

Additionally, in deciding whether to work with a particular rep or repping organization, ask about the type of accounts contacted, find out a little bit about the rep's track record (i.e., how long in the business; how long on his own; who are some major clients), and notice how willing the rep is to share this information with you, as well as what he says. Such openness and rapport can be quite important, because you want to feel you can trust and be comfortable with your rep. In addition, see how enthusiastic your potential rep seems to be about your product or product line. This enthusiasm can be a key factor, because if your rep is high on your product, he or his organization is more likely to push it; this can include featuring it in trade shows. But without this enthusiasm, even if you have one of the biggest and most powerful repping firms behind you, your product can easily get lost along with many others.

Key Questions to Ask

The following series of questions provides a kind of recap and summary of the major considerations in hiring a rep. Ask yourself:

- What is the commission and other costs involved?

- What territories does the rep handle? Where does he want an exclusive? Where is he open to an overlap? How well will the rep's territory and types of accounts fit with the other reps I have or am considering having in my network? (These questions are especially important if you are trying to set up a regional or national sales network, because you want to avoid conflicts over territory and accounts. In some cases, reps will make categories overlap in their outlying territories, so you can accommodate reps who both handle the same area. One way is that one might agree not to include a particular territory, or both might agree to a nonexclusive in that area. But try to avoid such conflicts when you can. Using referrals from the reps you already have can be one way to avoid this problem)

- How well will my own product or product line fit alongside the products currently handled by this rep? (There should be a good fit, though your products shouldn't be directly competitive with another line he represents. For example, if you have games, it's ideal to find a rep who handles other games too. But if you and another of the rep's clients both have games on money, the match may be too close—and many reps will turn you down if they feel the products are too directly competitive.)

- Are the rep's other products of high quality and/or from good or known manufacturers? (It's best if the rep represents some solid, established companies. That's a sign the rep has a good reputation. Also, your products will benefit by their association with other high-quality and well known products.)

- What is the rep's background? What kind of track record does he have? How long has he been in the business? How successful has he been? How long has the rep had his own business? Or if his repping firm is relatively new, how long did he work for someone else in this field? (If the rep is already handling several established product lines, his background may not be an issue. But if a rep is relatively small or new, you want to be sure he's experienced and knows what he's doing. Thus, a history of working for someone else is reassuring.)

- How well does the rep like my product? Is he really enthusiastic about it or not? (You want to be sure the rep will really push it and give it a good shot. Sometimes, this means a smaller rep may be better for you when you're just getting started or have a small line, because with a big rep your product line could get lost with all of his other products. On the other hand, a big rep who really thinks you have a terrific item might be able to showcase it and give it the push it needs. Thus, it can be very important to choose a rep who's really hot for your product, even if you have to make some compromises in other areas (i.e., paying a little higher commission, giving the rep more territories, etc.), than to choose a rep who's only lukewarm, because the more enthusiastic rep will work harder for you, whereas commonly the other will just add your product to his line to see how it flies. But in this day and age, most products don't sell themselves. They depend on someone behind them pushing—and your rep can be the key to making or breaking your product, by the extent to which he pushes it and tells the salespeople he works with to do the same.)

Finding a Rep

How do you find a rep? Besides referrals from one rep to another, already mentioned, three good ways are (1) going to trade shows; (2) going to a local merchandise mart or wholesale showroom center in your area; or (3) contacting stores selling your type of product.

If you go to a trade show (you'll find the dates and locations listed for these in your industry publications, or, if they're in your area, try the calendar for your local visitor and conventions bureau), one approach is to walk up and down the aisles until you see someone with a product line of similar items. If that's the booth of an independent rep or repping company, you can stop and talk about that person or company possibly repping you (or make an appointment to meet at a more convenient time). Or, if it's the booth of a manufacturer, he might be able to refer you to his own rep, who may have another booth at that show or may stop by at this booth from time to time during the show to assist. For example, this is what I did when I was in the games business. I went to a gift show in my city and found a few reps who had displays with some games, and later I did the same thing at a toy show in another city. Then, I spoke to the reps to find out if they might be interested in repping my product and asked some questions about their background, and I set up several independent reps in the field that way. Also, if one of your reps is in a trade show, this can be a way to find additional reps—by spending some time in his booth to call attention to your product and demonstrate it to other buyers. Not only will that help to increase sales at the show, but you may attract other reps from other areas who are interested in repping the line.

Similarly, if you go to a local merchandise mart or wholesale showroom, you can go up and down the aisles and visit various showrooms. Often, you can simply show a business card to get in, but sometimes you may need at least one contact already there. One way to get this is by finding a referral to a rep through other sources (i.e., from a department store buyer). Then, after that rep lets you into the mart or showroom center, you can visit other reps as well.

Finally, a good source of leads is contacting the buyers for stores in your area where you would expect your product to sell. Then, speak to the appropriate buyer, either by phone or by appointment. Sometimes, just dropping in at small stores works well. Then, briefly describe or show your product, and ask for suggestions on the reps the buyers deal with who would handle this. If you do this with a few buyers, you can collect a number of names and numbers, which will help you make comparisons. In addition, you may find that some reps get mentioned again and again, which suggests these might be especially good ones to handle your line. Then, call those reps, especially those who have received the most mention, and set up an interview. At the interview, you can ask various questions (such as those suggested above) to help you decide, and, all things being equal, choose one of the reps who got mentioned the most.

What to Give Your Rep to Get Started

Once you have decided to put on a rep, he'll usually need from you just a few product samples, plus catalog sheets and price lists. The rep can then usually sell on his own without much support from you, though your continuing assistance will, of course, help. Such assistance might take the form of additional samples, being present at trade shows when your rep has a booth, etc.

Find out how many samples your rep will need (commonly one for each showroom, and perhaps a few extras for trade shows), as well as how many catalog sheets and price lists. Perhaps start out with a small amount (i.e., 500 catalog sheets and 500 price lists); and be ready to supply more if the rep needs them. If you receive any publicity, let the rep know, and provide some press releases or a PR sheet showing the clips you have received. Plan to continue to keep the rep informed as you get more PR information or if you plan any promotional events.

Recruiting Sales Brokers

If you are in an industry where sales brokers can help to promote your service, there are a number of sources for finding such brokers.

One source is your local yellow pages. Look in the directory under the type of business you have. Besides companies that directly offer these services, you may find some brokers for these services. Some of these brokers also advertise in trade publications, and your local Chamber of Commerce may have a directory of business services as well.

Still another source is business network meetings, since brokers often come out in force for these, as these meetings are a potential source of new clients. In fact, if you have a brochure or flyer about your service that you can leave out at such gatherings, you'll find the brokers frequently may contact you. I found several people to represent my writing and marketing services that way.

Another possibility is a local business newspaper in some larger cities. Also, if you go to a conference or convention for your industry, you may meet sales brokers there in the course of general networking, and some may have a booth.

Normally, these reps won't want an exclusive in their area and will just expect to supplement your other sales efforts, so you don't have to ask as detailed questions as you might in hiring a rep who wants an exclusive territory in an industry. Accordingly, the main thing is to be sure that the sales broker seems to be reputable, has a good track record, and is representing other clients who you feel have a good reputation, so your own isn't compromised by being linked with other companies of dubious merit.

Then, find out what the sales broker needs to work with you (i.e., brochures, flyers, copy from you), clarify what percentages the broker wants in commissions, and go over other arrangements. Thereafter, it helps to keep in touch with your sales broker from time to time, particularly if you have any promotional news that may help the broker in promoting you, your company, and your service.

Recruiting a Sales Manager

If you have decided you would prefer to play only a minor role or no role at all in organizing a sales team to sell your product or service, then the key is to recruit a good sales or marketing manager who can take over this role. Or, at least start off in this position yourself and recruit and work with some salespeople until you can identify someone who can take over. You may find you can get quite good at this role if you follow the principles of good sales organization, even if you don't really want to be selling, and it may be necessary to do this for a while in order to get your project on the market. Then, once you have a track record, it becomes easier to get someone else to take over, just as it becomes easier to sell to new customers once others have bought.

So how and where do you find a good sales manager, and what incentives should you offer?

One consideration is whether this is someone you want to hire; perhaps a partnership may make more sense. In today's competitive environment, the role of the sales or marketing manager has become so important: he or she can make or break your company. So give careful thought as to what arrangement is best for you.

Hiring a Sales Manager

One advantage of hiring is that you are still in control and can easily make changes in who is your sales manager. But then you also have to make your arrangements appealing enough so you can recruit a good person to take charge.

Accordingly, consider some of the following questions to help you in presenting your project to a potential candidate:

- What are the major benefits of my product? How does it compare to the competition? What are its major selling features that can be used to make it easy to sell?

- What kind of sales volume is likely? About how much time and effort is required to achieve that sales volume?

- What are my commission arrangements for personal sales? What kind of overrides and bonuses are available if the sales manager brings in other salespeople to sell?

- Approximately how much is a person in this position likely to make, based on the commission offered and the likely sales volume achieved in a given amount of time (such as twenty or forty hours a week)?

- Am I willing to pay a draw to provide a base salary (a typical amount is $1,000 to $3,000 a month to new sales managers in small companies)? Or am I expecting the person to work on commission only?

You should be able to answer these questions in order to give the prospective sales manager a clear picture of the opportunity available, so he or she can determine if he or she can support the product, and if there is enough return to want to do it.

If you don't have a track record yet on the product's sales, work out a projected estimate, based on your assessment of how others are doing with similar products. Then, base your returns and commissions on that. There's a sample of how to do this on the following page. (Exhibit 2.)

As for deciding whether to pay a draw or go commission only, you'll find that it's easier to recruit someone when you offer a draw, since many good people don't have the resources to work completely on speculation. But if you're just starting, you may not be able to do this, and often some of the very best people prefer a commission-only arrangement, on the grounds that they can make more this way. And that's usually true, since the way most companies handle the draw-commission or commission-only decision is to pay a lower commission rate

Exhibit 2.   Sample Projected Sales Estimate

Average monthly sales volume per person: ×   Value of   =   Total
(List the number of expected or projected   Each Sale   Monthly
sales for each category of product or service)   Sales Value

_____   _____   _____
_____   _____   _____
_____   _____   _____
_____   _____   _____
_____   _____   _____

                                               Total Personal
                                               Sales Value: _____

Average time needed to achieve this
monthly sales volume   _____hrs.

Earnings from a ____% average commission on personal sales =   _____
(Multiply the total monthly sales value by
the commission)

Earnings from a ____% average override bonus based on the
personal sales of other salespeople.
(Multiply the total monthly sales value per person by the
number of sales people expected to be supervised by the sales
manager and the override bonus percentage)   _____

                                               Total Projected
                                               Earnings: _____

Average pay per hour   _____
(Divide the average time needed to achieve
this monthly sales volume into the total projected earnings)

than they would otherwise when they use a draw-commission system, since they are offering the salesperson a base security. Conversely, when a company seeks a straight commission sales manager, their commission offer will be somewhat more. For instance, a common arrangement might be a draw of $2,000 against a 25 percent commission, versus a straight 33 percent commission in a commission-only arrangement. Perhaps offer a prospective manager the option of either set-up. Just be sure that your projections or past experience show that a person is likely to sell enough to make at least or more than their draw when you offer that option—otherwise there's not enough money in sales to offer that arrangement. Then, note the person's reasons in making their choice. A really hot-shot, confident salesperson will take the commission-only arrangement if he or she knows it offers the prospect of paying more. On the other hand, the person may have some valid reasons for needing the draw, such as high debts and a low cash-flow situation at present. Consider these reasons, along with the other factors you use in deciding who you want in the job.

Also, I would recommend setting up any arrangements on a 30- to 60-day trial basis. Of course, the sales manager should get credit for any sales made or initiated during that period, whether you make this a permanent arrangement or not. But then, you both have a time to assess each other and decide if you want to continue to work together. In particular, you want to be able to look at the person's results. How have your sales done in this period? And, if there are other salespeople working with your sales manager, does he or she seem to be effective in working with and motivating others?

Creating a Partnership

With the right person, a partnership can make a lot of sense if you're just starting off, don't have much money, and want someone to take over the sales/marketing function.

One advantage of a partnership under these circumstances is that you don't have to pay any money in advance to a partner, and you may find a partner who is willing to invest some capital into getting the business started. The major caution, though, is to be sure you have the right person, since once the partnership is created you're locked in together. Alternatively, set up a founding partnership agreement, which sets up a provisional arrangement for the first few months. Then, should you want to break it up early, the agreement offers various options to split apart easily.

In any event, if you do want a partner, think out in advance what you expect your respective roles will be and what you propose for a split. A 50-50 arrangement is common, but it may be that after you work out who does what, a different arrangement might be fair. For example, if you're putting up the money as well as providing the product or the service, maybe it makes more sense to set up a 60-40 or 67-33 split. Or perhaps allow for a sliding split arrangement based on how the company evolves. In any case, it's a good idea to go over your proposed arrangements with a lawyer after you and your prospective partner tentatively agree, just to be sure there aren't some unexpected sticking points that could cause problems in your arrangement later on.

As part of your proposal to a prospective partner, you should also work out your expectations and projections for earnings as best you can, just as in seeking to hire a manager. (See the Sample Projected Sales Estimate, Exhibit 2.) This will help your potential partner decide if this represents a good opportunity, and what the possibilities are for business growth.

I would also suggest keeping some kind of commission plan as part of your partner's compensation, even though he or she will also be sharing in the profits. This way, there will be some immediate pay-off tied to sales, which will help to keep motivation high. If there's only a far-off profit down the road, this can be a damper on the motivation to sell. By the same token, include some ongoing source of pay-off for you.

What to Look for in a Sales Manager

Whether you decide to hire or seek a partner, there are certain qualities you want to look for in your sales manager. First, you want someone with those characteristics that make a good salesperson generally. Second, if that person is going to be hiring other salespeople to be part of a sales group, then that person must be good at leading and coordinating other people. Third, the person should have a track record of previous management experience, preferably in sales, and a few good references. Finally, look for integrity and a strong sense of ethics. Whoever is heading up your sales effort is going to be setting the tone for everyone else in how you present your product or service to customers. And for long-term growth, integrity and ethics are crucial.

More specifically, some of the qualities your sales manager should have—many of these are true for any good salesperson—are the following:

- **Persistence**—he is willing to stick to things and not give up.

- **Willing to Work Hard**—he enjoys the challenge of doing a job well and putting in the hours necessary to see it through.

- **Open to Risks**—he isn't scared off by difficulties and has the courage to try new things that promise a good chance of success.

- **Is Well Organized**—he has goals, a plan to achieve them, and is good at details and follow-through, so he or she can carry out a project from beginning to end.

- **Learns Quickly**—he has knowledge in a wide variety of areas and is receptive to learning more.

- **Has a Good Track Record in Direct Sales**—he has actively called people to make contacts and has achieved successful sales results.

- **Likes to Compete and Win**—he has entered competitions before, has won, and likes to take on new challenges.

- **Is a Good Leader and Teacher**—he has previously coached or taught others and has directed and managed people.

- **Takes Initiative**—he is creative in coming up with new ideas and activities, and follows through in putting them into practice.

- **Has Made Money in Other Fields**—he has a record of success in whatever he or she does.

- **Willing to Learn**—he is receptive to learning new information and new techniques for doing things, because this is the only way to keep getting better in today's world of change.

- **A Good Listener**—he wants to hear what other people need and want in order to give them satisfaction—the key to good sales and to effectively managing other people.

- **A Good Motivator**—he can inspire others by his or her words and example.

- **Likes Other People**—a trait that is crucial for anyone in sales management, as this is truly a people business.

- **Has a Positive, Optimistic Attitude**—a must for anyone in sales, and more so for anyone in sales management, because a sales leader has to be able to look constantly on the bright side of things and keep going, even when he or she doesn't get positive results. In turn, a sales leader needs this to keep the people he or she works with high and motivated, too.

So, when you talk to a potential candidate to see if he is appropriate to take over a sales management role, ask questions to learn if he has these qualities. A few years ago in a book, *Strike it Rich in Personal Selling*, I made up a chart listing the kinds of questions to ask to determine if the person has star quality as a sales leader. Well, here it is. Use it to help you assess the person you're considering for this role (see Exhibit 3).

Finally, apart from all these basics, you need someone who reflects your own style of doing business. You need someone who is going to represent you and your vision of what the company should be, because in a very basic sense, your sales manager, whether someone you hire or your partner, is an extension of you, and he will provide the role model for the other salespeople in your company. So, choose carefully, and here you should usually trust your gut level sense. Here, some of the things to note are the person's appearance, style, and personality. Are these qualities that represent you? For example, if you're a very polished, urbane, sophisticated type of person and want your product to appeal to this kind of person, then choose a sales manager who has this image. Conversely, if you are more of a down-home, folksy person, find someone who feels down home and folksy, too.

Exhibit 3.   The Qualities to Look for in Your Star Recruits

Qualities to Look For	Questions to Ask
1. Persistance and Willingness to Work Hard	
Has a strong desire to succeed	How much do you want to be successful?
Is willing to keep going, even when others give up.	What are you willing to do to achieve this success?
Invests time in hard, but productive work.	How do you feel about working overtime? Are you willing to work weekends, give up vacations?
Is willing to work long hours and do more than expected to achieve a result	Have you worked on any project which others tried to get you to give up, but you completed it successfully?
Is future oriented	What are your goals for the future?
Tries a little harder to offer more than the competition	Do you do any volunteer work? Why did you choose to do the volunteer work you do?
2. Well-Organized and Goal Directed	
Has goals	What are your goals?
Has a plan to achieve these goals	How do you plan to achieve your goals? What have you done so far to achieve them?
Sets up an organized work schedule and plans each day	Do you plan what you are going to do each day? How do you do this?
Is good on detail work	How do you like taking care of details? Have you managed an office?
Able to coordinate projects so they run smoothly; follows through from the beginning to the end of a project	What kind of projects have you been in charge of? What kind of responsibilities have you had on these projects?

Exhibit 3.   (continued)

Qualities to Look For	*Questions to Ask*
3. Interested in Learning and Self-Advancement	
Likes to learn	What is your educaticnal background?
Learns quickly and retains information easily	Do you learn fast? What are some examples of this?
Has taken special courses, such as home study, adult education, or correspondence courses, or has taught him/herself some skill	What sort of courses and programs have you participated in during your free time?
Reads widely	What have you read recently? What do you like to do in your free time?
4. Willing to Compete and Eager to Win	
Has a competitive spirit	Are you active in sports? Have you been involved in any sports competitions? How did you do?
Eager to take on challenges	How do you like corpetition? Do you look for opportunities to compete?
Willing to take on difficult jobs that seem almost impossible and make them work (such as tuning around a company that is losing money or helping a brand new candidate win)	What is the most diff.cult job you ever did? What was the outcome? How do you account for your success? Have you ever raken on an almost impossible task? What was it, and why did you decide to do it?
Has a record of entering and winning in competitions	What kind of awards have you won?
Has strong desire to win	How important is it to you to win?

Exhibit 3.   (continued)

Qualities to Look For	*Questions to Ask*
5. Works Will with People and Takes the Initiative in Working with Them	
Likes people and feels comfortable working with them	How do you like working with people?
Has previously made calls on people to get them to do something, such as vote or contribute to some cause	Have you been involved in any political or fund-raising campaigns? What did you do?
6. Good at Teaching and Managing People	
Has been a coach, teacher, or group leader	What kind of experience have you had in leading groups? Have you done any teaching? What did you teach?
Is good at and enjoys imparting his/her knowledge or skill to others	How do you like leading groups or teaching?
Is a popular or well-respected leader of people (as a committee head, political leader, office manager, etc.)	What kind of managerial experience have you had? How many people did you supervise? How did you like being in management? How successful do you consider you experience managing others? Why? Have you ever run for a political or other office? What were the results?

Exhibit 3. (continued)

Qualities to Look For	*Questions to Ask*
7. Has Creativity and Influence	
Is very creative	What would you do if you were marketing this program?
Comes up with new ideas easily	What kind of innovations or changes have you introduced on previous jobs or projects? What was the response to them? What did you do to see that these changes were carried out?
Is receptive to change and seeks new ways of doing things	How do you feel when someone tells you to do something differently? What do you do? Do you like doing things the way others do them? Do you frequently think about doing something another way?
8. A Previous Track Record of Success	
Has been successful in an outside sales job (such as selling cars, insurance, or consumer products), where he went to the customer and was able to sell the product	What kind of experience have you had in direct sales? What kind of success did you have selling different products?
Has made and accumulated money in other fields, including selling	What business ventures have been especially successful for you? How did you measure your success?

In short, besides making sure your sales manager has the basic qualities that contribute to success, you should feel there's a fit between your personal style, the image you want to present of your company, and the style of the sales manager representing you.

Where to Find Your Sales Manager

Once you decide whether you want to hire someone, or would rather get a partner, there are two key sources to tap—advertising or organizations with sales people.

Advertising. If you're looking to hire someone, your local newspaper classifieds are ideal, and if you have a business daily or weekly in your area, try that, too. Normally, plan to list your ad under Sales Management or Sales Manager. However, for certain specialty products or services, list the industry first, and then sales management—since people who want to be in that field will look there, though they may look under sales, too. But because there are so many different sales positions listed, your ad can be hard to find. For instance, I found this to be the case in advertising travel positions. I had more serious, committed people call when I advertised under travel, rather than under sales.

Briefly describe your product or service in the ad and what type of selling or management is expected. Note whether you are paying a commission only, or a commission and a draw, and what kind of background is expected. For example:

> Sales Management. Gift products. Must be exper. in direct sales. Sell to companies, organizations. Comm. only. Call:

It's important to be specific and state qualifications and commission arrangements in advance to do some prescreening in the ad, so you reduce the number of calls you get from inappropriate people.

Then, when people call, be prepared to do some additional screening on the phone, as well as giving some more details. I've found you can cut down the time you have to spend on the phone and can be more efficient in who you arrange to meet to talk with further if you are prepared with an organized response for your calls. For example, prepare a brief outline or script of what to tell the caller and the questions to ask. I would suggest responding with a sentence or two to tell the caller more specifically what the job entails; then quickly ask the caller to tell you a little about his own background in sales, so you can decide in a very preliminary way if the person might have the qualifications you seek. If so, set up an interview; for a sales manager, I suggest this be one-on-one, although in recruiting salespeople you can easily do a preliminary interview with several at a time.

If you want to find a partner, your ad should go under Business Opportunities, rather than in the Help Wanted section. In fact, advertising here, you may even find someone to put up some money for a share of the business, which helps to show the person is willing to make a real commitment. Even if you don't expect this, at the very least you'll find someone who is very willing to work on a commission only arrangement in return for a share in the business itself.

As in the help wanted ad, be specific in what you want the person to do, and note your partnership/commission offer. For instance:

> Partner with sales management background sought for small gift products business. Become sales manager. No investment req. Commission/partnership arrangement. Call:

As in advertising for employees, be prepared in advance with your response to calls. Say a few words to give more details on your company, and then find out about the caller to see if he or she has the background and the interest to make a good fit.

Organizations with Salespeople. Besides advertising, you may find certain organizations in your city that are for salespeople, or have a large number of members with sales backgrounds. Some of these groups even have jobs files, so you can indicate your interest in finding a sales manager. Some examples of groups with national organizations that may have a chapter in your city include the Association of Sales and Marketing Executives, and the National Association of Professional Saleswomen. Also, your chamber of commerce may have some business networking events and a directory of people in different fields. Other local sources include leads clubs, tips clubs, organizations for older business and professional people looking for work (such as 40 Plus in many cities), and civic groups of business people, such as the Lions Club, Rotarians, and Soroptimists.

CHAPTER 3

Recruiting Salespeople: Organizing Your Own Sales Team of In-House Salespeople or Independent Distributors

There are two ways in which you might decide to organize your own sales team. One is if you are hiring the salespeople to represent your company's products or service, whether on a part-time, full-time, or draw/commission/salary basis. The other is if you are setting up a sales network as part of a multi-level or network marketing distribution program. In both cases, you will have do much the same things in training, motivating, and supporting your people, and you will have much the same considerations on what to look for in recruiting people for your group.

However, there are a few key differences. In recruiting your own in-house sales group, you will generally expect to have a closer relationship with your people, because they will be working solely for you and representing your own company. You will also probably expect to be more selective, particularly if you expect to work on a draw against commission basis. By contrast, if you are recruiting independent distributors, you are essentially recruiting salespeople to go into business for themselves, with support provided by you (for which you get a commission override on what they sell). But then, once you recruit them, they are representing the company whose products you are distributing under your sponsorship—and they generally will have the right to change lines of sponsorship down the road if they are able to show good cause why they should do so (i.e., they aren't satisfied with the sponsorship support they are receiving). Another difference is that most MLM/network marketing companies today provide all sorts of back-up training, and motivational and support assistance in the form of company literature, tapes, videos, and sponsor-led or company-organized presentations, rallies, conferences, and the like, whereas when you are the company, you have to develop and provide your own materials. Then, too, since salespeople joining an MLM/network company see themselves as going into business, they will normally expect to spend something for their own sales kit and sales materials, as well as product samples (and even make some of their own purchases as a consumer). On the other hand, when you bring in-house salespeople into your company, they will normally expect you to put up the money for the sales materials they use, or at most they will expect to put up a returnable deposit for any materials they take, if the cost is sufficiently high, subject to a full return of their money if they drop out and return your material. Finally, because of these key differences, the usual approach in MLM/network marketing companies is to pursue a less selective, more inclusive, recruit-anyone-with-potential strategy. Then, sponsors put the most effort into cultivating those who show the most potential and interest. Meanwhile, others can still participate in the program to whatever extent they wish (i.e., just selling occasionally and attending occasional presentations and sales meetings; or even just being a customer in the program and dropping all or most efforts to sell).

Much of the following information will be useful for those working with distributors in an MLM program. However, because people organizing MLM/network marketing sales teams have special considerations, and often prefer to look at material designed specifically for people going into this kind of business, the rest of this chapter focuses on working with in-house salespeople (though most of these suggestions will apply in MLM/network recruitment efforts, too).[1]

Some General Guidelines in Hiring Sales People

The rest of this chapter assumes you have decided to act as the sales manager, either permanently, until your company gets large enough to create a separate sales manager position, or on a temporary short-term basis, until you find a capable person to take over this role (and possibly it may turn out that one of your salespeople may in time fill the bill; so in recruiting, if you are looking for a sales manager in the near future or down the road, think about each sales recruit as potential sales manager material, and perhaps consider grooming one of these people to take over this role, should you find someone who you think may be good).

Although you usually do want to be more selective in hiring an in-house salesperson as compared to an independent MLM/network marketing distributor, you normally don't need to do the kind of in-depth interviewing suggested in hiring a sales manager, particularly if you are just hiring someone to work on

---

1. Those who want more specific information on setting up this type of sales organization are referred to these other works by the author: *Get Rich Through Multi-Level Selling* (Self-Counsel Press); *Strike It Rich in Personal Selling* (New World Books, originally published by Avon); and *Success in Multi-Level Marketing* (Prentice-Hall).

salespeople first decide to come aboard, many of them will come and go, and you can't be sure of their commitment until you have a chance to see how well they perform (and they have a chance to decide if they are going to be sufficiently successful and make enough selling your product to stay with you). Thus, you don't generally have the time to do such intensive screening in the beginning, unless you are going to be recruiting someone to sell a very expensive type of product, where the salesperson is going to have a great deal of responsibility for these items (i.e., such as selling very expensive jewelry, custom art, tour packages, and the like).

But barring these special considerations, I feel it makes sense to determine that the person has some of the basic qualities of being a good salesperson, through using a brief application form and a short, perhaps five- to fifteen-minute interview. Then, consider the first few weeks a period of trial and testing to see how well the person works out (and be aware that the salesperson will consider this a time of trial and testing for himself as well, as he will ask himself if he wants to keep selling for you).

If the person can sell well, you'll start seeing some results in the form of sales or at least some strong prospects who seem likely to respond with some additional follow-up. If not, you can quickly terminate the arrangement, and very likely the salesperson will want to do this too. After all, if he or she runs into difficulty selling your product or service, and is depending on a commission, he or she won't stay around very long. So, the first weeks represent a kind of self-screening process, and in time, you'll find out from the field who's good and who's not. Then, you can work with the people who are good to build them up into a strong team, and let the others go. Later, when you bring in new salespeople, plan to integrate them with those you already have, so they can work together, either in nearby territories where they can support one another, or through an override system, where the oldtimers can supervise the newcomers.

Getting Ready to Start Recruiting

When you start looking for potential salespeople, be ready with all your sales materials and product literature, as well as your response to callers, so you're ready to go when people respond (see Chapter 8 on preparing this). When you're looking for a sales manager or partner, you can discuss all these things in the course of an interview, to get the person's input on what you need. Then that person can help you in developing those materials, since he or she will be actively involved in providing leadership.

But if you're just getting salespeople to sell for you, you need to get geared up, so they can get right out there and sell for you right away while their initial interest is still high. Otherwise, if you hire your people and take a few weeks to get organized after that, you'll find most of your new recruits have drifted away and gone on to something else.

Another key consideration in recruiting is what kind of person do you want, and whether you want someone to work on commission only or will pay a draw, which you should already have determined by now (as discussed in Chapter 1). The answers to these questions will affect how you advertise and recruit, and where you direct your recruitment efforts. In turn, your product will help determine the best type of salesperson for you.

For example, ask yourself:

- How complex is it to sell this product? If it requires extensive product knowledge (such as a computer or high-tech product), or if it requires good sales skills and training (such as a beauty product that must be demonstrated), then you need a more experienced person. If it's an easy-to-explain consumer product that requires minimal training, then a person with limited or no sales background could do it, as long as he or she has the people skills and personality that are the raw materials for making a good salesperson.

- Is the product directed towards a certain market (i.e., a certain age group, sex, lifestyle, income level, etc.)? If so, it's a good idea to find salespeople who have characteristics similar to the target group's; they're then better able to develop good rapport with their prospects and make a sale. For instance, if you have a product that appeals to college students, find college students or young adults to sell it. If your product appeals to suburban housewives, hire women. If you want to hit the business and professional market, use men and women with previous business experience. Certainly, many salespeople can cut across markets and sell to virtually anyone. But you'll up your sales generally if your sales force shares characteristics with the people you're trying to sell.

Deciding How to Pay and How Much

The other major consideration before advertising is how much to pay, and in what form. Should you pay commission only? A draw and a commission? Or a salary alone, with possible bonuses? It depends on what you want to do, and how much you can afford.

Normally, as previously noted, salespeople work on either a commission or a commission and draw arrangement. But under certain circumstances, a salary might make sense. For instance, if you plan to do the follow-up and presentations to customers yourself, it might be helpful simply to hire a person who will get on the phone and make lots of preliminary calls to find out the right person to contact and make the initial "we'd like to send you information" call. Or maybe this phone person's job might be to go through an introductory script in order to get the person to set up an appointment with a salesperson who will follow-up later. In this case, it might be appropriate to pay the person a small hourly wage—say $5 to $7 per hour. Possibly, this small wage could be combined with a bonus for every appointment that results in a sale—say $5 for the base salary, and perhaps 10 to 20 percent of every sale that results.

With a draw and commission arrangement, you have more control over your salespeople than you do with a commission only. In this case, they are more like regular employees, and you can expect a more regular commitment, such as a certain number of hours a week for a weekly draw. Or you can use a low base hourly rate, such as $4 to $5, and apply that against any commissions earned.

When you use this kind of a draw system, you should provide a place for people to work so you can supervise them and make sure they are in fact putting in the hours expected. Typically, this kind of system is used with fairly unskilled salespeople who are just learning the business or have had only a few low-level sales jobs before. Since the salespeople are drawing a base wage, the commission rate is much lower than it would be in a commission-only arrangement. But then, such salespeople usually need a base wage because they can't afford to work on spec; their cash flow isn't enough. Then, too, they may lack the confidence of the salesperson willing to work on commission only.

In any event, this draw and commission approach often works well when you have a fairly simple product to sell that lends itself to a direct sales approach to the general consumer (such as trips to Hawaii, photo portraits, or a membership in a consumer club). Then, the salesperson simply gets on the phone, possibly with the aid of some telemarketing equipment to do the dialing, and makes a number of calls until contacting an interested prospect. Or he or she may go door-to-door, or perhaps operate out of a booth at a flea market or fair. Such selling is fairly routine, and the salesperson needs a base pay to continue to do it. The commission provides an extra incentive for the salesperson to try to do well.

You'll find many more salespeople who are willing to work under an arrangement where they can at least count on a small base salary each week. But you'll also find that many of the best salespeople would prefer to have the opportunity to make more on a commission-only arrangement, if they like the product, since they know they are good and are confident they can sell. For example, the big earners in insurance, real estate, securities, travel, and other fields all work this way.

If you do use a commission-only system, however, your relationship to your salespeople changes, for then they are working for you as independent contractors. As such, they are free to choose their own hours, and you can make your office available to them, but they may prefer to work out of their home. Basically, whatever they decide to do is fine within the policies and procedures you set. What you should be concerned about are the results. You don't have to pay anything unless they sell; but then, you don't gain anything either, and you've invested your time and effort in the process.

Thus, in setting up a commission system, structure it so it encourages a salesperson to take the initiative to get out there and sell as much as possible. Also, design the commission rate to permit the person to earn an hourly rate that is greater than he or she would earn working in an equivalent job that offers a salary or a commission and draw. Naturally, the economics have to work out for you in setting up the commission so you can afford to pay. But assuming the pricing and costs are worked out on your product to allow a good commission, along with a good profit, keep your commission as high as economically feasible. Your company will be more attractive to good salespeople, and they'll be more motivated to work harder, resulting in more sales and more profits for you.

A common commission arrangement starts at around 25 percent of the retail price and then provides added incentives, so a top salesperson can make as much as 40 to 60 percent on direct sales. Or, if you have an override system, about 25 to 40 percent might go to the person who makes the sale, and another 10 to 20 percent to the other salespeople who are involved in sponsoring, supporting, and supervising the immediate salesperson. However you do it, it's important to build in incentives, so there are extra rewards for a good performance. Besides the sale itself, that's how salespeople measure their success, so build up your commission—rewards system to both attract salespeople and then motivate them to sell.

Recruiting through Advertising and Other Sources

Once your sales materials and product literature are ready, and you have decided on what to pay and how, the next step in the recruitment process is advertising through your local newspaper or local sales and business organization—and deciding in advance how you're going to respond, so you can plan your advertising accordingly.

Deciding How to Respond to Your Ad

It's important to do this advance planning, because when you advertise, you will get numerous calls from people who you will screen out or who will screen themselves out. There are three basic ways to deal with this screening process, which will affect how you word your ad: (1) screening yourself, (2) using a prerecorded message, or (3) hiring someone else to do the screening.

Many sales managers simply prepare for dozens of calls and work up a brief response explaining the product or service and what kind of salesperson the company is looking for. Then, if he is still interested, they ask the caller a few questions about himself to see if they feel they want to pursue the process further through an interview.

However, if you don't have the time or inclination to go through this routine repeatedly, I would suggest using a prescreening recorded message on a special phone line. When people call, your prerecorded message briefly—in perhaps a minute or two—explains what the position entails and the kind of person you are looking for. Then, if the person is still interested, he can call another number to talk to you directly. The advantage of this approach is that it gets rid of the callers who are clearly unsuited, and you don't have to spend the energy to screen them out. Moreover, when people who are still interested call, you don't have to spend a lot of time with them explaining the product or service they'll be selling; they've already heard that. Instead, you can quickly ask them a few questions about themselves to see if they sound like good, qualified applicants. Then you can quickly move into setting up an appointment if they are.

In my own experience, about 50 percent of the callers hung up, and most of the rest who called did want to set up an appointment. Thus, each time I used a prescreening message, I saved about three or four hours of time on the phone.

Alternatively, if you don't like recordings, but don't want to answer all of these calls yourself, another possibility might be to hire someone for a brief period to answer your phone, using a brief script provided by you to explain what the position offers and the qualifications required. Then, your employee can take the phone number of still-interested callers, and you can call back. Or, your employee can give the prospective salesperson the number to call to speak to you.

In short, think about the best way for you to handle the first cut of callers, and work out your ad approach on this basis.

Where to Advertise

Probably the most productive source of leads will be your local paper's "Help Wanted" Sunday section. For most products and services, an ad that starts off with "Sales" will be fine. But for certain types of industries, which attract people who want to sell in that specific field, an ad starting off with the name of that field will be a good draw, such as: "Computers—Sales" or "Travel—Sales." Or perhaps try an ad under both, and use a different name in the ad for respondents to call, so you can see how each ad pulls and the quality of respondents you get from each.

For example, when I tried this for a travel company, the "Sales—Travel" ad pulled about twice as many calls—around sixty in all—than an ad that said the same thing but started off saying "Travel—Sales." However, only about a third (twenty) of the Sales—Travel callers were interested in a further interview, and only about half (about ten) of those who scheduled an interview showed up, and then only about half of those wanted to market the program (down to five). By contrast, with the Travel—Sales ad, which was more closely targeted to a sales-person in a specific field, there were much fewer callers to begin with, only about thirty. But then, about half of those scheduled an interview (fifteen), and almost all of those showed up (twelve). And of those who did, virtually everyone wanted to sell the trips (ten). And in the long run, those who answered the Travel—Sales ad stayed with the company for a much longer time.

Thus, the more you can target your ad to appeal to someone who is going to be interested in selling your particular product, rather than interested in selling generally, the more your ad will do some of the screening process for you. You may get less calls, but you are likely to get a higher continued interest rate from those who do. However, to avoid screening out those who might miss your more specialized ad, it might still be a good idea to place the more general type of sales ad. Just be aware that you may get different types of callers from each ad, and pay attention to these differences to help you decide your best approach when you're ready to advertise again.

Besides your local daily paper, another good place for certain types of products might be a local weekly featuring local events and lifestyles. Most major cities have these (such as the San Francisco *Bay Guardian*, *Village Voice* in New York, and Los Angeles *Free Press*). The job ads here often feature unique sorts of work for small and growing companies, and are designed to appeal to people who are looking for alternative, out-of-the-ordinary kind of jobs. So, if you have a specialty product that might appeal to such a group, this might be a good place for you to advertise. Check the help wanted columns to see what kind of positions are being advertised, and see if your opportunity would fit in. If so, it's probably a good bet your ad will pull well, too.

Finally, some organizations in your area for salespeople may have a jobs bank or jobs coordinator, so you can list your job opportunities. For example, a national group called the National Association of Professional Saleswomen does this, and they may have a chapter in your area. Another possibility is self-help groups for older workers trying to find jobs, such as the 40 Plus Club in many U.S. cities. Many of these people are extremely competent and eager to get to work. A part-time or short-term sales job might be very attractive to some of these people as something to fill in while they look for a high-level business or professional position.

What to Say in Your Ad

Commonly, the bigger companies have the bigger ads for salespeople. But your ad can be short—only a few lines—and still get a good response, and you can keep costs down. What's important is to highlight what the person will be selling, and indicate the main requirements, conditions, and rewards of the job. For example, our five-line travel ad that pulled so well said only:

> SALES—TRAVEL (or alternatively TRAVEL—SALES)
> Sell trips to Kenya, Egypt, and China to groups and organizations.
> Part-time. Commission only plus free trips possible. Dir. sales exper.
> preferred. Creative Travel. 567-2747.

In those five lines, we covered all the basics, as follows:

1. What is the person going to be selling? (i.e., trips)

2. Any special method of selling? (to groups and organizations)

3. Is it full-time, part-time, or does the person have an option? (part-time here)

4. How is the person paid? Commission? Commission and draw? Salary? (commission in this case)

5. Are there any special rewards, bonuses, perks of the job? (i.e., free trips)

6. What kind of requirements are there to qualify? What kind of background does the person need? (direct sales experience preferred)

Finally, when it comes to having the person contact you, I would suggest putting down either the name of a firm or the last name of a person to contact, plus the number. Having a specific contact is more inviting than using a number alone. Plus, using a firm name or last name looks more professional than simply using a first name, as in "Ask for Joe."

Another advantage of using a specific person's name is that you can code your ads, so you'll know to which one people are responding without having to ask. Just use a different name in each ad, and then keep track of who calls which ad. You can use a simple tally for this. In addition, it is useful to keep track of the names of the people who make appointments and which ad they called, so you can determine the quality of responses from each ad, when you discover which ad respondents show up for appointments, who gets involved, and who turns out to be a successful salesperson for your company.

If you are using a recording for screening, you don't have to say you are doing so in your ad. People will find out when they call, and if you say something like "call for recorded message," this can be off-putting, as well as make the ad cost more. Simply leave any mention of a recording out. Besides, people are more and more used to dealing with recordings these days.

Finally, if there are only certain times when you or an assistant will be receiving calls or when a message phone will be on, specify a time to call in your ad. Normally, people assume the ad means Monday through Friday, 9 to 5, unless you say otherwise, though you may still get calls at other times. It's much better to set things up so people can get through to someone who can set up a meeting right away if there is mutual interest. Otherwise, it's easy for potentially good people to get lost if you have to call them back and they are hard to reach. You end up playing telephone tag, and their interest can easily flag in the meantime before you make connections.

Responding to Calls

Be ready with a prepared response when people call. You'll use one approach if you or an assistant is handling calls, another if you're using a phone message to do some screening. In either case, a high percentage of the people who call will not be interested, or they may say that they are, but then not call back to make an appointment, or they may make an appointment and not show up. So be prepared for this, and view the recruiting process as a kind of funnel, much like selling anything. From your initial approach to the final sale—which in this case is recruiting a successful sales person for your company—a decreasing percentage of those you initially speak to will stay involved. Thus, expect and accept this, and when people don't follow through as promised, just cross them off your list. Still, you can take steps to save some time and effort to compensate for this, such as setting up group interview situations for several people, or having other things that you can do during the time when an individual interviewee doesn't show. Some more specific techniques to compensate will be discussed later.

Handling Calls Yourself or through an Assistant

When you or someone else handles the calls, have a general outline or rough script to follow to expedite the call. You can identify yourself by any name you want, or use several names, if you are using a coding system, because you can always introduce yourself as someone else when you actually meet the people who come for interviews. In fact, I've found when you're a small or growing company that it's actually more impressive to sound as if you are setting up the interviews with someone else than to be doing your own prescreening. So if you're taking your own calls, perhaps use another name.

In any event, since people want to know more about the job and the pay when they call, and you want to know about them, a good way to do this is to divide your script outline into three major parts, and plan on your initial conversation taking no more than one or two minutes. If the person has a lot of questions, simply explain that answering such questions is the purpose of the interview, and try to set up an appointment. Don't let someone talk you into a long conversation on the phone. It will sap your energy, and a person who is that interested should be willing to ask you these questions in person.

The basic parts of your outline should be these:

1. *An introductory statement* indicating that you (1) want briefly to let the person know what the job is about, (2) would like to know a little about the caller, and then (3) if there seems to be a good fit, you'd like to set up an appointment for an interview. For instance, you might say something like:

   "Thanks for calling. I'd like to tell you a little about the job and then find out a little about your own background in sales and (name your industry). Then, if you're still interested and it seems like there's a good fit, I'd like to set up an interview with you."

2. *A brief description of the position.* You can repeat what's already in the ad and then elaborate a little. For example:

   "We represent a travel wholesaler and we're looking for someone to sell trips to our destinations—Kenya, Egypt, and China—to groups and organizations. It's a part-time commission position and we'll train."

3. *A few questions* about the caller to see if he or she would be appropriate selling for you. For instance:

   "Now, can you tell me a little about you? What kind of background do you have in sales or travel?"

   Now listen both to how the person answers and what he or she says. The person should be well spoken and articulate. That's even more important than if the person has a background in sales or in your industry, because so much of direct selling involves getting on the phone and talking to others. If the person has any trouble presenting himself, that's a good reason for screening him out.

Then, if the person does have a favorable background, comment on this supportively to add that personal touch and help create a desire in the person to want to meet with you. For example:

"Well, good. It sounds like you might be really good for this position, since you've done all that. We've got a complete training program, but it helps when someone already has some good background experience."

Or, if the person's background is less relevant, but he or she still sounds promising and you're open to training, say this too, and encourage the person to feel he or she can do well by learning what to do. For example:

"Well, even if you don't have a sales background, it sounds like you'd be good at sales, because you have done a lot of work with people before. Besides, as long as you're interested in learning, we can train you in what to do."

If you do feel the person isn't right for the position, and the person hasn't already decided this for himself and told you so, simply explain politely why you feel the person wouldn't fit the position, thank him for calling, and say goodbye. For example:

"Well, we really are looking for someone with more experience in the field. But thanks so much for calling."

4. *A response to any questions* the caller has. Even if you try to be complete, some callers may still have questions, so be open to answering a few of them if you can. If you've hired an assistant, it helps to make up a list of anticipated questions with answers, so your assistant can field most questions, too. This is much better than having your screener in the dark, because then people won't end up feeling frustrated because they have been talking to an answering service or someone without any information, and you won't have to call back a lot of people who want answers before they will set up an appointment.

   However, limit your answers at this stage to two or three questions. If the person has more, this is the time to suggest that he or she hold these until the interview.

5. *A request to set up an interview.* If the person is still interested and it sounds like a good fit, the final stage is the call for action—in this case arranging an interview. At this point, it's better to offer just one or two options as to when you would prefer to schedule the appointment. This also gives the person a feeling there is some competition for the position, and the interviewer has a busy schedule, so the position sounds more impressive, important, and appealing. If the person can't make it, he or she will tell you, and you can always offer to see if you can work around the person's schedule, if some other times are more convenient.

   When you set up the interview, tell the person if it's going to be a one-on-one meeting or whether it will be done in a small group. Emphasize that it's important for the person to call you back if he can't make it, because

the interviewer will be counting on him being there. People will then take
the appointment more seriously, and some people will call if they change
their mind. You still may get some no-shows, but not as many. Finally, ask
the person to give you his phone number, just in case. Then, if you need to
do any rescheduling, you can always call to make a change.

A typical request to set up an interview might go something like this:

"Now, if you'd like to discuss this further, we can set up an appointment for an interview. I've got some openings at 3 on Tuesday and at
4 on Wednesday. How would those be for you? . . . Well, good, let's set
that up. Now, if something else should come up for you and you
change your mind, can you please be sure to call? Otherwise, we'll be
looking forward to seeing you then. Finally, if I can get your phone
number, just in case we have to call you about something . . . Thanks,
and we'll see you on (repeat the day and time of appointment you have
just set up to reconfirm)."

Handling Calls through a Recorded Message

In using a recorded message, your goal should be to give the caller additional
information on the position, responsibilities, payment arrangements, potential
earnings, and the qualifications or background you require or prefer. Start with a
brief introduction to let the person know he has reached the right number, and
explain that this recording will tell more about the position. Then, if he is still
interested, it will provide another number to call to set up an interview. After you
describe the position, responsibilities, payment, and qualifications, detail any special benefits or bonuses, and what time commitment is likely. Finally, conclude by
asking the prospect to call another number to schedule an interview if he is still
interested.

If a person does call, you or an assistant can take it from there. Now, setting up
the interview should be fairly routine, since your caller has been prescreened and
is likely to have few questions, as your recording has answered the most usual
ones.

As an example, here's the recording we used for callers on the travel ad quoted
earlier:

Hello. You have reached Creative Travel. If you are calling about the
ad, this will give you some additional details on the position. And
then you can call the number at the end of this message to arrange for
an interview.

We are looking for five or six salespeople to market our trips
around the San Francisco Bay Area to companies and organizations.
We represent a major national wholesaler based in New York who
organizes trips to Kenya, Egypt, Greece, China, and Morocco. Your job
will be to contact the representatives of these groups to set up trips for

the whole group, so the earnings can be quite substantial. We will supply you with leads and you can develop your own.

You can work on this part-time and there are sales management positions available. You will receive a commission on all sales, and it will also be possible to earn free trips as a bonus.

We're looking for someone who has had previous direct sales experience or has enthusiasm and initiative and is willing to learn. We provide a complete training program.

We've scheduled some times for some small group interviews on Tuesday, Wednesday, and Thursday afternoon. If you're still interested, please call (415) 658-2747 and ask for Ms. Randolph to set up an interview. Once again, that's (415) 658-2747.

If you'll review the message, you'll see it has these key elements:

1. Introduction. This introduced the company and prepares the caller to listen to a message and take down a number to call at the end if he or she wants to arrange an interview.

2. Details on the position. It includes some of the following important details:

   a. Number of positions open

   b. Where the positions are located

   c. Who the salesperson will be contacting

   d. The background of the company

   e. How the salesperson will be approaching the individuals to be contacted

   f. Where the salesperson will get the leads

   g. How much of a time commitment is required

   h. The payment arrangement by commission

   i. The possibility of extra bonuses

3. The desired or expected qualifications or background of the salesperson.

4. The availability of training.

5. The types of interviews scheduled.

6. A request to call for an interview if still interested.

Interviewing

Once the interview appointment is scheduled, you can use the names and phone numbers of those setting up an appointment for tracking the effectiveness of your recruitment process, and in case you have to make emergency changes. But otherwise, there's no need to call people to confirm or for anything else. If people show up, fine. If not, that's to be expected, since in the interim, between the prospective recruit's call and interview, he may find another job, decide to do something besides sales, have a family problem—just about anything can come up. In general, I have found that about half the people who make appointments actually show up for group interviews; about three-quarters appear when they are one-on-one meetings.

When people do arrive, be prepared both to present your opportunity in the best possible light, and carefully assess the prospective salesperson—any interviewing situation involves a mutual screening. While you're deciding if you want that person to be part of your sales group, he is deciding if he wants to join with you.

For efficiency's sake, it helps to divide the interview into three parts, much like the phone call. In the first phase, you give a brief presentation about your product or service, showing what it is, why it's good, and how the salesperson will benefit from selling it. In the second phase, you get information about the prospect (or prospects in a group interview). Then, if you feel your prospect (or at least one in a group situation) is a likely recruit, you can go into more detail on your program and expectations. If not, you can diplomatically terminate the interview right there.

Using Individual or Group Interviews

Should you use individual or group interviews, or a combination of both?

It depends. Two key considerations are how many people you are hiring, and how complex your product is to explain. Another factor is how many people you have to talk to and how much time you have. Probably, the more people you are hiring, the longer the interview needed to explain your own program; and the less time you have, the more a group interview arrangement makes sense as being more efficient to do some initial explanation and prescreening.

Say you are seeking only one or two people. Then, individual interviews can make more sense, because you may only need to interview a small number to find some people you want, and these interviews also can help to give you a more personal feel for each prospect, which may be especially important because you'll be working closely together. On the other hand, if you want to hire a group of people to handle different territories or types of contacts, a group interview to select those you want to talk to further individually works well.

The complexity of your presentation can be an important consideration too, because if it's quick and simple, you can easily meet with prospects individually to explain everything. On the other hand, if you have to go into detail to show exactly what you're offering and how to sell it, then, due to time considerations alone, a group interview format can speed up the preliminary stage of your interview process. For example, in marketing the travel program, we had videotapes describing the countries where our trips were going, as well as some detailed information on our commission program and our approach to groups and organizations. It took about an hour to present this material, so it made more sense to use the group format; it would have taken too long to present the same complete explanation and demonstration to everyone.

Finally, look at the response rate you're getting in deciding what type of meetings to have. If you only get a small number of replies, then one-on-one meetings might be the way to go, barring other considerations. On the other hand, if you're overwhelmed with too many callers, it's probably best to use a group, so you can meet most or all of your callers who still want to talk after going through your phone screening process. The advantage of this combination prescreen and interview approach is that this way you don't have to cut off potentially good prospects so soon because you have simply run out of time to interview more people. Thus, you can more effectively interview and decide who would be best for the position.

In short, if you're debating between which interview format to use, individual or group, the following are the key factors to consider in choosing one or the other. Weigh them according to what is most important to you.

Key Considerations	Factors Favoring an Individual Interview	Factors Favoring a Group Interview
Number of positions	1-2 positions	3 or more positions
Complexity of explanation	Quick and simple	Long and involved
Amount of response	Small number of prospects	Large number of prospects

Whichever you use, be flexible as circumstances arise. For example, if someone sounds like a really enthusiastic and qualified prospect, but can't make a group meeting during the times you have scheduled, perhaps meet with that person individually, or consider setting up an additional group meeting at this time. That way, you may get a good person you wouldn't be able to meet otherwise.

Setting the Stage for the Interview

Much as in other situations today, impressions and images really count when you're doing an interview. So whether you're interviewing one person or several at a time, it's important carefully to stage-manage the interview setting, so your prospect gets an image of a successful, growing, dynamic company. Also, you can use this pre-interview time to learn about your prospective salespeople by asking them to fill out a form about their background. Another good use of this time is to provide some literature about your product or service that prospects can glance through while they wait to talk to you—it not only helps to give some more details on the company and what salespeople will be doing, but it is useful to have in case you are running late and they have to wait.

If you have an attractive, impressive-looking office for individual interviews or access to a nice conference room for group interviews, that's ideal. But if not, there are offices and conference rooms you can rent on an hourly basis from companies that provide a full range of office and secretarial services. Sometimes you may have to pay a monthly retainer to maintain a minimal presence in the office (often as low as $25 to $35 a month), but some companies will rent the space on an available basis. It's an easy way to appear successful when you're first getting started or have limited funds, and this image is important in getting good salespeople to represent you.

When people first arrive for the interview, it's helpful to have some material on your company or product available for prospective recruits to look through; they can then be learning a little about your opportunity as they wait. Also, this is a good time to give out a background information sheet or questionnaire for them to fill out. Later, if you are doing individual interviews, you can go over this with the person. Or if conducting a group interview, you can hold onto these forms and review them after the introductory presentation, to help you decide with whom you want to talk further. As noted in Chapter 1, such a questionnaire will give you an idea of each person's background in sales, where he prefers to work now, and how much time he wants to commit. In a group interview, a sign-up list is a good way to track how many of your callers have shown up, and from where.

In preparing for one of these presentations, it helps to use a checklist, to be sure you have all the materials you want to show or hand out and any equipment you need. You can use the checklist (Exhibit 4) for this purpose.

Once everything is set, you're ready to do a good interview.

For example, in setting up the travel company sales team, we used a rented conference room, and we set up the room so that when people arrived, they picked up a background information questionnaire to fill out, along with various brochures on the company, the trips, and the marketing-commission plan. We used a checklist to be sure all of the slides, projectors, travel books, and presentation folders we wanted to show were on hand.

All this advance preparation does take extra time, but it's well worth it, because it helps to make your interview go smoothly, and it helps to impress your prospects with your company and your professionalism, so they're more likely to want to work for you.

Initiating the Interview by Establishing Rapport

As in any meeting with someone new, start off with a few minutes of rapport-building. This gives you a chance to help the other person feel comfortable and feel comfortable yourself. Additionally, you can use this as a chance to get to know a little about the other person and feel more of a connection.

For instance, in the one-on-one interview, start with some small talk. Did the person find your office easily? Is he or she busy with lots of interviews now? Or maybe make a few comments yourself about something, such as how much re-

Exhibit 4.   Checklist for Interview

Equipment Needed

> VCR _____
> Monitor _____
> Slide Projector _____
> Screen _____
> Slide Trays _____
> Extension Cords _____
> Other (list)
>
> _____
> _____
> _____

Handouts and Introductory Information

> Brochures _____
> Flyers _____
> Marketing or Commission Plan _____
> Product Information _____
> Catalog Sheets _____
> Other (list)
>
> _____
> _____
> _____

Other Materials

> Sign-up Sheet _____
> Background Questionnaire _____
> Marketing Techniques Book _____
> Sales Training Tapes _____
> Samples of Sales Aids _____
> Video Tape _____
> Audio Tape _____
> Slides _____
> Other (list)
>
> _____
> _____
> _____

sponse you've been getting, or how glad you are the person could make the interview at this time and get through the traffic without any problems. Another possibility, if you've been able to review the person's questionnaire or resume, is perhaps to comment on something here that impresses you, and then follow up with a few more comments based on the person's response.

In the case of the group interview, making brief introductions can help to break the ice. My own approach is to start by introducing myself briefly, to set the tone. Then I ask everyone else in turn to give their name, and say a few words about who they are, what they do, their experience in sales if any, and why they answered the ad. This approach helps to make everyone feel at home, and the brief response provides a little bit of insight into each person. You have a sense of who you're talking to, so you can orient your presentation accordingly.

Also, start this introduction process on time. Even if you have only one or two people, and some of the people you expect haven't shown up, it's best to wait no more than five or at most ten minutes beyond the scheduled time, out of respect for the people who have come on time. The latecomers can always talk to you later about what they have missed, and, of course, some of the people who are missing may be no-shows.

Presenting Your Product or Service

Consider the first part of the interview as your own sales presentation to your prospects. You want to show why they should want to market your product. Also, besides selling that, you're selling the advantages of working with you.

This way you quickly deal with some key questions the prospective salesperson wants answered to help him decide if he wants to work with you:

1. What am I going to be selling, and why is it good? What are the benefits of this product or service, and how does it compare with the competition? What are the credentials of the company?

2. How am I going to be selling it—by phone, by personal contact, by referral? To whom am I going to sell it—to individuals? groups? companies? What kind of sales materials will I have to sell it (i.e., catalog sheets, promotional pieces)?

3. What am I going to make by selling it—how am I going to be paid?

4. How are you going to help me sell it? What kind of leads, training, coordination are you going to provide?

Thus, the initial stage of the interview should be designed to quickly (in about five to ten minutes) provide answers to these issues. And this is where all the sales materials and training materials discussed in the first chapter become important—to show that you not only have a good product or service to sell, but you have the back-up materials and support the salesperson needs to sell it.

If you are using a one-on-one interview format, you can cover these questions informally; in a group situation, plan on a more structured and formal presentation dealing with each of these points. More specifically, I suggest covering each of these four issues through an informal conversation or organized presentation, as follows.

The Product and the Company Behind It

This is the time to show your product or service and any literature you have developed that describes it. If your product needs to be demonstrated, such as a mechanical device or book on time planning, do that. If you have brochures or catalog sheets or a background sheet on the company, give these out. If you have acquired promotional clips or testimonials about what you're doing, show these too.

One approach might be to give out this product/company and promotional material as handouts to people who come to the interview. Alternatively, put a set in a presentation folder that people can look at.

Then, as people are reviewing this material or afterwards, briefly talk about your product, making sure to cover the following points:

- The major benefits
- How it compares to the competition and in what ways it is better
- The track record of the product or service to date, if any
- The credentials of the company

In short, you're selling your company and your product to the prospective salespeople. They need to feel it's saleable in order to sell it themselves.

The Sales Approach to Be Used

Now, in talking about your company's sales approach, you want to highlight your vision of your prime target market and how you envision your salespeople reaching it. If people are already experienced in direct sales techniques, you may not need much detail here, since they will already know what to do. But otherwise, clarify some of your specific sales ideas, so people can feel comfortable with what's expected of them. For example, some people may feel perfectly fine about calling people on the phone—they've done plenty of phoning before—but if they have to make a personal presentation, they can't do it. Alternatively, other people hate cold calling on the phone, but love meeting with people in person. So let them know the parameters. Will salespeople have to do both? Can they use the technique they prefer themselves? Can you coordinate people with complementary skills to work together as a team? Clarify briefly what they have to do, and show them any sales materials they will use to do it, such as catalogs, price lists, telephone sales scripts, presentation books, etc.

In brief, this section of your introductory presentation should, in a sentence or two, cover these major points:

- The target market for the product (i.e., age, income level, lifestyle)
- The types of groups or individuals the person will be contacting (i.e., associations, companies, nonprofits, individuals)
- How the person is usually going to be contacting these groups (i.e., by cold calling, by personal presentations, by referrals, etc.)
- How the person will get the leads (from you, from his or her own initiative, or both)
- The sales materials the person will have (i.e., catalog sheets, price lists, scripts, presentation books)
- Who will provide the materials (are you supplying the materials at no cost; does the salesperson have to make his or her own copies; is there a charge for sales materials?)

By going over these issues, you show your prospective salespeople that you have carefully thought through how best to sell your product, and that helps them feel confident they can do it, too.

The Payment Arrangements

Now comes the real meat-and-potatoes question: what's in it for me? Now go into your commission or draw and commission plan, and show how that translates into hourly, weekly, or monthly earnings.

This is the time to hand out your marketing or commission plan, so your prospects can see what's possible in black and white. Then, briefly explain how it works, and possibly use a flip chart, poster, or blackboard to help you. The kinds of points to cover here include:

- What is the base commission (and draw if any)?
- What are the earnings on an average sale?
- How many sales are likely on a day? In a week? About how many sales can be made in an hour? Or, for a more expensive product, how many hours are typical for a sale?
- How do these typical sale patterns work into average earning per hour? For ten/twenty/thirty/forty hours a week?
- What kind of bonuses are possible for good sales?
- Are there overrides for supervising or recruiting other salespeople? If so, go into the structure of your sales network, and use a chart to illustrate.

- What sort of track record, if any, do other salespeople who have worked with you or others in the company have? If there's no track record, because it's a new company or new way of selling the product, what makes you think sales will reach the level you project?

- When or how frequently will people get paid?

You don't have to go into this information in great detail. In fact, you might just cover the highlights, and wait until you have found out more about your prospects and feel they may work out, before you spend a lot of time and effort on the details. The point is to explain just enough so your interviewees feel working for you will be financially worthwhile, assuming you feel they would be good selling for your company. You can go over the specifics later.

Your Training and Support

Few salespeople can simply go out there and sell. They need to have continual direction, motivation, and support. Now's the time to show the back-up help you'll provide.

For example, if you have worked up sample phone scripts, letters, and price comparisons, show these. If you will be putting together product updates and newsletters, publicity releases, or ads, use examples to illustrate. If you plan a training program, such as using sales and motivational tapes in your meetings, explain what you plan. And if you've worked out guidelines for selling or have a marketing training manual, or other support materials you are providing, show these, too. Perhaps include these in a presentation book you can flip through in your presentation.

The key types of support your prospects will want to know about include:

- What kind of guidance will you give on how to sell (i.e., sample phone scripts and letters)?

- What kind of promotional support will you provide for your product or service (i.e., publicity releases and ads)?

- What sort of data will you provide to keep your salespeople well informed on the market generally (i.e., sample price comparisons, surveys of the competition)?

- What kind of creative marketing ideas do you offer (i.e., a list of suggested marketing ideas)?

- What kind of coordination will you be doing to provide leads and prevent conflicts due to overlapping sales efforts?

- What kind of company image back-up do you offer, in the form of letterheads, business cards?

- What kind of day-to-day support do you provide in the form of the use of an office, typewriter, phones, etc.?

- What kind of training do you offer through written materials, training meetings, etc.?

- What kind of regular meetings do you plan to have to provide motivation, guidance, and general coordination?

Obviously, you don't want to spend a great deal of time on the particulars of all the support materials, meetings, and training techniques you offer. The main thing is to show that all this support is available, so you can impress your prospects with the ways you can help them. To a great extent, you can demonstrate the range of help you offer by flipping through a presentation book and showing examples of phone scripts, letters, PR releases, ads, price comparisons, marketing idea lists, letterheads, and the like. Then, you can quickly list the other types of back-up programs you offer, such as meetings, training aids, and the availability of the office, if they need it.

Getting Information About and Assessing Your Prospects

Once you've completed your brief introduction to your company, you can swing into the second phase of the interview—finding out about your prospective salespeople and assessing whether you would like them to work with you, assuming they want to do this. There are five main areas in which you want to get information, using both your questionnaire and personal questions and observations to obtain this.

Appearance. The person should look neat, well dressed, and well groomed. That's basic. But beyond this, consider if the person presents the appropriate image you want for your company. In a company with a consumer product with broad appeal, this image could be broad, too—perhaps anyone who looks businesslike and professional might be suitable. But in some companies with a specialized product line, you might want a special look—such as a certain air of authority to sell to high-level executives or a sophisticated career-woman image to sell a beauty product line for career women.

General Attitude. Here you are looking for the kind of traits associated with success in sales. You may notice some of these qualities as the person talks and expresses himself. For instance, the person may have a very optimistic, people-oriented approach that you pick up right away through his friendliness and upbeat comments. But to find out about other qualities, such as the person's willingness to persist, do hard work, and be organized, you might ask questions such as: "How many hours a week do you usually work?" or "Would you say you like detail work or not?"

The main qualities to look for that make a good salesperson include the following:

- Having a positive attitude towards life
- Being willing to work hard
- Showing persistence
- Being well organized
- Paying attention to details
- Being outgoing and liking people
- Enjoying competition
- Being open to challenges and willing to take risks
- Having a strong interest in getting ahead

General Skills. Certain skills are associated with success in sales, so note if the person has these skills, too. Again, you will pick up some of these by observation, or just ask. The key skills to look for in this category are:

- Being articulate—any salesperson needs to be able to express himself well.
- Being a good listener—the key to finding out what others want is listening; a salesperson who talks too much, even if he talks very well, can easily talk himself out of a sale by saying the wrong things.
- Willing to learn and be taught—you need someone who can take direction from you and is interested in personal improvement, as that's the way to get better and move ahead.
- Being good with people—you want someone who can work well with both customers and the other members of your team.

Sales Experience, Interest, and Potential. Here you have to decide how much sales background you require and how much you're willing to train. Usually, the more sales background a person has, particularly in your field, the better, because that person will be equipped to be more productive, since he already knows what to do. But with training, other people with the enthusiasm and interest—and the skills associated with good selling—can have excellent potential. If you're willing to spend the time in training, consider them. Otherwise, stick with experienced people, and look for the following to assess experience:

- Years of direct sales experience, including: experience with phone sales, experience in making personal presentations, and experience in your particular field, if possible.
- Track record of success in selling, as measured by previous earnings, and any awards for good selling.

- References and recommendations.
- Participation in any sales and business groups (suggests an even stronger commitment to sales).

Fit with Your Sales Team and Sales Approach. Consider how well you can work with this person and how well he will fit in with the rest of your team. To a great extent, the importance of this fit depends on how you're setting up your organization. For example, if you are recruiting a large number of people who will be working fairly independently, this question may not be very pressing. But if you want to work closely with a small group, having a good fit matters a lot. Assuming it does, the kinds of factors to look at include:

- The geographic areas where the person wants to work—this is important if you plan to assign territories, since you'll want to choose people for your team in different areas. You may need to choose between two people who want the same place, or perhaps one of them can be persuaded to work in a different spot.

- The types of groups or organizations the person wants to contact—you need to know this if you want to split up the types of groups people contact within the same area. Then, too, if a person has strong contacts in a certain market segment you want to reach, this can be a key person to have on your team.

- Special skills the person may have that can complement your sales program—for instance, if a person has experience in giving talks and presentations or PR, this experience might be tapped to benefit the whole group, so they would be important to have on the team.

- Amount of time the person wants to commit—does he want to work part-time? Full-time? And if part-time, does this person have enough hours to make the kind of commitment you need for your program? For example, he should be willing to spend at least five to ten hours a week if part-time, and either meet with you and attend a meeting at least every two weeks or more.

- Personality considerations—these are very subjective, but ask yourself, do you like this person? Do you feel comfortable with him? Do you feel he will make a good team player with the mix of people you want on your team? Then, trust your gut-level feelings or intuitions. If you feel any hesitations or feelings of mistrust, you're probably right, and you shouldn't work with this person.

In the one-on-one interview, you can usually get this range of information in talking with the person and reviewing the answers on your questionnaire, and perhaps looking at a resume. Then, if you do feel the person might work out, you can let him know, so if it's mutual, you can go on with the next phase of the interview—going into your program in more detail and explaining the logistics of coming aboard. Or if either you or the prospect have decided "no," you can simply conclude the interview. Should either of you be unsure, go on with the interview and make your decision later.

In the group situation, you normally will want to talk one-on-one later with those people who are still interested and who seem to be possible candidates, based on your initial impressions. You can do these talks right after the formal group interview with those who want to stay around, or set up an appointment for later. In this type of interview, it helps to glance quickly over the questionnaires when they are first turned in before you start your initial presentation; that will give you an initial sense of who is there. Then, as you speak with the group, observe and listen carefully to get a general impression of each person's appearance, attitude, skills level, sales background or potential, and personality. If anyone seems a possibility at this point, go on to the final phase of the interview and ask the people who are still interested to stay around to talk with you further or to set up a one-on-one appointment. Or, if you feel nobody's quite right, politely wind things up to save time.

Going into Detail on Your Program and Expectations

Once you have established that your prospective salesperson is still interested in the possibility of selling your product, and you are still possibly interested in having him sell it, or aren't sure, it's time to move to the final phase of your interview. This involves going into more detail on your program and expectations, and winding up with arrangements about where you go next.

How much detail will depend on the complexity of your program. The idea is to give the person a better sense of what he will be doing in selling for you, and how you plan to work with those you recruit.

For example, in this final phase of describing the travel program, we showed people about fifteen minutes of videotapes on our destinations, to illustrate the places the company went to and show how people would be selling the program by doing presentations for groups and organizations. Then, we gave out and discussed a marketing techniques manual that those who joined our sales team would receive, went over the marketing and commission plan in further detail, described our plans to develop and distribute leads to people, discussed our plans to have regular weekly meetings for coordination and training, and reemphasized our expectations for a minimum time commitment each week. In addition, we invited questions, and, finally, we asked those people who were still interested to let us know after the meeting. Then, if we both agreed there was a good match, they could attend an orientation meeting to go over the program and selling approach in more detail, and after that they could join our sales team and begin selling the trips.

Likewise, in your interviews, I would suggest covering these main points:

- Provide more complete details on your products or services and their market. Use a tape, video, or demonstration to help you explain.

- Provide additional information on the marketing approach you are using and the commission you are paying. If you have prepared marketing materials or a booklet of techniques, you can give this out and discuss this now (though point out this is only for those joining your team).

- Describe what you will be doing now and in the next few weeks to provide back-up and support, such as distributing leads and having regular meetings.

- Restate any requirements or expectations you have for those joining your group, and ask for a commitment from those who come aboard (for example, an agreement to participate for at least five or ten hours a week and attend one weekly sales meeting).

- Invite people to ask questions and clarify any points as necessary.

- Let people know what they need to do now if they still want to join your sales group (such as attend an orientation meeting to prepare them to sell your product, or go out on a sales call with you).

- If this is a group interview, make arrangements to meet with those people who do want to join your group, so you can discuss this with them and decide if there is a good fit. If so, they can get involved right away.

- Ask those still interested to fill out your background questionnaire if they haven't already done so, so you can go over this when you meet with them.

Deciding Who to Recruit and Planning for the Future

Sometimes, by the end of the interview, you can make a recruiting decision, and so can the prospective salesperson. But often, one or both of you may want to think it over. If you can, it's preferable to come to this decision on the spot, while the prospect is there and has just heard your presentation, since now he is likely to be most enthusiastic and ready to go.

But, if necessary, allow that space for either or both of you to think it over. For instance, a person may be going on a few other interviews and wants a chance to decide which he prefers. Or maybe the prospect wants to review his commitments for the next few weeks to be sure he or she has the time to commit. Then, too, it may be that you have to choose between two people for a certain territory and you can't decide on the spot; you want to talk to each person individually first.

In any event, once you decide who to recruit, have the next step already planned, so you can immediately involve the new recruit in your sales effort. There are three major ways to do this: (1) inviting a person who is ready to go right out and sell; (2) having the person accompany you or an experienced salesperson on a sales call; or (3) inviting the person to attend an orientation, where you will go over the program in more detail and discuss how to sell it. I would suggest using these approaches under the following circumstances.

Inviting a Person to Start Selling Right Away. This typically happens with an experienced salesperson. He feels ready to go out and sell, and if you have a relatively simple product or service, and he has a good sales background, probably he can. In this case, take advantage of his knowledge and enthusiasm by encouraging him to go out and sell right away, while his level of excitement is high. Let him know you are open to other possibilities, such as having him join you on a sales call or attending an orientation. Also, invite him to call if he has any questions. But otherwise, if he wants to sell right away and you feel confident he can do it, by all means, let him do so.

Having the Person Accompany You on a Sales Call. This approach works especially well when you are just recruiting one or two new people, and have the time to work with them personally. Then, you show them what to do by having them watch you do it. This way, they can listen in when you're making some calls, or they can come with you to watch you do a presentation. You can then discuss what happened, and perhaps they can do the call or presentation next time while you observe, until they feel comfortable going out on their own.

This is also a good approach to use later, once you have gotten a sales team organized and are adding additional recruits. In this case, the new salesperson can team up with an experienced person to show the novice the ropes. This is also an ideal arrangement if you are using an override system, in which the experienced salesperson is sponsoring or supervising the newcomer in return for a bonus on his sales.

Inviting the Person to Attend an Orientation. This approach works best when you have recruited a number of new salespeople at the same time. At the orientation, you describe your product or service at length, and further explain some techniques, so the new person can get out there and sell it. Afterwards, you can offer individual help to people who want it. But very often, after such an orientation, people will feel ready to start selling immediately, so you can move into more of a motivator-coordinator-administrator-trainer role, as will be discussed in the next chapters.

Moving On

Your recruiting decision is a key one; your sales program is only as strong as your salespeople. Thus, the critical first step is making sure your new recruits are good.

Then, after you've got them, it's important to swing right into the next phase, which is the focus of the rest of this book—working with your people as a motivator-coordinator-administrator and trainer. That way you keep everyone motivated and your sales organization running smoothly, and you help your people to know exactly what to do.

CHAPTER **4**

Orienting and Motivating
Your Salespeople

Once you've decided to bring a new salesperson aboard, you need techniques to assist that person quickly to get out there and sell, and help to keep the momentum going. A good way to do this, and part of your initial training, is to begin with an individual or group orientation, or one-on-one field demonstration to discuss your program and how to sell it. Then, depending on circumstances and the person's experience, you can provide additional individual or group training.

What to Include in Your Orientation

Whether using an individual or group orientation, focus on describing your product in more detail and on the main selling points and techniques, so the person feels ready to start selling. Whatever orientation approach you use, include some discussion of the following.

An In-Depth Presentation of Your Product to Build Product Knowledge and Confidence. This helps your salespeople fully understand what you do, so they can explain it to others, and feel confident the product is good, so they can share this conviction with others. To this end, underline the main benefits and important features of the product and how it compares with the competition. If you have multiple products, first go over the program as a whole, to provide a view of the big picture; then deal with each product individually.

For example, if it's a product line, go over the various items in the line, and explain how they are used and by whom. If it's a jewelry line, show the pieces and describe the typical customer (i.e., a middle-income woman in her thirties or forties). If it's a service, discuss the types of services offered and the usual buyer (i.e., large corporations, small businesses, doctors and professionals). Outline the prices for various services.

Your Presentation Materials for the Customer or Client. Go over any catalog sheets, flyers, brochures, testimonials, price lists, videotapes, presentation books, publicity handouts, etc., that will be used to show off your product to the customer or client. Go over the contents, and how and when to use these.

For example, if you recommend that the salesperson put together a presentation book from your materials, illustrate how you have done this, and how the salesperson might best show this to the customer. If you have copy masters the salesperson can use to make his own copies, hand these out and suggest how to use them (i.e., print on colored paper and add in your name and phone number). Or, if you've got a demonstration video, show this and comment on how to use it; if the tape runs more than ten or fifteen minutes, perhaps invite the salesperson back when convenient to view the tape on his own.

Your Ideas About Techniques for Approaching the Customer and Closing the Sale. The amount of detail in your orientation depends on the experience of your new salesperson. If he or she is relatively experienced in sales, you need to say much less and can leave more to his or her discretion. If the person is new to sales, you have to explain much more.

Minimally, plan to go over your specific policies for selling, based on past experience with what works best. For instance, if your salesperson will be contacting corporations, and companies in certain industries are more likely to buy, pass this on. Likewise, if a certain sales approach works better for your product (i.e., making a call, sending out information, and making a follow-up call to set up an appointment), describe and recommend this technique.

If you have written guidelines and policies, hand them out at the orientation, and go over the major highlights to underline that these materials are important. At the same time, note your willingness to be flexible, so that any salesperson should feel free to suggest changes to you or to adapt your general approach to his own style, as long as he follows the basic policies, which can't be changed now or at all (such as a policy of getting a 25 percent deposit for any customized work).

Your Plans for Future Meetings and Trainings. Describe your own plans for regular meetings and trainings, and what attendance you expect of the salesperson.

For example, it is usually good to have at least weekly or biweekly meetings, with you personally or as a group, to keep salespeople involved and motivated. If you plan to have these, let a new salesperson know, so he can plan accordingly. Also indicate if you expect attendance at these meetings, or if this is optional, although it is preferable to have some regular contact, since those who come to meetings are more likely to stay involved and committed. Without regular meetings, salespeople on commission only are likely to lose their connection with you and gradually drift away.

Likewise, if you offer a training program of any type, explain what it will feature. For instance, note who will lead this, whether it will use sales tapes, if you will bring in special speakers, etc. Also, get some input from your new salespeople about what they need, so you can incorporate this into the training if needed, or modify the planned training based on people's experience. This way, you can find a good balance: you don't want to spend time on specific sales techniques that people already know, yet you don't want to leave anything valuable out.

Your Sales Commission and Bonus Program. In this part of the orientation, cover how your payment plan works. If you have a written policy sheet or marketing plan describing this, review it with your new salesperson, so you know everything is clear. Perhaps use a flip chart or blackboard to explain.

Although you may have covered the main parameters of your commission and bonus arrangements in your initial recruiting meeting, now is the time to review pay arrangements in detail. Also, you can use this discussion to motivate with some incentives, by emphasizing the benefits for good performance. Specifically, the points to highlight here include:

- The basic commission and bonuses for high volume;

- Overrides, if any, for sponsoring and supervising other salespeople;

- How this commission translates into real money based on a typical sale;

- How much money is likely to be earned in a day based on the number of sales likely;

- How this commission rate translates into an approximate hourly income.

This detailed discussion of your payment program will help your salesperson estimate his likely return, so he can better decide how much time to commit to selling for your company.

If there can be a more long-term commission pay-off, make this clear, so the person can plan ahead. For instance, in some fields, there is a high commission on a single sale—but it usually takes several months before the sale is finalized and the money earned, such as in real estate, where there is a wait for escrow to close, or in travel, where the commission usually isn't paid until the person returns from a trip.

Additionally, go over any procedural arrangements, such as how to get credit for a sale (i.e., put one's own code number on an application; fill out a form; list the name of a referral for subsequent credit if that person becomes a buyer).

Finally, if possible, explain how you will handle multiple contacts by two or more salespeople (i.e., will you split the commission based on each person's contribution, or will you give credit to the person who closes the sale).

Your Sales Aids and Training Materials. Go over any sales aids and training materials the person will be using right away, and briefly highlight the contents of any other materials you are handing out for future use.

You want to focus on what the person should do to get started now, so he isn't confused by too many ideas or information.

For instance, if you have a suggested phone script and follow-up letters, give these out and review how to use them. If you have a how-to-get-started list, go over your recommended steps so the person has an immediate plan of action to start. If you have a leads list of contacts, give this out. Or, if the salesperson is expected to develop his own leads, you might suggest some step-by-step guidelines on what to do, unless he already knows.

Other possible sales aids to give out include sample price lists, ads, additional marketing ideas, and a list of recommended resource materials.

Your Letterhead and Business Cards. Some companies give the salesperson his own business card right away; others wait a short time until the salesperson seems to be working out. In either case, you can start by providing some blank business cards the salesperson can use until he gets his own personalized cards. Also, if he wants to send out letters, you can provide some stationery (or give out a copy master, so he can make his own).

Other Materials to Hand out at Your Orientation. Another good addition to the orientation materials you hand out are copies of any newsletters or updates you have, if you are doing this. A current issue, and possibly some back issues, are useful to let your new salespeople know what you have been doing.

Also, if you have several salespeople, and it's appropriate for people to work together, you might hand out a list of your current salespeople and make some recommendations on who people might like to team up with and how. For example, someone who is experienced might team up a with newcomer and work out a commission split accordingly. However, let the decision to work together come from your people; you just provide the suggestions.

But there is one caution in doing this. The technique may help you in creating powerful sales teams when you feel confident your new people are really going to stay with you. But if you have any uncertainty about people's commitment to your program, it may be better to wait, because you may find that instead of using your list of salespeople to form teams, a salesperson who drops out may use this list to try to recruit your new people away from you to do something else. Use your own judgment in deciding what's best for you.

Using an Individual Orientation

This approach is appropriate when you are recruiting only one or two new people, and have the time to talk with each person individually. Also, it works well when you already have a strong sales group and an override system, because then you can assign one or two of your new people to someone already on board for orientation and supervision.

An ideal way to use this orientation is in tandem with the one-on-one field demonstration, where the new recruit goes on a sales call or observes what a more experienced salesperson does. Depending on your style, you can do this orientation in several ways: (1) do a demonstration first, then follow with a discussion about what happened and what the person should do; (2) combine the demonstration with an orientation; or (3) go through a more detailed introduction, and then take the person out in the field. Or, if a person is experienced and you have done a comprehensive orientation, further demonstration may not be necessary; after an introductory orientation, the person is ready to sell right away.

In the course of the orientation, cover the topics previously mentioned. However, in a one-on-one discussion, you can go over these topics informally, and personalize your presentation to suit the person. For example, if the person wants to target a certain market because he feels more comfortable with that group (i.e., a woman teacher doing part-time sales wants to contact educational organizations and schools), emphasize those aspects of your product line that will appeal most to that group.

Or, say the person would rather use a sales approach without phoning. Show that person ways to get started right away using non-phone techniques, such as talking to program chairmen at meetings, sending out letters, or passing out flyers at organizational events.

Also, allow plenty of time for questions, and encourage them to gain insights into what your new salesperson needs and stimulate further inquiry. Then, knowing what's needed, you can arrange to supply it, to help give your salesperson the necessary tools—which will translate into even more sales.

In short, use this individual orientation to get to know your new salesperson, as well as detail the product or sales information he or she needs to know. You can then adapt your program so your recruit can best use his own strengths to promote it. Then, too, this personal touch helps build rapport, which contributes to motivation. The money that comes with each sale is certainly important. But equally important, perhaps more so for many, is each salesperson's desire to feel competent, powerful, productive, and appreciated. In turn, your support can help your salesperson feel this way—and feeling good will contribute to more motivation to perform and higher sales.

Using a Group Orientation

The group orientation format is ideal when you have just recruited a group of salespeople to market your program, or you expect that only some of your new people are likely to stay with the program. In this case, your orientation not only provides information and motivation, but is part of the winnowing process to build a solid team.

Indeed, any orientation serves several purposes:

- It helps to create a team spirit among the people working with you.

- It enables you to do some preliminary coordination of your sales group: by finding out where people are most interested in working, you can provisionally divide up your territories.

- You can use the orientation to do some additional screening to determine who really is serious about working with you of those who initially expressed of interest.

For example, the following approach worked well for me when I was organizing a sales group. At my initial group interviews with about two to five people each, I invited those people still interested to attend an orientation, and I found out what times people preferred. I set tentative dates for two orientations at the interview—one in the morning for people with days available, and one in the evening for people with full-time jobs. Then, several days later I called everyone to finalize arrangements and confirm who still planned to attend.

Next, I made a list of the people I was expecting for each session, and I organized the materials I planned to hand out (marketing plan, flyers, brochures, marketing techniques manual, sample phone scripts and letters, etc.) into piles on a table for distribution. As people arrived, I invited everyone to take a set of everything, and explained we would go over these at the orientation.

Then, using an agenda for what I planned to cover, I began with introductions. I used these to help everyone feel comfortable with the group and also to learn more about who these people were and where they might work well if they remained involved. Specifically, I asked people to share briefly about their background in sales and in general, say where they were from, and indicate how much time they wanted to put into selling the program (i.e., under ten hours a week; ten to twenty hours; or more).

Next, I covered the topics previously described, referred people to the handouts as appropriate, asked for questions, and worked out details for when people would like to attend an ongoing series of sales and training meetings each week. Finally, I concluded by giving out blank business cards and letterheads to those who were still interested, and I worked out times when those who wished could use the office to make phone calls and send out letters.

In short, if you are planning a group orientation, the following arrangements are suggested:

- Invite the people who you want to recruit from your initial interviews to attend a group orientation.

- Work out the preferred times, and set up one or two orientation meetings for about three to eight people. Do any follow-up necessary to let people know when the meetings are.

- Make a list of the people you expect to come, and unless someone has a good excuse, eliminate any no-shows from from your sales team. You'll find those who are casual about attending this initial meeting are likely to be casual about marketing your product.

- Organize in advance the materials you plan to hand out, and lay it out so people can easily get a complete set. (Either organize it in complete sets yourself, or have separate piles for the different items you are handing out, so a person can take one of everything.)

- Plan an agenda, listing what topics you want to cover in what order. One possible sequence might be the following, though adapt this agenda to your own style and preferences:

  - An in-depth presentation of the product or service

  - A review of presentation materials for the customer or client (i.e., catalog sheets, flyers, brochures, testimonials, price lists, order forms, video tapes, presentation books, publicity handouts, etc.)

  - Ideas about how to approach the customer and close the sale

  - Plans for future meetings and trainings

  - Sales commission and bonus program

  - A review of sales aids and training materials

  - A distribution of the latest newsletter and current sales representative list

- Begin the meeting on time; if anyone is late, wait no more than five to ten minutes, to show respect for the people who came on time, and fill in any latercomers as necessary after the meeting.

- Start with introductions to help everyone feel at home and find out about the people in your group, for future planning. Briefly say who you are and describe your plans for the company. Then ask people to introduce themselves briefly. Suggest that they might do so by sharing the following information: their name, their background in sales and in your product field, where they are from, and how involved they want to be in marketing the program (a few hours a week, ten to twenty hours, more than this).

- Go over the major topics listed in your agenda, and ask people to ask questions, if they have any, after you finish each topic or at the end of your formal presentation.

- If you don't already have background questionnaires, ask people to fill these out now, and indicate when and in what part of the area they would like to work.

- If your office is available for your salespeople to use, work out the appropriate arrangements. (For example, find out who wants to work at home and who wants to use the office; and if you need to, schedule times when different people can use the office, and ask people to sign up to use it.)

- Work out arrangements for the best time to conduct your regular sales meetings and trainings. Find out, based on people's past sales experience, who is interested in an ongoing training program, and schedule that, if appropriate. A good time to do this might be for thirty minutes to an hour before or after the regular meeting. Then those who want to can come for the training as well as the meeting. Also, get a sense of how often people are willing to come to meeting. Once a week is ideal, but if that turns out to be tough for a number of people, perhaps schedule a meeting every two weeks—the minimum, in my opinion, for keeping a sales group together. Have some discussion to decide on the best time or times for the most people, and schedule the meeting now. Preferably, have just one sales meeting. But if it's difficult to get everyone together, which it may be with many people working part-time, schedule two—perhaps one in the morning or afternoon for the people who are free days, and perhaps one in the evening for those who work days and are free at night.

- Give out a letterhead and blank business cards to those who are still interested in working on your program, assuming you still feel they will fit in.

- If people feel ready and you feel they are, too, let them know that they can now go out and sell, and quickly review the steps they can use for immediate sales.

- If people don't feel ready or want some additional selling tips, indicate that you will be glad to work with them individually or in a group, to provide further training. Suggest a follow-up training meeting or invite people to join you for an in-the-field demonstration of your own sales techniques.

- Indicate that you are always receptive to further questions and want to do all you can to help your people be successful. Also, say you welcome their feedback and comments. Then, end the meeting. At this point, everyone should have a plan for the future and be ready to go.

Using a One-on-One Field Demonstration

A one-on-one field demonstration is an excellent orientation and training tool to use in combination with an individual or group orientation. You or your sales manager can do this, or have an experienced person in your sales group do it—an ideal approach if you have an override or sponsorship system, where new recruits are brought in under an experienced person. This demonstration can be used for both phone calls and regular sales presentations.

The purpose of the demonstration is to give the new recruit a first-hand look at how someone who knows how does it, so he can learn from this role model. Then, after some observation, the newcomer can try to sell himself, while the experienced person looks on. As part of the demonstration, include some discussion about what the newcomer should especially watch for in observing the more experienced person sell, what happened in the sales presentation, and how he did if he tried to sell himself.

The following example illustrates using such a demonstration for a telemarketing approach, after I recruited some new people to market a savings club program. I invited them to listen in on an extension when I made a series of initial cold calls to potential customers. Then, I gave them a rough script, suggested they use this as a guideline, and asked them to try a few calls on their own while I listened to them. Afterwards, we talked about how and why I did what I did, and I asked them how they felt about what they did. Also, I made suggestions and asked them to suggest what they might do better next time.

In another example, showing a sales call demo, I went along with one of the two regular salespeople for a collection agency service, which regularly used this hands-on approach to train new salespeople. I observed while the salesman made a call to confirm his appointment. Then as we drove to the first stop—a hotel where he hoped to persuade the bookkeeper to turn over all her collection accounts to the agency—he explained what he was going to do. "I'll make a little small talk first to establish rapport," he said, "and then I'll swing into my presentation. I'll emphasize why the hotel needs our service and how much time and money they will save as a result." Then, he showed me a book of details on the services offered, along with some testimonial letters about the company. He also described some sales techniques he would be using to establish rapport. "I'll repeat her name frequently as we talk," he said. Thus, by the time we arrived at the hotel, I had a complete briefing on what to expect.

When we went in, he introduced me briefly as his assistant, and then, just as he had described, he went into his presentation. Since he had already prepped me on what to look for, I was especially aware of the sales methods he was using, and I noted how he moved from stage to stage of the presentation, starting with the small talk opening, and then going on to some questions to learn about the bookkeeper's collection problems and needs. Next, he went on to a brief highlighting of benefits, a more detailed discussion of the programs the agency offered, a discussion of how they could be tailored to the hotel, and finally he asked some questions leading up to the close. Afterwards, when we stopped for coffee, we went over exactly what he had done in more detail, so I could better understand how to use the techniques myself, had I planned to become a salesperson for the company.

This demonstration approach also is commonly used when the salesperson uses a demonstration to sell a product, such as a cooking demo to sell pots, a facial demo to sell beauty products, or a product-tasting event to try out a food product. This way, the salesperson can see for himself, in dramatic form, exactly how to do it. An alternative that some companies use is a videotape of a hands-on demonstration. Still, there's more impact when the new salesperson goes out into the field himself. Also, the conversation about the demonstration before and after the event helps to focus the newcomer's attention on some key techniques used in the field, so these have even more impact.

In some cases, after the initial demonstration and discussion, a new person will feel ready to go out and sell. But often, especially with a person with little sales experience, a few demonstrations are necessary until the person feels really confident. Then, too, if you have a relatively complex product to sell, a few demonstrations may be needed.

It's also a good idea to use more than one demonstration, to involve the new person gradually in presenting more and more of the presentation, as many companies do. For example, the experienced person can initially handle the opening, close, and the more important parts of the demonstration, such as discussing the major benefits and answering objections, and let the trainee show some of the details. Then, if the trainee seems comfortable with this, the next time he or she can do a little more, and perhaps a little more at a subsequent demonstration, until he or she is ready to go out on his or her own.

In some companies, after a single observation stage, the new salesperson might be turned out on his own and be ready. But in other cases, more time and direction might be preferable, say because the product line is more complex, or the salesperson needs more experience. If so, the trainee should expect to have someone come along on his first presentation (or series of presentations) to observe and give some feedback, and this may continue until both feel the salesperson is ready to go on his own. Or in some cases, a new person may prefer to team up with a more experienced salesperson and work together in this way.

In short, there are lots of options. It depends in part on your personal style, the complexity of your product, and the background of your new salesperson. If a person is relatively experienced to begin with, he probably won't need as much assistance in learning exactly what to do. Yet, even so, the experienced person may want to observe how you or your salespeople sell, since he is representing a new company, and may find it helpful to see your own approach.

Thus, in using a one-on-one field demonstration, adapt it to suit your own circumstances. Some of the major points to keep in mind are:

- Spend some time before and after the demonstration discussing what you are going to do or how you have done it. Before the demonstration, alert the observer on what to look for and what role he should play (e.g., your assistant who will be taking notes). In particular, advise him to note the phases of your presentation, the sales materials you will be using, and the sales methods you will employ. Afterward, review what you have done, and highlight the sales techniques that have been particularly effective. This is also a good time to ask the new salesperson to describe his own observations and reactions, and how he can use what he has seen in his own sales approach.

- If this is an in-person demonstration rather than a phone call, let the client or customer know who the new salesperson is (e.g., your assistant who will be taking notes). This way, the client or customer won't be sitting there with unanswered questions, while you are trying to get him to concentrate on your presentation so you can make the sale.

- Do the demonstration exactly as you would do an ordinary sales call on the phone or in person.

- To help the person recall what you've done later, possibly provide a phone script or sales presentation agenda as a guide.

- Recommend the parts of the presentation the new person should keep in mind when he does it himself. Suggest that the person should also feel free to adapt your approach to best suit his own style.

- After the first presentation, if appropriate, suggest that the new person do parts of additional demonstrations. Then, you can discuss what the person should do in advance, and afterward discuss how he did it. Be sure to get feedback from the person on how he felt about what he did, and how he can use this information in the future.

- If appropriate, accompany the new person when he does a presentation or two himself. Then, use any discussion sessions before the presentation to help the person get ready. Afterward, offer feedback and suggestions on how it went, and discuss what the person can do to improve.

In doing these demonstrations, your role should be not so much that of judge or critic; rather, you want to help the person by offering your advice and support.

Not every salesperson will feel this kind of help necessary, particularly if the person is experienced and feels he knows what to do. Therefore, if both of you feel comfortable with the new recruit going out and selling on his own after an orientation, fine. But otherwise, this demonstration approach is an excellent way of getting anyone, whether experienced or not, introduced to selling your product. It's a way to get the newcomer out in the field right away.

Keeping Your Sales Group Motivated

Besides training and coordinating your people, keeping everyone motivated is critical for effective selling. People have to feel enthusiastic to take more initiative, and that enthusiasm helps to make the sale.

Such repeated motivational efforts are necessary because selling includes dealing with plenty of rejection. A certain percentage of people will say no—even 90 to 95 percent is expected in some sales programs. Thus, salespeople need to remain up and inspired even during those down periods, so they can put day-to-day negative feelings and obstacles aside to focus on their ultimate success.

While some salespeople can motivate themselves, many need support from their sales leader or other salespeople to stay on track. Then, too, this assistance can help those who are already motivated do even better.

Some things you can provide, depending on the size of your group and the responsiveness of your people, are the following: (1) individual and personalized shows of support; (2) motivational and inspirational meetings; (3) awards and incentives for improved performance; and (4) special events to provide recognition.

Individual and Personalized Shows of Support

This approach is ideal when your sales group is still small, though you can use it with other methods as your sales team grows. The key is showing your personal interest, recognition, and approval on a one-on-one basis. Let the person know you are behind him and want to help.

For example, make an occasional phone call to see how things are going, and do so in a positive way. Let the person know you want to help, not that you are checking up to find out how many sales were made. Another possibility might be to offer a suggestion about a new sales approach you found effective, or maybe share information about an upcoming talk, article on sales, or inspirational book that might be of interest. Still another option might be to ask if a certain sales approach or leads referral list is working well—if so, good; if not, you'd like to offer your help to improve this.

When you call, your tone should be friendly and supportive, while the call should be direct and to the point. Your call is not to just chat, but to spark the person, to get him excited and motivated to sell.

If the salesperson does talk about any difficulties in response to your call, use this opportunity to discuss what to do to improve. If the problem is relatively simple (such as: "What can I say to get past the secretary?"), you can usually handle it immediately with some tips on what to do. But if the expression of concern indicates some deeper problem that needs talking over (such as: "I'm having trouble locating and contacting non-profit groups. What do you suggest?"), set up an individual meeting—or perhaps bring up this topic at your next group meeting, if others seem to be having this problem, too.

Another approach is to meet with a person individually to praise him if you feel he is doing well, or otherwise show support. Such meetings might also be used to get general feedback on how the person thinks things are going. Ask if there are things he would like to see changed or improved (a positive way to ask for criticisms or complaints), and if there are, indicate that you would like to take some remedial steps. What does the person suggest? Or, if you have some thoughts on the matter, share these and see if the other agrees. Maybe have a mini-brainstorming session to come up with new ideas. These motivational support meetings can be quite short—perhaps ten to thirty minutes—since your main purpose is to provide encouragement and show your desire to offer support.

Typically, a meeting in your office or over coffee is fine. But should you want to provide some special recognition or say thanks to the person for doing especially well, perhaps make the get-together a special occasion, such as providing a dinner or lunch on you to show your thanks.

Motivational and Inspirational Meetings

Once your sales group is large enough for regular group meetings, motivational meetings become important. Set these up as special meetings, or set aside a part of your regular weekly meeting for some motivational activities.

Using Sizzle Sessions

One type of meeting is the small "sizzle session," basically a get-together of about five to fifteen people, with a mixture of inspiration, training, planning, brainstorming, and perhaps a little socializing. The main purpose is to create enthusiasm or "sizzle," as well as come up with plans and ideas. Participants should leave feeling charged up and ready to go.

These sessions can be organized in various ways. One successful sales leader meets with the top leaders of his sales team in a restaurant during off hours—generally midmorning or early afternoon—and each person relates something positive that has happened with his or her sales effort. Then, people share ideas about how to create even more sales.

Another possibility is to have a different person in charge of leading each meeting and rotate the responsibility. Then, at the meeting, the leader guides others into thinking up new sales strategies and solutions to any problems, and then seeks to build enthusiasm to "go do it."

However you structure your meetings, the key to a good session is keeping everyone involved, thinking positively, and focused on coming up with ideas to deal successfully with the current topic. At such meetings, seek to avoid negative gossip about people not at the meeting, or about other companies and products. Such talk will only bring down everyone's energy. Furthermore, your emphasis should be on finding solutions, not on sharing problems. This way everyone feels that creative "sizzle," and feels part of a warm, supportive, positive, dynamic group.

Using Inspirational and Motivational Speakers

Another kind of motivational meeting is one that features an inspirational and motivational speaker or discussion. Some sales leaders occasionally have special meetings that feature this. Others may combine this approach with their regular meeting—designating perhaps fifteen to thirty minutes for a special speaker or discussion.

A good way to start off such a meeting or meeting segment is with some high-energy, upbeat activity. For example, in one sales group I belonged to, the leader—a Southern gospel type—began the meeting by having people introduce themselves or preface whatever they wanted to say with the statement: "I'm the Great So-and-So, and I'm . . . ('. . . excited to be here,' '. . . going to sell $1,000 this week,' '. . . raring to go out and contact at least ten people today.')." The approach may sound corny to some, but it worked. In fact, at some meetings, people outdid themselves with enthusiasm to say how great they were, because the sales team leader offered a reward—usually a $20 or $50 bill—to the person with the highest energy. For instance, one a man won by standing on his head as he yelled out "Well, I'm the great ___ and I'm going to break all records this week."

You may not necessarily find the "I am great" approach your style—I know it's not my own approach. But however you do it, the goal of getting people's adrenalin going is a good one. It intensifies motivation. It's like adding a fuel additive to the engine of a car to give it more kick. And you can use a more subtle approach to achieve this aim, too.

For example, a more subdued way to the same result might be to ask people to start by describing what they are really excited about right now, or what they are enthusiastic about doing in the following week.

Then, as everyone moves into a more enthusiastic, positive frame of mind, shift into the focus of the meeting. Some possible approaches might be:

1. *A Motivational Speaker.* Try bringing in an outsider if your group is large enough, or maybe have group members volunteer to be the speaker and talk about a motivational subject for about ten to twenty minutes. Such topics can be related specifically to sales (i.e., "How I Made My Sales Goals for the Month" or "How to Turn Nos Into Yeses"). Or the talk can deal with success themes generally (i.e., "Why Being Positive Guarantees Positive Results").

2. *A Motivational Tape or Video.* As an alternative to a speaker, try a motivational tape or video. To hold attention, keep this up to about fifteen minutes for a tape, twenty to thirty minutes for a video. Use either sales-related or general success-oriented topics, as noted above.

3. *A Report on a Motivational Book, Article, Film, etc.* Make this report yourself, or have a volunteer do it. Select the book, article, or film to review the preceding week. Then, at the meeting, the reporter both summarizes what he read or saw, and personalizes the report by expressing his reactions. Next, the reporter or the group discusses how the message of the book could be applied by group members to become more successful. Plan on about five to ten minutes for each report.

4. *A Discussion of the Message of the Motivational Speaker, Tape, Video, Book, Article, Film, etc.* Lead this yourself, or ask for a volunteer. The purpose of this discussion is to get everyone in the group reacting to the motivational message they have just heard, and thinking how they might apply it themselves. Each person in the group should be encouraged to say something, and the leader can either ask volunteers to comment or ask everyone say something in turn. Use the approach that feels most comfortable for your group. About fifteen to twenty minutes makes a good discussion.

5. *A Motivational Show-and-Tell.* Try a kind of motivational show-and-tell to get everyone motivating one another. Set up the meeting in advance by inviting everyone to bring in anything they think is motivational—stories, poems, illustrations, photographs, ideas, etc. Then, during the meeting, the meeting leader asks participants to describe what they have brought in. For example, one might to read a motivational poem and share his reactions; another might read from a short book with ideas for success; still another might describe a recent inspirational talk he heard. About ten to twenty minutes is a good time for this.

6. *Other Possibilities.* The possibilities for putting on creative, exciting motivational meetings are endless. The key is to keep everyone actively involved by varying the pace, getting people to contribute, and making any motivational ideas personal, so people see how to use these ideas themselves.

Then, conclude any meeting on a positive, uplifting note, so people feel ready to apply to selling what they have learned in the meeting.

A representative motivational meeting might go something like this. It's about an hour long—organized into these six segments:

- Opening Kick-Off—Introductions, Positive Remarks—five minutes
- Motivational Show-and-Tell—ten minutes
- Report on a Motivational Book—five minutes
- Motivational Tape, Video, or Speaker—fifteen minutes
- Discussion of Motivational Tape, Video, or Speaker—twenty minutes
- Concluding Remarks; Final Message of Inspiration; Song, Chant, etc.—five minutes

In summary, whether you use sizzle sessions, motivational meetings, or part of your regular meeting to motivate, do something to keep your group motivated. Your people will not only find the meeting content helpful, but will welcome your support in just putting these meetings on. Plus, they will get stimulation to go out and sell from each other. A way to view the motivational meeting is like a triangle, where the salesperson in the center gets three types of benefits—from you, from the meeting, and from other salespeople, as indicated below. And the results are more motivated salespeople—and higher sales.

Sources of Motivation

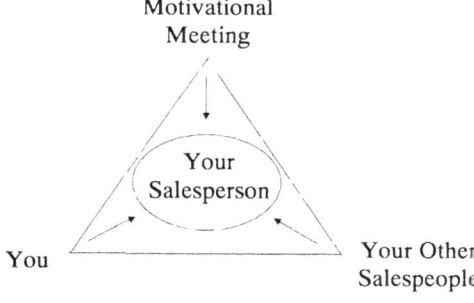

Awards and Incentives for Improved Performance

Another key motivator used by virtually all sales organizations is awards and incentives, to give the person recognition and often a financial bonus for having accomplished something. These also provide a reward to aim for.

Such motivators can become extremely elaborate as a company gets large, and some companies use spectacular awards and recognition ceremonies to present them. For example, Mary Kay has gala celebrations at exotic locations, where top performing beauty consultants are honored, and the highest achievers get the keys to a pink Cadillac. Other companies combine awards ceremonies with an elegant dance or party. Some give cruises and vacations to top salespeople. In fact, an incentive travel industry has emerged that helps to wine, dine, and pamper successful salespeople with luxurious vacation in glamorous locations.

Regular monthly award ceremonies are also used by some companies to combine recognition with providing tips to salespeople. For example, at one jewelry company where I was invited to speak on strategy tips, the Master of Ceremonies began the awards part of the meeting by introducing the top performers of the month, and the crown of achievement was passed from the top salesperson of the previous month to the new one. In addition, he handed out certificates and awards for those who showed the greatest increase in sales, the most improvement, the best attitude, and other improvements in the past month.

Sometimes, too, companies introduce special sales promotions, where they set up special sales goals during a certain time period. Then, those salespeople who achieve these targets can make extra commissions and get bonus gifts and premiums, for making these goals.

If you are still a small company and have only a few salespeople, you probably can't go all-out with this kind of pizazz. But you should still develop some kind of small awards or incentives program, and as your sales group grows, expand on it. Then, as you introduce different awards and incentives, notice which ones are most effective for your group, and develop additional incentives of this type. For example, some people respond more to financial bonuses; others more to recognition; some prefer special events and ceremonies; still others may be attracted by premiums, vacation packages, and trips. So get a sense of your group's wants, and tailor your incentive program accordingly to be more motivating. One way to find out these desires is to include some questions about them on a feedback questionnaire from time to time.

Also be aware that as your group grows, the types of motivators that are attractive are likely to change, since in the early stages of growth, financial incentives are especially important, while recognition and prestige-type awards become more powerful later on.

For example, some incentives that can be effective in the earlier stages of sales group development are:

•   A financial bonus for making a certain sales goal by a certain time

•   An increased commission rate for all sales made in a certain month

- A thank-you dinner or night on the town for your top performers
- A bonus gift when a person achieves a certain sales volume in a given month

These first-level incentives are all essentially financial in nature or involve a bonus gift. These kind of financial benefits pack more power in the early stages, because you don't have the group network established that makes recognition awards, ceremonies, and events so powerful. But as your group grows, you can start adding other types of incentives and rewards, such as:

- An award certificate (preferably framed)
- A plaque or cup signifying a certain achievement level
- A listing of the award or achievement in your newsletter
- A bi-weekly or monthly awards program as part of your regular meeting
- A special party or meeting to honor top performers (perhaps every few months to start; eventually every month or two).
- A specially made bonus gift, such as an engraved watch, leatherbound book for photographs, personalized luggage, etc.
- A weekend trip to a nearby location associated with having fun (such as a trip to Palm Springs from Los Angeles; a trip to Las Vegas from San Francisco)
- An extra bonus and perhaps a gift for having the highest sales volume, initiating the most new accounts, etc.

Use your creativity and knowledge of your sales group in deciding what would be an appropriate award. For example, if a salesperson is particularly interested in something, relate an award to that. (i.e., give a selection of tapes and records as a bonus to a a real music buff).

Similarly, consider the interests of your salespeople in shaping an awards event. For instance, if you're selling jewelry, a glittery, elegant event might be appropriate. But if you're selling health items, and your people tend to be more casual in style, maybe a picnic or an open-air festival in a tent would be more appropriate.

Another possibility, as your group grows, is getting a quantity of gift and premium items from an advertising specialty company. (Try under "Advertising Specialties" in your local phone book.) These companies feature all kinds of premiums and promotional items, including buttons, pens, key tags, glasses, mugs, certificates, t-shirts, trophies, executive gifts, recognition awards, watches, just about anything you can think of. You can order these personalized with the name of your company or the name of the person getting the award.

For additional ideas, ask people at other companies what kinds of awards and incentives they use. Use your own network of contacts, or try calling the sales department at other companies about your own size or a little bit larger, so you can learn what companies with similar resources and a similar sales force are doing, and what might be some future possibilities as you grow.

In turn, setting up an effective awards and incentives program will help your expansion by stimulating your salespeople to do that little bit more to gain increased commissions and recognition, which will result in increased sales and profits for you.

Special Events to Provide Recognition

Recognition events can run the gamut from acknowledging a salesperson at one of your regular meetings, to organizing an awards gala for an evening, to staging a few days of recognition activities combined with sales training, speakers, and more. In the beginning stages of organizing a sales group, you will be concerned mainly with giving recognition at regular meetings or at an occasional evening ceremony, so only these types of recognition events will be discussed here.

Using a regular meeting to recognize someone's achievement is a good way to begin. When you do, play it up. Make that part of the meeting special, so the person getting the award or attention really feels he or she is in the limelight. This approach serves several purposes. Besides making the person being recognized feel good, it helps motivate him to do even more. Also, it motivates the other salespeople observing the event to want to do more, so they can get recognized for their accomplishment, too.

A good way to provide this recognition is to save the awards until the end of the meeting; then have a break between the regular meeting activities and the recognition/awards part. This way, whatever you do feels more special.

You might also distribute an agenda at the beginning of the meeting that indicates when the regular meeting will end and when this special part will occur. Another possibility might be to create a brief program booklet on your typewriter or word processor, listing the people being recognized and for what. When you have only a few people, it may feel a little silly to do this, but people will still enjoy it. For example, I have been at meetings with only a handful of people, where it looks like everyone is giving awards to everyone else. But the people still feel very good about doing this, because they value the opinions of the other people there, even though they are a small number. Furthermore, the small ceremony can have a larger effect, because people can express their pride when describing their recognition, and can show off their awards to others, thereby reinforcing their feeling of commitment and motivation.

Providing special refreshments also helps to provide some extra pizazz for a small meeting. For example, get a cake and embellish the icing with the name of the person or people being recognized. Perhaps put in a candle for a certain level of sales volume attained (i.e., one candle for every $1,000). Maybe have some champagne. And consider using buttons, streamers, or other party favors to create a celebratory mood. Another possibility is to invite people to bring their own dishes, and encourage them to bring something special. Or maybe reserve a table in a nearby restaurant and move your celebration there.

Naturally, take into consideration the tastes and style of your own group in planning any recognition event. Just keep in mind that your goal is to do something special to make this more than a regular sales meeting, so that at least part of the event involves a recognition ceremony or celebration, and each person being recognized feels sincerely honored, and others can see you care about your people, too.

As for the recognition ceremony, provide a little ritual to make it feel special, such as saying a few words when you hand someone a certificate, premium, bonus check, or gift, to show your appreciation. Maybe say a little speech to describe what the person has done and how. Perhaps ask the person to say a few words about how he feels about the award or the accomplishment, and what he did to attain this. Getting the person to describe how he did it is a good thing, because it gives others some guidelines about what they can do, as well as inspiring them to work harder to gain recognition, too.

If you are giving recognition to several people, honor the person getting the highest recognition last, and do a little bit extra to recognize this. The advantage of this approach is it builds up to the high point of the event.

Finally, conclude with some time for conversation and refreshments—a good time for people to congratulate anyone who has been recognized and ask more questions about how he did it.

Should you plan a separate recognition event, a similar format is fine—just make the ceremony a little more elaborate and add on some extra socializing or other highlights, such as a speaker.

Different groups use different formats. Some start with dinner or a potluck, others with cocktails, still others with coffee or conversation. In any case, about a half-hour to an hour for arrivals and socializing works well. Then, if you have a program, cover this before the awards to save the recognition part of the program for last, so the occasion builds to this.

Several possibilities for a program might be: an inspirational speaker; a speaker talking about sales techniques; a report or slide show by you featuring recent highlights in selling your product; demonstrations of the sales techniques used by members of your sales team; etc.

Then, to highlight the biggest awards, build up to these by giving out any smaller awards first. Save the biggest one (i.e., "Salesperson of the Month," "Salesperson of the Year") for last. As you give out each award, mention the person's accomplishments, and perhaps give a little of the human side of the person, too (e.g., "You may be amazed at how much Sylvia has been able to do when she really decided to commit herself to this program this past month. Not only did she up her sales volume 50 percent, but she has a husband, two kids, a dog, and belongs to a church singing group on the side."). Then, prominently show the award you are giving out. If it's a certificate, hold it up and read it; if there's a note of congratulation, read it. Finally, if you are giving the person any symbols of recognition, invite him to show them off, and perhaps arrange for a photographer to take photos for group members or for your company publication. For example, at their monthly awards program, a jewelry sales leader would take the crown of leadership from the last month's winner and crown the new monthly sales winner, and then put a red velvet cloak around her shoulders. Meanwhile, the group's photographer was there snapping photos for the partici-pants who wanted them, and for the group's newsletter.

Even if you don't take photos, if you have a company newsletter, be sure to include a report of the event and a listing of everyone who won awards.

Still another way to add to the occasion is by having a group member or outside professional contribute a musical accompaniment, and perhaps you might even arrange to have the ceremony recorded on video.

Then, following the program and ceremony, include some time for socializing, or perhaps couple the event with a party or dance.

Such events can become very memorable and important for your salespeople. They feel truly recognized for their efforts, by you and by other salespeople in your company, and as a result, they are apt to want to try harder. At the same time, their recognition presents them as a role model for others in the group to follow. So, everyone usually leaves the event feeling good and more committed to achieving personal and group goals.

In sum, however you do it, effective award and recognition ceremonies can be a real aid to keeping everyone directed and motivated. They help everyone feel even better about working together, and this increased commitment, motivation, and good feeling translates into more sales.

CHAPTER 5

Setting Up a Training Program

A training program, in conjunction with regular sales meetings or held separately, can help your sales organization grow and perform more effectively. First, many new salespeople will need such training, and some may be attracted to work for your company because of the training you offer. Second, you can use it as a good refresher for experienced salespeople, as well as making sure that the people you hire apply your own sales approach or philosophy, which can differ from company to company. Third, during the training, you may acquire many new ideas for selling yourself that can be incorporated into your overall sales strategy. Further, a training program can be a source of inspiration and motivation itself, as your people get together on a regular basis to work on ways to sell better.

There are three key methods of training you can use, individually or in combination, depending on the needs of your sales group.

1. You can use written materials, including books, articles, and checklists, along with cassette tapes and videos, with sales techniques or product information.

2. You can use role-playing, in which you set up situations your salespeople may encounter, so they can practice good approaches and responses.

3. You can act as a role model by accompanying salespeople into the field to show them how to sell or to see what they are doing, so you can offer helpful feedback.

Individual Versus Group Training?

When you are first starting your sales organization and only have a handful of people working with you, individual training is especially appropriate. This way, you can meet with each person individually and engage in role-playing, or accompany the person on sales calls on an as-needed basis.

But once you have three or four people, it makes sense to start shifting over to a group training approach. This may be more suitable, because you can find yourself stretched in too many directions if you try to train everyone individually. Second, at this stage, the peer group process takes over, and your salespeople will be motivated to work on improving their sales skills through training, because they will be in training together and will stimulate and inspire each other.

If you find that some people need some extra attention, you can always set up separate meetings or go on sales calls with them. Likewise, if some people can't attend a meeting, you can always fill them in later or let them go through the sales training materials you are working with on their own.

Setting Up Your Program

When you set up your program, you can make the training program a regular part of the job if you are paying a salary or a draw. However, if you are only paying a commission and have people working for you on a part-time or independent contractor basis, it may be wise to keep your training program optional and flexible in format and content to best suit people's needs. However, if you do make it optional, keep your training separate from your sales meeting, which you use to coordinate activities. These sales meetings do need to be required, so you can keep things coordinated effectively.

Keeping the training optional works well for several reasons. First, as long as you keep the training separate from the sales meetings, the training program is designed to help the individual improve his or her own abilities; thus, people should decide for themselves if they need to improve in certain areas (though you can always give them some feedback to show why they may need improvement). Then, if they feel the training is valuable, people will want to do it. In fact, you'll find that good salespeople appreciate the need for continuing training to improve their skills.

Accordingly, seek ways to develop your training to meet your salespeople's needs. To find out, get feedback as you go along. Find out where people feel weak and where they would like help. What sales techniques would they like to learn? What sales approaches are they having trouble with? Do they need help in locating leads? Ask questions of your people, or perhaps use an evaluation questionnaire from time to time, to find out what people want and need.

Also, in getting feedback, find out what kind of training approach your people might prefer. Would they like meeting in a group? Would they like to work more closely with you? How much time would they like to devote to training? One hour a week is a common amount of time, but check with your people. Maybe some would like to spend more time; others feel perhaps a half-hour would be enough. Adapt your program accordingly.

Another consideration is whether to combine your training with your regular meeting, perhaps as an optional half-hour or hour program before or after the meeting. If you do combine the meeting and training, it's probably best to keep the training relatively short (for example, a half hour), since people's attention spans are limited; if your sales meeting lasts an hour or so, a long training may be too much. Alternatively, if you have a separate time for the training, an hour to an hour and a half is fine. You can go into more depth since people are coming to the training fresh and don't have to stay alert for another meeting after the training.

Finally, consider how to apply your training to what your salespeople will be selling. For example, if you're using generic sales training materials, discuss how these ideas can be adapted to the situations your people encounter, or use these trainings as a time to share the sales methods that have worked for you, and encourage others to share their own ideas.

In short, to set up a good training program, be aware of what your people need and adapt it accordingly in format, content, and time the program is offered.

Using Written Materials, Tapes, and Videos on Sales Techniques and Product Information

In your training meetings, you can use materials you develop yourself, based on your own experiences in selling. Or, you can draw on a wealth of books, articles, tapes, and videos developed by sales trainers who have workshops and seminars all over the country.

There are numerous trainers. Some are associated with major seminar organizations such as Career Trak. Others have public seminars or set up special training sessions for companies, such as Tom Hopkins, who has a complete series of tapes, videos, and a book under the title, *How to Master the Art of Selling;* Tony Alessandra, who has books and materials on power selling; and Sheila Murray Bethel, who has written dozens of articles in numerous sales and motivational magazines. You will also find that many sales trainers are members of the National Speakers Association, which is based in Phoenix, Arizona, and has chapters in dozens of U.S. cities. The group has a membership directory that it sends out to organizations interested in hiring speakers.

Another source of training materials is articles on selling from some of the sales-oriented business publications, such as *Entrepreneur, In Business, Success, The American Salesman, Professional Selling, Salesman's Opportunity Magazine,* and *Selling Direct.*

The kind of materials you use depends on the level of skill and the interest of your people. For instance, if you have a number of new people, it might be good to start with a step-by-step program. They can still be out selling while the program is going on, but the training will help them improve, and you can use the training meetings as a forum for discussing any difficulties they might encounter in the field.

For example, when I set up a training program for new salespeople, I specify a half-hour after our regular meetings as a time when people who want to can listen to a series of twenty-five-minute sales training tapes that are part of a complete series of twenty-four tapes, using one tape per meeting.[1] These began with some introductory tapes on the profession of selling and the characteristics of a good salesperson, and then covered specific sales techniques, including how to use questions, how to work with the emotions, ways to deal with failure and rejection, prospecting through referrals and without referrals, telephone techniques, planning a sales presentation, making contact, qualifying the buyer, using visual aids and demonstrations in presentations, handling objections, making test closes, strategies for closing effectively, time planning and organization, and goal setting.

After each tape, I spent about ten minutes talking about how the methods discussed in the tape could be applied in the field.

This approach of listening to a tape or watching a video in a group is ideal. However, keep any tape or video around fifteen to thirty minutes, so people stay attentive. It's also a good idea to preview any material first, so you can note the main points in advance, and use these in a discussion after the tape. This discussion afterwards is important; it emphasizes the key things you want to be sure people learn from the tape.

Also, it gives you and your salespeople a chance to discuss how they can apply those techniques in the field. By previewing you are in a better position to lead this discussion and flag what you consider the most important points.

If you use books or articles, a good approach is to make arrangements so everyone reads a chapter or a few articles in advance of the meeting. (Use inexpensive books or perhaps photocopies of selected chapters to do this.) Then, at the meeting, go over the main points, based on what people have read. As in discussing tapes or videos, focus on how people can apply these techniques themselves.

If you're ambitious and experienced in selling, you can also create your own materials. One approach is to write up your ideas on a handout, which you can copy and distribute at the meeting. This is especially appropriate if you can give suggestions on applying valuable techniques in the field.

For instance, say your salespeople plan to follow up on some ads or are going to participate in a trade show. You might put together a list of how to use good telephoning techniques to follow up on the leads obtained.

Another approach is to involve your salespeople more actively in the training process by having one of them lead each training meeting. This person, after a tape or video, would then lead the discussion. Or, perhaps a salesperson might report on some sales books or articles he has read, and then lead a discussion on how others can use these methods.

The format is very flexible. However, from time to time, make sure you are on the right track, by getting some feedback before or after the training meeting, perhaps by using a questionnaire. You want to find out the following: Do people like what you are doing? If so, should you continue doing it? What else would people like to see you do? Do they have specific ideas about the content format, or sales materials you are using? Then, take these comments to heart and make

---

1. I used the Tom Hopkins program: *How to Master the Art of Selling Anything.*

any appropriate changes to improve the training. You'll see the results down the road in the form of better trained salespeople, and therefore better sales.

Using Role-Playing to Set Up Test Situations and Practice Techniques

Role-playing is another powerful sales training technique. Here you set up a simulated situation and then participants act it out—a good way to try out new techniques or practice old ones.

For successful role-playing, begin by explaining what you are going to do and how role-playing works. Then, because role-playing works most effectively with voluntary participation, explain that participation is optional. This way, people don't feel suddenly on the spot to perform. Instead, stress that this technique is a powerful way of learning what to do through playing the part, and encourage everyone to participate. You will find that most will.

Once people are prepared to try the technique, find out what sales areas your people feel they need help with so you can role-play that, or use the technique to demonstrate how to do something new. For example, if people are having trouble making a cold call or making a close, set up some sample situations around that. Or if you have found an excellent way to do a presentation, try a scenario to demonstrate it.

Once you have decided what topics to role-play, select one and describe the situation. Commonly, these role-plays just involve two participants, the salesperson and the customer, although if it's appropriate to your sales situation, you can increase the number of roles, such as creating a scenario with two or more customers or a scene where two salespeople work together as a team. When you go through the preliminaries of describing what happens, keep the scenario brief, so the participants can be spontaneous in playing their roles and the scene as they see fit. Also, if your salespeople haven't role-played before, demonstrate how the process works by using a fishbowl technique, where you play the salesperson yourself and choose another person to be the customer or vice versa (though usually you will be the salesperson if you're the one showing the technique; if you have someone who is especially good at something, you can use him to show this).

In your explanation, point out that there will be a discussion of the experience afterwards, and plan to include this. This after-the-experience discussion is an important part of the process; it is a way of getting reactions from both the people who were role-playing the scene and any observers. You can note and discuss your own reactions, too. Through this feedback you can learn such things as how comfortable the "salesperson" felt in using the technique; how the "customer" reacted; and what the observers felt about the "salesperson's" approach and effectiveness. You might also use this discussion period to talk about how the salesperson might do the scene again to make it better. Then the person can perhaps role-play the situation again, using the ideas from the discussion to improve. If so, follow up any replay with more discussion. If you feel the person playing the sales role has mastered the technique or has improved, note this, since this kind of positive feedback helps learning and motivation. Or, if the person still needs more practice, state this too, along with any suggestions on what to do to get better to inspire further effort.

Preferably have this discussion after each team does a role-play, or after a series of role-plays using the same scenario. Then, at the end of the role-playing process, a summing-up discussion to review the main points helps people learn the key points you want to stress. You might also ask for suggestions on what to role-play at a subsequent meeting, so you can prepare some situations in advance, as well come up with future role-playing suggestions yourself.

A typical role-playing situation might work something like this.

- You begin by announcing that you are going to do some role playing. You explain it will help people make better phone calls, and they can try out some techniques you have found useful in making sales. Then, to describe the technique, you note that they will pretend to get on the phone with a potential customer and try to set up an appointment. Further, you announce, you will demonstrate how the process works first, and then everyone else will get a chance to do it. Afterwards, everyone will have a chance to discuss the experience.

- Next, you demonstrate what to do. You ask a person to volunteer playing a business executive, and explain that you will be the salesperson who has just reached this potential customer on the phone. Then you invite the volunteer to join you in the middle of the group so you can demonstrate. (Perhaps set up some chairs in front of or in the middle of the group for this purpose.) Now you simulate how you would make the call and ask the "business executive" to respond however he wishes. You show how you open the call, what you do to keep interest, how you answer objections, and how you close by seeking to set up a meeting. Meanwhile, the other person can choose to be cooperative or not—and you respond accordingly to be persuasive and make the sale.

- After the demonstration is over, you mention briefly what you did to highlight the techniques you hope people will learn. Then, you ask for volunteers to try out the exercise. A good technique here is to have participants play out the situation once, and afterwards switch roles and do it again. Before the volunteers start, you review the basic situation to be sure they understand what to do (i.e., the salesperson is calling a business executive to sell a new service, say a computer management service, and has just been put through by his secretary). Then, you ask the "salesperson" to start the call, reminding him that his goal is to set up a personal meeting with the executive so he can demonstrate the system. Participants should improvise from there.

- After the role-play is over—typically with the salesperson making the sale, with or without resistance and objections from the customer, you ask the "salesperson" and the "executive" to comment on their experiences. How did the salesperson feel about the call? What did he try to do? What did he feel comfortable doing? What was uncomfortable, if anything? What worked? What didn't? Then, you ask the customer for his own comments and reactions. What did he think was good or not good about the salesperson's approach? How did he feel the salesperson handled his objections? Did he feel like setting up an appointment? Why or why not? If the participants switched roles, you ask them both for their reactions in each role. Then you ask those who watched what they thought, and give your own reactions.

- Now, if you feel it's appropriate, you can ask the same participants to do the simulation again, incorporating what they have learned from the discussion; afterwards, you discuss what they did briefly. Generally, this repeat role-play will be much more on target, so there's less to discuss. Rather, if there's improvement (there usually is), it's a good way to affirm that the salesperson is doing better, and the customer is more responsive as a result.

- Now you ask for more volunteers, and they play out the same scene, or, if you prefer, you suggest a few modifications, such as: "Okay, try doing the same situation as before, but this time, the executive is an extremely busy person," or "Okay, let's use the same situation as before, but this time, the executive wants to get all the answers on the phone instead of meeting with you in person."

- You try out a few more scenarios in a similar fashion. Then, at the end, you ask people to discuss what they learned from the role-playing session, and you summarize the main points yourself.

- Finally, you ask if anyone has any suggestions for situations to role-play next time, and you conclude the role-playing part of the meeting.

How much time should you spend on role-playing? It depends on your situation and the response of people in your group to this technique. Some salespeople will feel very comfortable with the technique, and may have used it before; they like the chance to try out new approaches and get feedback. Other salespeople may resist it, sometimes because they feel uncomfortable about being on stage, or being tested or judged by their peers. Some may resist because they feel they already know what to do and so don't need to go through the routine. Still others may simply go along with whatever you decide to do to be agreeable. So, get some reading of your group before you institute role-playing into your training. Encourage everyone to do it, but also find out who really wants to do it, to be sure your group is sufficiently behind this approach to make it work.

If you do decide to go ahead with this method, another factor to consider is whether to include role-playing in your regular training meetings, or to set up a special workshop to go over sales techniques using role-playing. Check with your people to see which they prefer, if they are receptive to doing this.

If you do incorporate this in a regular training meeting, have it last about fifteen to thirty minutes, since this permits time for both acting out the scenes and some discussion. Or, if you set up a special role-playing workshop, one to two hours is a good time for this, because it enables you really to work with this approach in depth.

Being a Role Model for Salespeople in the Field

A third good training method is acting as a role model for your new salespeople by either accompanying them in the field yourself, or having your experienced salespeople do this. Whoever is the role model should have had some successful selling experience with your product or service. If you have a salesperson do it, work out a joint commission arrangement, so the experienced salesperson has a pay-off and therefore a motivation to do this. One good approach is to say that if sales result when the experienced salesperson makes his usual presentation to show the newcomer what to do, the experienced person will get full credit. But once the new salesperson starts setting up appointments and making presentations, with the experienced person helping him, a fifty-fifty commission split seems fair. Another approach is to use an override system, where a new person is assigned to an experienced salesperson, and the experienced person gets a regular override on all of that new person's sales.

In any event, the role model approach provides the advantage of giving the new person a hands-on experience of what to do, using the experienced person's actions as a guide to how to act. Some experienced salespeople may not need this, but it's ideal with all new people, and experienced people may find this quite helpful if they haven't sold your kind of product or service before, or if you have developed special approaches for selling.

If you've had some successful selling experience with your product, you can perform as the role model yourself. Alternatively, you might appoint a sales manager or top salesperson to do this kind of training and negotiate the appropriate compensation arrangements to cover this.

Commonly, the role-modeling technique involves three stages: (1) being an observer only, (2) joint participation, and (3) making a presentation with support.

These stages represent a gradual turning-over of responsibility for the presentation and sale from the experienced person to the newcomer. More specifically, what happens in each stage is the following.

The Observer Only Phase. In this stage, you (or the experienced salesperson) take the newcomer out in the field as an observer. His job is just to watch, and he is introduced to the prospective customer as an assistant. Or if you're working with telephone techniques, let the person listen in on the call, either on an extension or an open room receiver.

Begin with some discussion before the call to give the new salesperson an idea of what he will observe. This will help him notice the specific techniques used.

This introduction can be given quickly. If the presentation means a drive some-where to give it, this can be a good time to tell the new person what to do.

If you are demonstrating cold calling techniques, no special advance introduc-tion to the customer is necessary. You simply bring the newcomer along and explain that this is your assistant. However, if you are making a presentation to a pre-set appointment, it helps to check with the prospective customer in advance, so he knows you will be bringing an assistant with you. This advance checking can help in establishing rapport and making the sale, because it's a courtesy to let the prospect know what to expect, so he can be prepared for your call—and perhaps have an extra chair in the office to be ready for your meeting. Also, this checking helps to show your respect for the prospect, and can create a more receptive meeting as a result.

Then, at the presentation, the newcomer should primarily (or strictly) observe. Tell him what to expect in advance so he does this, and doesn't interfere in ways you don't want. It's all right to ask the person to do a few minor things, like put up any charts or get out your presentation materials. But otherwise, he should just observe, and he should not ask any questions of the prospect or offer infor-mation. Be clear about what you want, since the person is new and you don't want him interfering with the flow of your own sales techniques and possibly derailing the sale.

Plan a short discussion or debriefing session for after the presentation—or, if you are doing a series of these, perhaps wait until the end. Some sales leaders do this in the car while driving to and from appointments or returning to the office. But it's preferable to set aside some special time to focus on this discussion—per-haps over coffee at the end of the presentations for the day.

During this discussion, go over what you did. Explain why you used certain techniques, and encourage the newcomer to ask questions and give reactions about what happened.

The number of presentations the newcomer should observe in this phase de-pends on your product or service and the person's experience. If your product or service is fairly complex—say a computer system, you may need to have him observe several times, before he feels really comfortable to share in the presenta-tion or do it himself. But with a simple program, a one-time observation might be sufficient. Then, too, a more experienced person will need less of an introduction; the novice will need much more. So, in deciding on how much training to give, take these two factors into consideration: (1) the nature of the product, and (2) the person's background.

The Joint Participation Phase. In this stage, the newcomer gradually assumes more and more responsibility for the sales call. Encourage this transition as rap-idly as feasible.

To do so, have some discussion with the newcomer before the presentation to find out what he feels most comfortable doing. However, reserve the more critical parts of the presentation for the experienced salesperson. For example, the experi-enced person should handle the opening and the close. Then, plan in advance who is going to do what and stick to this. This way, your presentation will flow smoothly, because you're both certain of what to do.

Initially, in this phase, you can have the newcomer do some limited support activities, such as doing a demonstration of your product or service, after you do a brief introduction of what he is going to do. Also, if you are using a presentation folder, flip charts, overheads, or other materials, perhaps have the newcomer present these, while you do any explanation.

Then, once the newcomer feels comfortable with these limited support activities, you can turn over additional parts of the presentation to him. For instance, now he might do the explanation as well as demonstrating or showing the materials.

Through this process you can shift more and more of the presentation to this person until he feels comfortable handling the whole thing and you feel confident about this, too.

After the presentation, allow some time for discussion and feedback. In particular, point out what he did that was good and what can be improved. If the person makes any mistakes, be supportive. Point them out in a constructive way to show how he can improve or do things differently next time. Ask him how he feels about what happened—what he liked and what he didn't. Also, ask what changes he would like to make in the future. The discussion is designed to help the person improve and be prepared to take on more responsibility next time.

Use your judgment to decide how many joint presentations are necessary before the person can take on more responsibility for the sale. For some newcomers, one or two joint participation presentations may be enough; others may need more. It depends on the product and the person's own background and abilities. Use your own perceptions and feedback from the person to help you decide.

The Presentation with Support Phase. At this stage, the new salesperson is about ready to fly on his own. The purpose of his doing the presentation with some back-up support is to give both the newcomer and experienced salesperson a chance to see the newcomer in action to be sure he is ready to do it alone. At the same time, the presence of a back-up person offering support gives the newcomer a chance for some final feedback so he can further polish his presentation.

Now, in this phase, you (or the experienced salesperson) become the observer. The newcomer does the whole thing. You might assist a little at his direction, such as doing a demonstration or turning the flip chart, but otherwise it's his show, and you're the one who's introduced as the assistant.

Use this opportunity to observe closely what the person is doing. Notice how he does the opening, maintains interest, creates rapport with the customer, deals with objections, handles the close, etc.

Then, at your discussion after the presentation, give your reactions on the person's strengths and areas for improvement, and ask him to share his feelings about how things went.

If you both feel the presentation went well, the new person may be ready to go out on his own, or you may both want to do one more presentation with support to be sure. Should there have been any problems, use the discussion to plan how to improve for next time, and do a presentation with support again.

As in many other sales training situations, play it by ear in deciding when the new person is ready. Your goal is to get the person off on his own as quickly as possible, yet allow for additional support if it seems necessary.

Training Your Salespeople to Train Others

After you have a sales team successfully selling your product, the way to expand further is by training your salespeople to train others. After you have grown beyond a certain point, you or your sales manager can't handle the coordination, motivation, training, and support all by yourself. You need others to take over these roles, and there are tremendous growth possibilities when you do, since your sales group expands exponentially as you increase the number of sales leaders working with others selling your product.

A key consideration here, of course, is whether your product lends itself to this kind of growth. If you are selling something that has a specialized market or that you are limited in providing, you may need to have a small, specialized sales force to keep up with demand or production. But if your product has broad appeal, and you can provide it in larger and larger quantities, then you can expand exponentially.

One way to expand is to do so gradually within the structure of your existing company, by training a few people to become leaders. Another approach is to restructure, using the established methods of creating a marketing network—through franchising or organizing a multi-level company. In franchising, you sell the rights to sell your product or service in a certain territory, using your sales approach, name, and other proprietary features. In return, you provide training and support so the purchaser of your franchise learns how to do this successfully. In multi-level marketing, you create a pyramidal structure of distributors who are independently selling your product and are recruiting and training others to do the same. You provide the guidance and the policies that govern what the people working for you can or cannot do. But otherwise, everyone is an independent contractor, who can sell your product or service anywhere in return for a commission from you, plus bonuses or overrides on the sales of the people they recruit into their sales group. Since these are complex undertakings, requiring specified legal procedures, they are beyond the scope of this book. However, you can incorporate some of the principles these approaches have used successfully, such as the emphasis on training others to do what you do successfully, and showing them how to teach others to sell.

Deciding When to Train New Sales Leaders

You can make the decision to train sales leaders to train others when you first start organizing your sales group or after your sales group has grown to a certain point. In either case, it helps to start delegating and creating new managers once your sales team has grown to more than five to ten people, in order for it to effectively grow further. Otherwise, as the size of your group grows, you are apt to be less able to supervise and motivate your people effectively because you lose that personal touch so necessary to good sales management. Thus, work out your plans to develop team leaders in advance, or take steps to develop them once your sales group reaches this critical point.

One approach is to hire new salespeople specifically to assume a sales management role. Or, notice which of your salespeople seem to have leadership abilities, and help them develop into a sales manager role.

Hiring People to Build Your Sales Force

One easy way to spark this growth is to hire people to become sales managers in advance. Many multi-level companies and distributors do this—for example, when they advertise for someone to get involved in their business opportunity, they're looking for someone to become a distributor too and also train others.

In selecting people, use the same criteria for selecting a single sales manager, discussed in Chapter 2. You want someone who is good in working with people, takes initiative, is very positive, has a background in direct sales, and has a good track record in leading or managing others. Chapter 2 provides a detailed breakdown of the qualities to look for.

The main difference now is that you are not just seeking a single sales leader to take over the sales function; rather, you are hiring a few managers to split up the responsibilities. Since these tasks are being split, make clear divisions of who is handling what to avoid conflicts. One good method is to divide up the sales area into territories or to split up the types of markets you cover (i.e., sales to corporations; sales to retailers and wholesalers; sales to individuals and group; sales to churches and educational institutions).

Preferably, hire people who already have some background in sales management or have shown strong initiative and aggressiveness in the selling they have already done. This way, your new people can fit more easily into a management role, and your main responsibility will be showing them the kind of leadership style you prefer in working with your people.

Hiring Sales Managers When You Get Started

When you hire people for management before you have a sales group created, you can turn over much or all of the recruiting function to them. Your role is to provide the product, plus the sales materials and training materials to be used by the salespeople working with them; their role is to recruit and train the people who will work under them. To this end, they might do some advertising or contact potential salespeople they know themselves. Or, another approach might be for you to run an ad for salespeople yourself, and then assign callers to your sales leaders for follow-up.

For example, one company that imported clothes from Italy did this. It advertised for sales managers, and after some interviews, selected seven people to become managers. The company then provided these people with a list of its policies and commission arrangements, plus catalogs, order forms, and other sales materials. The company also had several training meetings and made its offices available for these managers, so they could make calls, type letters, and have small meetings with their salespeople. However, the managers had the responsibility of finding their own salespeople, and they were instructed to put in ads to do their own hiring. Meanwhile, the company continued to do its own advertising for salespeople, and it referred callers to the managers who were already successful in creating their own sales team. The results were spectacular. Within months the company had a strong team of four managers from the seven it initially hired, and these managers each had about a half-dozen salespeople going out and making sales through party plan presentations. When it started, the company had just a few clothing samples, catalog sheets, and order forms. But by skillfully creating an effective sales organization with a few key managers, in a few months the company was grossing nearly $10,000 a month.

Bringing in Outside Sales Managers

You can also hire outside people to be sales managers if you already have a going sales group, want some managers to provide leadership, but aren't sure you have strong enough people to hire all you need from within. Before going outside, carefully consider whether any of the people who are already selling for you can take over a leadership role, since it will be smoother if you can advance them into the manager position. But if not, bring in outsiders. However, be sure to prepare the way by working closely with the people you already have, so they feel comfortable working with newcomers as managers and don't resent them for their sudden appearance. For example, you might personally introduce the new people to everyone, or ask their input on who to hire. At the same time, when you do talk about these people, emphasize the past sales management experience they bring to the job, so your current salespeople see them as leaders who can help them and guide them, not just upstarts suddenly coming aboard with more money and status, and perhaps an override on their own sales, too.

Bringing in outsiders is a tricky business, but there are ways to smooth their entrance and early days on the job. One entry technique that works well is introducing the new people at a regular sales meeting and giving them a chance to describe their own backgrounds. You might even do this while you are still deciding who to hire, and use the reactions of your salespeople as a guide in making your decision. Then, after the new or prospective sales leader says something about himself, you might invite your own people to introduce themselves, and provide some mingling time after the meeting. Notice who seems to mix well together, and use any information you have about the interests and backgrounds of your new leaders and your current salespeople to decide who would work well together. These data can help you make decisions about assigning certain of your salespeople to each of these managers.

Still another possibility might be for you to continue to work with some or all of your present salespeople, but bring in these managers to develop their own sales groups in other areas. In this case, the transition will typically be a little smoother, since you don't have to help your current salespeople in making the transition from working directly for you or your general manager to developing loyalties with another. However, still be sure to explain to your current people what you are doing and how these new people will be incorporated into the organization, so they can feel reassured about what is happening. Moreover, be careful to assign these managers to territories or markets that are not already covered, if they are going to be developing their own sales teams. Alternatively, if they are simply slipping into a management role to provide leadership for a group already there, you can assign them the appropriate regional or market group title, such as the regional manager for a certain city or metropolitan area.

Promoting People in Your Own Organization

The alternative approach to hiring outsiders directly into a management role is to select people from your sales group who have leadership potential. Then, you can promote them directly. Or, perhaps set up certain conditions that a salesperson must meet to move into management—such as achieving a certain sales volume in a month.

When you do advance someone into a management position, it's important to do any necessary groundwork to assure that he is accepted by the others already there. This is especially important to smooth relationships if you assign any of your current salespeople to work with this new person. You want to be sure there is mutual acceptance and that the salespeople accept this person in the higher management role. A major source of conflict in any organization is the feelings of resentment that may arise when one person is promoted over another, since the person not promoted may feel disappointed that he is not doing as well, may feel lowered self-esteem because the other's promotion reminds him he didn't achieve as much, and he may envy or resent the person who has moved ahead, even though he may also admire that person for doing well.

Thus, to reduce the possibility of such feelings or help people get over them quickly, it helps not only to recognize the person being promoted, but emphasize the reasons for the promotion. You want to show that this promotion is appropriate and fair, that this sales manager has worked hard and is really good for the role. For example, at a regular sales meeting, after you announce the promotion, you might go over the achievements the person has made to earn this, or you might do this at a recognition ceremony, as described in Chapter 4.

It is also important to explain what this promotion means to the group as a whole, so people feel reassured about their own positions in the organization. A major concern that salespeople have is that someone else is going to be moving in on their territory (unless you are involved in a direct sales or multi-level company, where every potential sale is fair game), so you need to clarify if there are going to be any changes in territories. Then, too, it's important to put this promotion in as positive a light as possible for the organization itself. One way to do this is by pointing out the benefits this new person can provide to the group in this new role. For instance, mention how the new managers are going to provide extra training and coordination. Point out how they are going to help operations run more smoothly. Note how they are going to be exploring new markets and developing leads, which will be turned over to everyone else.

In short, turn any promotion into a big plus for the organization, and show how it will help each salesperson, as well as the person being promoted. This will facilitate acceptance by your sales group, and it will make it easier for the promoted person to perform his new role.

Working with Your New Sales Leaders

Once you have selected your new sales leaders and have worked out procedures for easing them into your organization, the final step is training them so they can work with your salespeople, and perhaps, down the road, train other people to work with their own sales group (which is the principle that makes some multi-level companies so successful).

Essentially, in training them, show them how to do what you have been doing—the focus of this whole book. If your sales leaders have already been in sales management before, your main task is helping them adapt their skills to your particular approach. If they haven't, you will need to give them more help in developing management skills. But in either case, you can use the following strategies in training your new sales leaders.

1. Hold regular sales management meetings in addition to any regular sales meetings. Design these to plan overall strategies for the organization, so your sales leaders can pass this information to the salespeople with whom they are working. These meetings provide an opportunity to get feedback from your sales leaders about what is happening in the field, so you can make decisions about what to produce and how best to sell it. These meetings can also be used to determine what kind of training your salespeople and your sales managers need, so you can provide it. Then, too, these meetings can be used to plan joint sales activities, such as participating in trade shows and setting up large-scale demonstrations and events. Another strategy is to use these meetings to plan what sales materials and product literature you need and to work out details about the content and method of presentation.

2. Invite your sales leaders to join you at product or service demonstrations, at sales presentations, and at your regular sales meetings to use you as a model to guide them. This way, your sales leaders can get ideas from you on how and what to do, though they should also develop their own leadership style. To use you as a model, your new sales leaders can start off by observing. Afterwards, allow them some time for discussion and feedback, say after a demonstration, a presentation, or meeting. Then, gradually, you can ask them to participate in various parts of the program, until they feel free to do it themselves.

3. Ask your sales leaders to set up their own meetings and organize their own training activities for their own salespeople. In this approach, you still provide some overall meetings, presentations, trainings, rallies, conventions, and other large-scale activities for everyone in your organization. However, your sales leaders take over when it comes to having smaller-scale meetings, presentations, trainings, and perhaps even rallies on their own with their own sales team. They should report to you on what is happening, and they should get your suggestions at the sales management meetings, so you still provide overall guidance and direction. But otherwise, they should feel fairly free to use their own ideas in deciding how to manage their own group. This way, you encourage your people to take initiative. And when people are able to use their own approaches (though within your own policy limits, of course), they feel more involved and committed.

4. Provide your sales leaders with regular training on sales management. When you hold these training sessions, design them to help your sales leaders in recruiting and working with members of their own sales groups. Perhaps set up an ongoing training program that follows the basic steps for running a sales group outlined here or use this book as a primer. In addition, allow plenty of time for feedback and discussion on any problems your managers are having in leading their group, so you can work out ways to resolve such difficulties.

In short, in working with your sales leaders, think of your organization like a pyramid structure with a chain of command spreading out from you to the sales leaders and then to the salespeople under them. You provide the general direction and guidance. You set the tone for the types of organization you want to have. And then you convey this approach through your meetings and training, so your leaders can pass this information on to their own sales people.

Yet, while you lead, remain open and responsive to feedback from the salespeople in your organization. To keep things operating efficiently, set up channels of communication, so your salespeople communicate through their sales leaders, who communicate to you. But also be flexible, so if there are any communication breakdowns, you can communicate directly with people in someone's sales group, and they can communicate with you. Normally, people shouldn't expect to do this—encourage people to use the usual channels, so your sales leaders feel they have a central, important role in leading the people in their group. Yet, if problems develop, you need to be able to hear about them, and that's when people should know they can come to you, and that you will, if necessary, deal directly with them. Later, as your organization gets even larger, use this basic model to move to the next organizational step—working with sales managers who are working with their own team of sales leaders and helping them know how to work with their salespeople, too.

CHAPTER 6

Time and Territory Management

When you first start organizing a sales groups in a growing company, a loose and informal structure works well because you only have a small group, and you aren't sure how well different salespeople will work out. But even when things are small and informal, have a plan for organizing a more formal structure in the future. Then, you can gradually introduce this structure to your group as it grows. Or you may find that it helps to mention in advance some of these procedures you plan to introduce subsequently, so people are prepared to accept the added procedures when you introduce them.

This chapter describes a number of organizational procedures that you can use. Choose those that suit your style and the stage of your company's organizational development.

Coordinating Contacts

It is extremely helpful to coordinate the leads or contacts your salespeople make. As your sales force grows, a major problem that can develop is your people stepping over each other and making the same contacts.

In some companies in which salespeople are organized into a multi-level or network marketing structure, there are no territories, so anyone can supposedly work anywhere. Moreover, this permitted territorial free-for-all is supported by a philosophy based on ideals of American freedom and independence. However, while such independent, survival-of-the-fittest ideas may be fine when people representing a company are hundreds of miles away or in different cities, as a practical matter, this does not work well when salespeople are working in a local area. This is because this freedom combined with a lack of coordination is not only inefficient, but it can breed jealousy and internecine warfare over contacts, leading even to secret sabotage as salespeople try to beat each other to make the sale and recruit others to assist in their own sales efforts.

Thus, it is important to set up some guidelines, if not territories or categories for contact, so people don't feel like they are spinning their wheels, or, worse, start engaging in territorial battles with each other. At the very least, establish some general policies about how your people should handle situations that occur from joint contacts. This way, they know who gets the commission for a sale or when it is shared, and feel the outcome is fair. (For example, if one person makes the contact and the other closes the sale independently, a policy of splitting the commission might work well, provided that the closing occurs within a reasonably close time of the original contact, so the initial overture can be seen as having some influence on the result. Another approach might be simply to split the commission between whoever is involved.)

One good technique for setting up territories or categories when your sales group is first getting organized is to create these boundaries based on the interest of the new people you hire. To do this, begin with a general idea of how you want to organize a sales force in the area—i.e., divide them into downtown, certain neighborhoods, and outlying areas or into categories—i.e., into business and professional groups, singles and social groups, nature and environmental groups, factories, and the Spanish-American community. Then, after you describe your initial thinking, ask what your people think of this and what they would like, so you can modify your plan accordingly.

One way to find out what people want is to ask some questions about this when you interview new people. In fact, you might use these preferences as a basis for making hiring decisions, in order to bring aboard a mix of people working in different geographic or interest areas. Another way to create those territories is to ask your people to fill out a questionnaire indicating what areas they would prefer to handle themselves, and then it helps to keep these territories flexible, so you can modify who does what as your own product line expands and as salespeople come and go from the group, or as they change their outside activities. To gain this continuing flexibility, perhaps ask for people to fill out these questions every six months or so, to see if and how interests have changed. Specifically, some of the questions to ask include:

- What neighborhoods in the city would you like to work in?
- What types of groups do you currently belong to?
- What types of groups or companies would you prefer to contact?

Then, as you review the answers to these questions, decide how to assign people to your previously created categories, modify these current categories, or create new ones.

In light of this continuing possibility for change, it's good to leave arrangements fairly flexible. One way to keep this flexibility is to let people know that you have recorded their primary areas of sales effort, and let others know who is working in which area. Then, as it becomes clearer who is doing what, you can gradually demarcate firmer boundaries between areas (i.e., dividing up the city by specific streets; specifying that one person will be handling all the churches in a city; etc.). Certainly, allow for exceptions when appropriate (say, one person has close friends in someone else's area), and invite feedback at your sales meetings on how you are splitting things up. Point out that you are receptive to making changes when this seems advisable. In turn, as long as they can see that you are considering their interests in setting up the system, your salespeople will like your efforts to create some structure, because otherwise they may feel some annoyance that they might waste time contacting someone who some other salesperson has already contacted; they may get into "who-gets-the-commission?" disputes, which can easily end up with hard feelings, demoralized salespeople, lost sales, and a high turnover when frustrated people quit.

Another approach to avoid overlap is for each person to fill out a Contacts Form listing each company or organization he or she is actively working with in a specific category or area. Then, other people will know not to contact that business or group. File these so others can refer to them by setting up a filing system by the name of each salesperson and by the categories or areas of contact. Ordinary manila folders or hanging files with labels are good for this purpose. File one copy under the name of the person, and another alphabetically by category, geographic area, or both. Other salespeople can then refer to these files to see who not to contact. A sample Contacts Form, Exhibit 5, is on the following page.

Before setting up such a system, make sure your people would like to do this, since it needs their support to work. They have to agree to use the system, which requires some paperwork and filing. Some people may not like to do this or may become lackadaisical about keeping forms up to date. People have to be willing to follow through.

Thus, explain that the system can help avoid overlap, but only if everyone is behind doing it. Tell them that you will take care of making copies and filing the reports, but they will need to fill out a Contact Form for everyone with whom they are actively working, so no one else will contact them. Then check what people want to do. Some may really like this system because there's less chance of double or multiple contacts. Others may prefer not to do this because of the bookkeeping needed and would rather take their chances with making an overlapping contact. If there appears to be a general consensus that your people want to do this, use the system. If not, don't use it—if only some people are filling out forms, the system won't work.

Additionally, it helps to let everyone in your group know who is contacting what types of businesses or groups or working in what area. This way they know what areas are being covered, and they can at times assist each other through referrals or working together on an area of common interest. When your group is still small, you can share this information at a meeting. But as your group grows, to keep track, make a list of everyone in your group, where they are working, and their areas of special interest. Exhibit 6 is designed for this purpose.

Exhibit 5.   Group Contacts Form

Please fill out this form for each business or group with which you are actively in contact, so you can be appropriately credited, should someone from this organization contact the office directly. Also, this form can be used to avoid or resolve any problems that may arise from multiple contacts of the same group. It can also be used for general follow-up by the office.

YOUR NAME _____

NAME OF GROUP LEADER/CONTACT _____

NAME OF GROUP, COMPANY, OR INDICATE IF AN INDIVIDUAL

_____

TYPE OF GROUP AND SPECIAL INTERESTS _____

_____

ADDRESS _____

CITY, STATE, ZIP _____

PHONE (Indicate if home, office, day, or evening, and when best to call)

_____

DATE OF INITIAL CONTACT _____

OUTCOME OF CONTACT _____

PRODUCTS/SERVICES INTERESTED IN _____

ADDITIONAL FOLLOW-UP (Indicate date, outcome, topics discussed, special interests, etc., here and on back of form)

Exhibit 6.	List of Sales Associates and Areas of Current Interest		
Name/Address/Phone Number		Geographic Areas	Business and Group Interests

Setting Up a Message System

Another type of coordination is a message system to field phone calls for people and handle mail.

Some people may prefer to work independently and use their own phone and address. If you are agreeable, you won't need a message system for them. But others may prefer to use your office as a base.

Of course, if you use a receptionist or answering service, the receptionist can readily take and direct any messages. However, if the receptionist is out or if you don't have one, which is sometimes the case in smaller companies, you can set up an answering machine to field your messages. If so, it helps to specify clearly the kind of messages callers should leave; further, request that they specify for whom. Moreover, if the phone is handling two or more businesses at the same time, use a combined message to explain that the caller has reached the following businesses, that he should indicate which products or services he is calling about, as well as for whom he wishes to leave the message. Ideally, it's better to have one phone per message for a business, rather than trying to coordinate more than one business with the same phone and message.

In preparing your message, you can include the following elements both to sell your program and to ask people to leave a clear message for a particular salesperson. These elements to include in the message are: (1) the name of your company, (2) a brief description of your products or services, (3) a brief mention of any presentations or sales demonstrations you do, (4) a request to leave a name, phone number, reason for call, and best time to return it, (5) a request to specify the particular person the message is for, (6) a statement that someone will return the call as soon as possible, and (7) a reminder to name the person they are calling.

Exhibit 7 is an example of a message used effectively by a travel sales group. People usually *did* leave a message, and normally they *specified who* it was for.

This identification process is critical for good coordination, and it keeps your salespeople satisfied that the message system is working well. That's why it's important to stress naming a particular person on the tape. Otherwise, potential customers who have heard about your product often will leave a message that they heard about your product somewhere (say from a poster or flyer), but they don't mention anyone's name. But with a reminder, they are more likely to check the information they have and provide a name.

Such information, if it can be obtained, is necessary for you to give the appropriate credit, so your salespeople can be paid their commission when a sale comes through, which motivates them to sell even more. Also, this information is useful to let you know what ads or sales approaches are pulling calls.

If someone calls without specifying which salesperson they want, you can return the call yourself to try to find out, to give appropriate credit. If the caller doesn't know offhand, probe to find out how he or she learned of your product (i.e., business card at a mixer, poster on a wall, a flyer at a meeting), and where or when this occurred. This way you may be able to trace back to determine who handed out that business card or distributed that poster or flyer. If you can't determine the source of the call, treat it as an unsolicited lead and distribute it to the person who is handling such companies or groups or is covering that geographic area. (See the discussion on Coordinating Leads in Chapter 7, on Providing Support, for details on how to organize a leads referral system.)

Preferably, write down the messages on the tape on a regular basis. It's best when the head of the sales group does this; then he is the coordinator. This also avoids the problem of one salesperson being tempted by a call and taking someone else's lead. If people are working outside the office at home, they can always call in to retrieve their messages, or someone from the company can always call them to report outstanding messages. Alternatively, for salespeople using or able

---

Exhibit 7.   Creative Travel Phone Message

Hello . . .

You have reached Creative Travel. We are currently offering trips to Kenya China, Egypt, Greece, and Morocco. We will be adding trips to Australia, New Zealand, Fiji, Tahiti, and Tibet this spring.

We are also putting on regular travel nights around the Bay Area, and if you would like us to put on a presentation for your group or organization, please let us know. We have both group packages and individual trips.

Please leave your name, what you're calling about, and which Travel Associate you want to reach. Also, when you leave your phone number, please indicate the best time to get back to you. If you want us to send you information, please leave your address and the destinations you are interested in. And be sure to let us know the Travel Associate you want to contact.

Someone will be in touch with you as soon as possible.

And now, please wait for the beep to leave your message.

---

to stop by the office, set up a file for each person and put the message in the appropriate person's file for him to retrieve himself.

Apart from the usual slips for recording messages, a good approach is to use a message record book—sometimes called an "Executive Message Record," which provides for message-taking in duplicate, since there is a page for original messages with an attached carbon, and the following page makes a copy. (Such message forms typically provide space to record who the message was to, from whom, from what company, the date, time of call, person's phone number, message, and miscellaneous data to check, such as call back, returned call, wants to see you, will call again, urgent.)

The advantage of using such a book is that you can slip the original message into the person's file, but you still have a record of it. As a result, if the first message gets lost or the salesperson doesn't act on it, you can use the copy to possibly follow up yourself later, or assign it to another salesperson for follow-up.

To make the file, there are several possibilities. One is to get manila folders and put each salesperson's name on one; another is to use hanging folders and put a name on each folder, or perhaps slip a series of manila folders into each one of these. Then, file alphabetically.

As for storing the files, one easy-to-use approach is using an open filing system, which may be preferable to an ordinary filing cabinet drawer, since it can be located on a desk, near a phone that can be used to return these messages. One such system is the Crate-A-File, commonly available in both stationery, office, and art supply stores. Another system is a collapsible rack that sets up to hold about a dozen hanging folders.

Use whatever system works best for you. What's important is having some sort of organized message-keeping system, so that people efficiently get their messages—and ideally you should have a record of the messages received as well, in case something gets lost or you need to follow up or reassign the message yourself later.

Then, once the system is set up for phone messages, the same files can be used for any letters that arrive for your salespeople or for any messages from you to them.

Distributing Sales Materials

As you develop new sales materials, training aids, commission plans, etc., the sales meeting is the ideal place for distributing and explaining them. Preferably, spend some time going over each item you develop to make sure everyone understands it and feels comfortable with it. If not, listen to feedback and make any modifications necessary, so everyone can feel supportive of your sales materials and approach. This feedback process is described in more detail later in this chapter.

An efficient way to handle distribution at meetings is to place piles of the new material at a central spot at the meeting location. Ask everyone to pick up a copy as they arrive for the meeting, and indicate that you will review this at the meeting. The review should, of course, be included on your meeting agenda.

Besides this initial distribution, it's also a good idea to have a file for such materials accessible to all your people, so if people don't make the meeting they can obtain this information later. The Crate-A-Files and collapsible hanging file systems mentioned earlier are ideal for this purpose. Create a folder for each item you distribute, label it, and place it in the file. Also, include a master for making additional copies in the file, so if someone runs out of materials or needs an extra copy after the original run is gone, additional copies can easily be made.

A good way to organize this file is to put the most recent materials (i.e., those handed out at the last meeting) in the front of all of the files. This way, someone who has missed a meeting or otherwise needs the most recent materials can readily locate them without having to ask you. Keep this material up front until after the next meeting (since people who miss one meeting are likely to want to catch up at the next one), and then refile it into the general file.

It is also helpful to organize the file system into logical categories, and use a divider with a tab to indicate this. Some typical categories might be: ad copies, sample letters, masters for flyers, masters for stationery, articles, marketing policies and procedures, marketing ideas, order forms, and newsletters. Set up the files according to the categories that are relevant for you.

If you have distributed quite a number of materials, a list of all the materials you have prepared and distributed will help your people know if they have obtained everything. Plan to update your list every few weeks to keep it current, and perhaps keep a copy of it in the beginning of the file. (You'll see a sample of an Available Handout form illustrated in Exhibit 8. You'll notice it lists everything that's available by major category, and includes the date when it was put together.)

This kind of filing system is also useful for distributing current materials to new people, since you can easily distribute copies of everything everyone else has to the newcomer. Just pull one of everything out of the file yourself, or invite the newcomer to go to the files and do so. Then, go over everything with this new person in your orientation, as previously discussed.

Using a Newsletter or Update to Keep Everyone Informed

A newsletter or update is an excellent tool, in addition to regular sales meetings, for keeping a sales group informed. With a small group, an update in memo form makes more sense. But as your group grows, a more formal newsletter with a special title looks more impressive. In fact, such a newsletter can be a tool for recruiting new salespeople, since it shows what you have been doing to support and guide your group.

Some of the topics to cover in your newsletters and updates include:

- Dates of upcoming sales meetings, and, if you know in advance, any special topics you will be covering (such as techniques for finding leads)
- Dates of upcoming presentations, talks, etc. you or others in your group might be giving—or which people might find of general interest
- Plans for new materials you will be developing, and a request for suggestions on materials needed
- New marketing and promotional materials available (at the next meeting or in the sales materials file)
- Upcoming advertising
- Highlights of a planned publicity approach
- Arrangements for an upcoming sales party or special event
- Availability of new brochures, flyers
- Sales tips from a recent meeting
- A list of new salespeople (or perhaps a welcome to newcomers)
- Guidelines for follow-up after a planned promotional event
- Current commission arrangements

Exhibit 8

Creative Travel

6537 Chabot Road • Oakland, California 94619 • (415) 658-2747

AVAILABLE HANDOUTS

July 22, 1991

The following materials have been distributed at recent sales meetings. If you are missing anything, you can pick it up at your convenience.

Masters (for copying or for presentation book)

Travel Earn Money Flyer
Customized Travel Program Flyer
Travel Nights Flyer
Overseas Program List with All Trip Dates
Kenya Adventure Flyer
Egyptian Odyssey Flyer
16-day Tour Flyer
13-day Tour Flyer
China Odyssey Flyer
Greek Odyssey Flyer
Registration Form
Creative Travel Response Letter (Dear Travel Enthusiast)
PR Release on Trips to China and Kenya
SF State Catalog Listing
SF Examiner Article on Kenya ("Into Africa")
East Bay Times Article on Trips
Palo Alto Times Review Article on Trips
SF Magazine Ad ("Discover the Splendors of Ancient Egypt")
Kenya Adventure Brochure Showing Sponsorship by Vermont Alumni
    Association or Boston Museum of Science

Brochures (for distribution to interested people)

China Odyssey
Greek Odyssey
Egyptian Odyssey
10-day Cruise
7-day Cruise
Kenya Adventure & Wildlife Trails

Sales Aids (for your own information)

Questions and Answers on Kenya and Egypt
Marketing Techniques Manual
Marketing and Commission Plain
Current Newsletter
Current List of Travel Associates

- New products and services now available
- Reports of achievements of other salespeople
- A report on an awards or recognition program

Use a short headline or underlined lead to introduce each topic. That way the key points covered jump right out.

About two to four pages is a good length for your update or newsletter. A few samples from some different programs I have been involved with are included to illustrate some ways you might set these up. (See Exhibits 9 and 10.)

Notice that both are very simply set up—you can do them on an ordinary typewriter or word processor. One is presented as an ordinary update; the other has a headline title to turn it into a more formal newsletter. You can easily create a headline title yourself using rub-on letters, such as Letraset or Pres-type (described in more detail in Chapter 8, on materials). Then, for future use, make some master copies of your head on a blank sheet of paper, and when you are ready to write up your newsletter, type or copy it onto your master or paste up your copy on the master later.

To show when your update or newsletter has come out, date it. To show this is part of a continuing series, number each one—or identify it by volume and issue number (i.e., Vol. 1, No. 1). Also, keep back copies of your newsletter or update on hand, to show what you have been doing to new people.

As for how often to do these, that depends on the size and activity level of your group. When you are first starting your sales network, a one- or two-pager every three or four weeks is probably fine. But as your group grows, you will probably want go go to a larger format, because you have more news to report. Also, you will probably want to do this more often, perhaps every two or three weeks, because there is more going on.

Initially, you or the head of the sales group might do all the writing yourself, when your group is still small. But as your group and newsletter grows, consider asking your salespeople to make relevant contributions, such as "sales approaches which have worked for me." This helps to keep your people more involved, and these by-lined accounts can also serve as a form of recognition among peers that serves as a motivator, as well as conveying useful tips to others.

There are all sorts of possibilities for a newsletter, depending on your own interests and talents in this area, and the needs of your group. Use an approach that works for you in your own situation.

Getting Feedback

It is also important to get feedback from your group from time to time to help coordinate what everyone is doing and find out what people need from you. Then you can prepare the necessary materials or adapt your support activities accordingly.

Exhibit 9

The International Foods Group

The Universe Traveler

⊫ₒ

September 1983 Vol. 1, No. 2
Edited by Gini Graham Scott, Ph.D. President, MLM Marketing Specialists
6537 Chabot Road, Oakland, Ca. 94618

INTERNATIONAL FOODS GROUP DOUBLES IN ITS FIRST MONTH

Now that we have finally received our first shipments of food and new
distributors have received their starter kits, we have started to grow rapidly.
There are now about 20 of us in the International Foods Group, up from about
10 in the beginning of August. And with the strategies we have planned, we
should start growing even faster.

IFG SPONSORS A COOPERATIVE ADVERTISING/PROMOTION CAMPAIGN

Now that we have key distributors all over the Bay Area, we are launching a
cooperative advertising/promotion campaign, featuring large ads and flyers
with the names of these distributors and the areas they are covering. Then,
prospects can call the distributor in their own area, and leads will be passed
downline from there. As we get new distributors in other parts of the Bay
Area, they will be added to this campaign.

The advantage to this approach is it makes each distributor seem to be part
of a strong well-organized team. And so prospects are more likely to be con-
vinced of the value of the program and sign-up.

UNIVERSE AS IN OCTOBER/NOVEMBER LIFESTYLE - LEADS GO DOWNLINE

Our August/September ad produced several calls and at least one new
Universe Foods distributor, so we'll have another ad in the October/Novem-
ber issue—and this one will list our key Bay Area distributors. The ad will
accompany my column on multi-level marketing—this column to be devoted
to what makes a good ad!

Exhibit 9. (continued)

IFG DISTRIBUTORS CONTINUE TO FOLLOW UP ON LEADS FROM SF FAIR

We're continuing to pass on leads from the SF Fair held July 30-31 to IFG downline members. We got about 400 leads who expressed interest in Universe Foods, and have new distributed about 150 of them, by area, to our key distributors. Everyone has been waiting until the food and sales literature arrived to make contacts. Now that they have arrived, the follow-up process is about to begin in earnest.

Since it's about a month after the fair, we're suggesting this kind of approach. Just call the person in an informal, casual way; say you got their name from a friend who was at the SF Fair doing a booth with Universe Foods; and since they expressed some interest in gourmet foods, you wanted to invite them to a small dinner or tasting party in their area. (And you might note that you got their name since you live in their area.) They'll have a chance to sample some of these foods, meet a nice group of people, and find out how they can get these foods which taste great, are super convenient, inexpensive, etc. (And if it seems appropriate, mention they can make money letting others know about these foods, too.)

Use whatever approach feels most comfortable to you in following-up. The main thing is to be friendly and informal, so people feel they are coming to a casual dinner, not just a business meeting. Or alternatively, offer to put on a small tasting party or dinner in their home if they would like to invite a few friends over. Yet, even though you keep it casual, do get their commitment to participate—or call you if they can't make it. Make sure they understand there will only be a small group at the dinner or tasting party and that their presence is important.

IFG SPONSORS ITS FIRST DINNER PARTIES; WRITE-UPS GO TO IFG MEMBERS

We had our first dinners to try out Universe Foods and then talk about strategies for promoting Universe in the Bay Area August 22rd and 23rd. We had 6 to 10 people at each event, which seems to be a good size to work with when you put on your own Universe dinner. Most of the people were already in Universe, and the guests there either signed up after the dinner or indicated they plan to sign up. We've written up a detailed description of this event: "Recipe for Putting On a Successful Tasting or Dinner Party," so others can do the same. Also, we have a list of costs of individual items, so you can figure dinner costs.

NEXT IFG DINNER/STRATEGY PLANNING SESSIONS SET FOR SEPT. 13 & 26

Since our first two meetings in August were so successful, we'll be having more dinners to try out new products followed by a training/strategy plan-

Exhibit 9.   (continued)

ning session for all 1st, 2nd, and active 3rd level IFG members every two weeks. Get-togethers for September are scheduled for Tues., Sept. 13 and Mon., Sept. 26 from 7:30–10:00.

PRELIMINARY PLANS TO GET A LOCAL WAREHOUSE

Since one of the keys to a successful Bay Area Universe program is having a local warehouse, we have been discussing some ways of getting a warehouse here as soon as possible. We are currently considering the possibility of financing a warehouse cooperatively, if we don't have a single person who wants to invest in a warehouse (it requires an initial order of 500 cases—approximately a $13,000 investment). However, if we get a group of say 20 people together to order 25 cases each—about $600 a person—that might be a way to proceed.

So as you get people in your downline, explore this possibility with them, and let us know if people are interested. We can coordinate the plans to organize a warehouse from here. Then, once we get one warehouse, we can set up sub-warehouses around the Bay Area, so that using a warehouse becomes very convenient.

PLANS FOR SPECIAL EVENTS IN THE FUTURE

While we see the small dinner get-togethers and one-on-one presentations as the primary way of promoting the Universe program, we are also exploring the possibility of organizing special events in the future as we get larger and more organized. One possible approach might to to have large events, perhaps one every month or two, featuring Universe Foods, special speakers, maybe entertainment, awards, etc. The purpose of these events will be to bring together everyone in the area for a kind of celebration combined with training in MLM techniques. Also, these could be a way of recruiting new people, too.

We'll be looking for ideas and assistance on organizing such events, so if you have suggestions, let us know.

IFG STARTS A UNIVERSE MARKETING TECHNIQUES MANUAL

This month we're starting a Universe Marketing Techniques Manual for members of the IFG downline. The manual will include ideas for promoting the program successfully. As we try out new approaches, we'll write them up and you can add them to the manual. Current write-ups deal with putting on a dinner party, one-on-one presentations, setting goals, prices of individual products, etc. While we suggest giving out copies of this newsletter to prospects as a promotional aid, we ask that you only give copies of the Universe Marketing Techniques Manual to people who actually sign up. After all, we don't want to give our best secrets away to the competition.

Exhibit 10

Creative Travel

6537 Chabot Road • Oakland, California 94619 • (415) 658-2747

TRAVEL NETWORK UPDATE

CURRENT SCHEDULE OF SALES MEETINGS

The following schedule of sales meetings has been set up for February to accommodate everyone through a weekly evening and morning meeting, and a bi-weekly meeting for people out of town (or who miss a regular meeting). Feel free to come to the meeting which is best for you, or make special arrangements to pick up the latest handout if you miss a meeting. These times are:

Mondays—5:15-7:00 (Arrivals—5:15-5:30; Meeting—5:30-6:30; P.M.
Sales Training—6:30-7:00)
Tuesdays—9:15-11:00 (Arrivals—9:15-9:30; Meeting—9:30-10:30; A.M.
Sales Training—10:30-11:00)
2nd & 4th Tuesdays—5:30-7:00 (Meeting for out-of-towners or if you can't
make regular weekly meetings)

NEW MEMBERS JOIN SALES TEAM

As a result of our recent Travel-Sales ad, several new people have joined the Creative Travel sales network, and over the next few months, we will gradually be creating sales teams to coordinate activities around the Bay Area. A welcome to: Sabrina Gogos (San Francisco), Tom Rinaldo (San Francisco), Ellen Sarbone (San Francisco), Michael Ziegler (San Francisco), Jill Ireland (Oakland), Marilyn Radojcich (Portola Valley), and Chris (Palo Alto).

EAST BAY RESOURCE CENTER STARTED

In order to make things easier for people in the East Bay, David Ganelin is in the process of setting up a resource center there, which will include copies of videos and extra brochures and masters. Also, at some point, the sales training tapes are expected to be available there, too, and other East Bay activities may be coordinated from there as the Creative Travel network grows and evolves.

NEW LISTS AVAILABLE OF FILMS, HANDOUTS, TRAVEL ASSOCIATES

The following lists are now available to help you keep track of the films in our library, the various materials handed out in sales meetings, and the travel

Exhibit 10.   (continued)

associates who are working with us. These lists, which will be updated regular include: 1) AVAILABLE VIDEOTAPES, 2) AVAILABLE HANDOUTS, and 3) CURRENT TRAVEL ASSOCIATES.

GROWING FILM LIBRARY

We now have over a dozen films in our film library and it's growing weekly. Three of these films come from the Tourist Offices of Kenya (*Holiday of a Lifetime*) and Egypt (*Cairo* and *Upper Egypt*). Another film comes from a person who went on one of our trips (*Kenya* by Roy Maloney). The rest have been taped off the air from KQED, which has been offering some wonderful educational films, mostly on Africa, though there will be more programs on some of our other destinations shortly. We will also be previewing films from the China-American Friendship Association, and may be transferring some of these onto video.

If you know of films or videos that you like on any of our destinations, let us know. Besides our current destinations (Kenya, China, Greece, Egypt, and Morocco), we are collecting films on the destinations we will be adding shortly (Australia, New Zealand, Tahiti, Fiji, Tibet, and hopefully Russia).

PR CAMPAIGN BEGINS

About three weeks ago, we sent out a mailing to 60 newspapers and magazines around the Bay Area, and there has been at least one listing that we know about—the *Palo Alto Times Review* listed our trips in their Sunday Travel section last weekend. There have been about a half-dozen calls as a result, and a handout showing the write-up is now available.

If you notice additional write-ups anywhere, please keep copies, so I can add them to our files and make up additional flyers.

VISIT TO THE METCO IN NEW YORK—PLANS BEING MADE NOW FOR NEW DESTINATIONS

As some of you know, I made an unexpected trip to New York last week to be on the Phil Donahue Show, and, of course, I made arrangements to meet with Metco—with Program Director Ed Williams and Sales Manager Joe Mangiacotti. I filled them in on the developments here in creating this network, and I picked up some additional brochures, including the new brochures of China, just out. We'll be getting the retail brochures from Metco very shortly—they're just waiting for their new Africa brochures to come in.

Joe also told me about the plans to add the new destinations in the South Pacific—Australia, New Zealand, Tahiti, Fiji—plus Tibet. He's currently meeting with the airlines, and will be going over to these countries in March to meet with suppliers. By June or July we should have brochures on these desti-

Exhibit 10. (continued)

nations and be ready to promote them. Russia is also under consideration as a new destination.

SOME MORE MARKETING IDEAS

Carry flyers with you wherever you go. For example, on the plane to New York, I got into a conversation with the person sitting next to me about our trips.

Think about how new marketing outlets might be able to sell these trips. For example, I've started talking to some hotels about letting their guests know about our programs.

One source of feedback is, of course, day-to-day conversations with individual salespeople, and your regular sales meeting. For instance, as part of every meeting, ask people what they need from you now.

Also, as your group grows, it helps to develop materials to get feedback, such as a Feedback Questionnaire or Comments Sheet. One advantage of these materials is that handing them out can get people thinking more specifically about what they want from you, or what they would like to improve. Also, this shows that you seriously want to know what people think so you can incorporate this into your organizational activities. Additionally, you may obtain important feedback that people may not share with you otherwise, because some people may not feel comfortable stating certain objections openly to you or in a meeting. Then, too, as previously noted, it is generally not advisable to bring up negatives about how things are working in a general group meeting, because this can turn into a big gripe session and lower morale. Certainly, you want to know if there are serious gripes, but it is often better to deal with these quietly or on a one-on-one basis, so you deal with the problem without making it worse. By using these feedback materials, you can provide people with a way to quietly express what they feel— and if they wish, let people fill out the questionnaire or comment sheet anonymously. This way they can feel even freer to say what they think, because they won't be afraid that you will get upset with them for bringing up any problems.

Exhibit 11 is a sample questionnaire. It asks questions on these key areas:

- Additional materials needed

- Help in sales training desired

- Types of obstacles or problems encountered in the field

- How sales meetings can be more useful

- Reactions to newsletter and information provided and suggestions for changes and additions

- Help needed with leads

- Overall feelings about sales management and coordination and any suggestions for improvement

These questions are designed to get feedback in a positive, constructive way. While some ask for comments about possible problem areas, they are designed to get suggestions for improvement. You can't avoid looking at what's negative if you want to change things, but then you use the negatives you get as a basis for change.

One good way to distribute these questionnaires and be sure everyone answers is to take about ten minutes during a general meeting to ask people to fill them out. An alternative is to distribute the questionnaires at the meeting, and ask people to fill them out and bring them back next time, stressing the importance of bringing them back. It's important to stress this if you expect people to return these questionnaires later, because commonly people forget or don't want

Exhibit 11.   Sample Feedback Questionnaire

This questionnaire is designed to learn what you need or would like to see improved, so I can best support you and coordinate the activities of this group. Please answer the questions to the best of your ability. You don't need to sign your name, since I will be looking at these questionnaires as a group to get a sense of what everyone wants generally.

1. What kind of additional materials do you need (i.e., sales literature, training aids, advertising and promotional materials, etc.)? Please be specific:

    _____

    _____

2. What kind of help would you like in sales training?

3. What types of obstacles or problems, if any, are you encountering in the field (i.e., in locating leads, in contacting people, in follow-up, etc.)?

4. How can our sales meetings be more useful to you? What would you like to see added? Dropped? Changed?

5. How do you find the newsletter/update? What else would you like to see included in it? What changes would you suggest?

    a. How often would you like to receive this newsletter/update?

6. Do you need any help with leads? If so, what kind of assistance would be helpful?

7. How do you feel generally about the way things are being coordinated? Do you have any suggestions for improvement?

to take the time to fill out questionnaires. That's why it's usually more effective, if it won't take too long, to get these questionnaires filled out and returned on the spot. However, under some circumstances, this take-it-home approach may be good, as when you feel there are some serious problems to deal with, and you feel people may be uncomfortable writing down their comments in a group or in front of you, because they will feel put on the spot and would prefer to turn in their responses anonymously. If you are using this anonymous approach, you can collect the responses by putting a file for Questionnaire Responses in your sales materials file set-up, and ask your salespeople to put their filled-out question-naires in that.

However you handle distribution, it's important to emphasize the value of this feedback for the group as a whole and for each person. Point out that you will be using it to make decisions about how better to help members of the group, such as by using their guidance to prepare the materials they need and make the sales meeting even better. Also, note that you want to see if you should make changes in the way you are coordinating things, or whether everyone feels things are fine as they are. In short, you want to emphasize that you are using these materials to improve things for everyone. Then, once your salespeople realize how this infor-mation will help you help them, they will be receptive to providing this feedback.

Once you get the forms back, review them question-by-question to get a gen-eral sense of what people want. Note where there are common criticisms about how something is done, so you can change. Likewise, if a number of people mention the same wants or needs, be prepared to respond. For instance, develop the requested materials; add the areas of sales training people want; provide more leads if people need this; and so on. If only one or two people make a comment, you might mention this at your next sales meeting, to show you are aware that some people want something in a certain area. Then, at the meeting you can see if others express a similar need, and if so respond accordingly. If not, perhaps simply help the people who have expressed that need on an individual basis. In any event, in the meeting you hold after you get this feedback, include a report on the major responses you received, and your plans to respond to these comments, to show you have seriously considered the suggestions received. Then, as soon as possible, put these plans into action.

How often should you seek feedback? That will depend on how things seem to be going with your group. If things seem to be going smoothly, about once a month is fine. But if you sense there are some problems, or you are considering making some changes in how you are coordinating things, perhaps do this more often—say every one or two weeks until you feel things are going smoothly again.

Summing Up

In summary, when you are coordinating the sales activities of your group, plan to coordinate activities in these key areas:

- Coordinating contacts
- Setting up a message system
- Distributing sales materials
- Using a newsletter or update to keep everyone informed
- Getting feedback

The decision to help people with leads is optional. Some sales leaders do it; others leave the development of leads up to their people. For a detailed discussion of coordinating a leads program, see Chapter 7 on Providing Support.

CHAPTER 7

Providing Support

Besides training, coordination, and motivation, other types of assistance might include the following:

- A leads referral system, where you develop some lead sources yourself, coordinate the distribution of leads, and help people develop their own leads;

- The development of sample telephone scripts, letters, and sales presentation guidelines to illustrate effective approaches;

- Providing tapes or videos or a chance to observe sample sales presentations;

- Putting on your own presentations or demonstrations to which your salespeople can bring customers;

- Creating sales presentation books for your people or showing them how to create their own;

- Establishing a regular feedback system to find out what other types of assistance and support your people need, so you can provide that, too.

Organizing and Coordinating a Leads Referral System

Since leads are the heart of any direct sales effort, your people need to be able to develop good leads—either on their own or with your support.

Setting up a leads referral system to help them do this can be very effective for several reasons: first, some new salespeople may not know much about developing leads and prospecting, so they will want your guidance. Second, some prospective recruits will be drawn to selling your product if you supply the leads or

assist in finding them, since they know leads generation can be very time-con-
suming, and they want that extra support. So, your leads system can be a factor in
being able to recruit top salespeople. Third, your leads and coordination assistance can help to avoid the problem of your salespeople contacting the same
people. You may not be able to avoid the problem entirely because of overlapping lists from different sources, but your guidance through leads management
will reduce the problem.

To set up a leads referral system, the first step is to do some research on your
target market to obtain lists of names of individuals or organizations within this
market. One obvious source of this research is any relevant to which groups you
belong, have been to as a guest, or have close associates who are members. If you
are a member, you may already have a membership directory or can get a list by
asking. You can also get lists from some other groups with likely prospects. One
source is the membership lists that some groups provide to non-members—sometimes for free to potential customers. Some groups offer their membership lists
for sale.

Here's an example of how acquiring membership lists might work. Say you
have a product that would be especially appealing to professional career women
in corporate management positions or heading their own business. You might
gather together the membership rosters of the businesswomen's groups throughout your area (i.e., the local chapter of the National Association for Professional
Saleswomen, National Association of Female Executives, etc.). Second, you might
get membership lists from business groups with a large professional women's
membership, such as a business breakfast group, the Sales and Marketing Executives, the local chapter of the National Speakers' Association, and so on. Still
another source might be the members of a singles or social group catering to a
business and professional membership.

Besides lists of individuals, you might also gather the names of likely groups,
organizations, and companies. A good source for this might be your local Chamber of Commerce, which might have a directory of all its member companies, and
perhaps a list of local associations and organizations. Special business directories
may also be useful, and these may be available in your local library. Some possible directories might be the following:

- A local Better Business Bureau directory for its members

- AT&T's Business Buyers Guide in some cities

- Specialized yellow page directories, such as directories for senior citizens
  (the Silver Pages), for ethnic groups (such as the Asian-American directory), and for minority groups (such as the Gay Businesses Directory in
  San Francisco)

- Another source is an organization of organization and company leaders,
  such as the National Association for Association Executives and the Young
  President's Club

Magazines and newspapers may also be a source of company and organization lists. For example, some business publications, such as *Venture Magazine, California Business*, city business papers, and your newspaper business section, may occasionally run lists of companies in different categories, along with the names and addresses of company officers.

Other sources are published guides by commercial publishers, some available in your own library, such as *Contacts Influential*, listing high-income individuals, and the *Corporate Meeting Planners Directory*, listing the people who plan company programs.

You can also obtain lists of individuals and companies from list brokers, by specifying exactly what type of person or organization you want to contact. You'll see these brokers listed in your local phone book under "Mailing Lists." There are additionally specialty list brokers, who specialize in lists of a certain type, such as New Age Mailing, which has lists of New Age, spiritual, peace, and environmental groups.

Trade shows and conferences are another source for lists. Often these are easily obtained from a program with a list of exhibitors, or they may be available for purchase from the show organizer.

Also watch current newspapers, magazines, and other media for possible leads, which can appear in ads or articles. Check for those relevant to your product line. For example, when I worked with a health program, I looked for ads from people selling other health products, as they were potential salespeople for my own health program. When I was marketing travel, I regularly checked the travel section listings of groups sponsoring a trip; maybe they might be interested in going on or marketing one of our trips, too.

In short, there are numerous sources for lists of individuals and organizations. Once you determine what kind of lists would be useful for you and your group, research those that are available by contacting your local library, business associations, associates, or list brokers who might have lists. Also, collect likely lists when they appear in magazines and newspapers.

Then, as you gather these materials, organize them into a file you or your salespeople can use for easy reference. For example, in marketing a health program, I made up a manila folder for each category of leads, which included lists of: Speakers, Women's Groups and Businesses, Writers and Media People, Singles Groups, Nature and Environmental Groups, Communications and Media Groups, Health Professionals and Therapists, Personal Development and Social Groups, and Miscellaneous Leads. Then these were in turn organized by city or area in the territory we covered.

Choose the categories that make sense for your particular product or service, based on the types of markets you expect to target and the different geographic areas covered by your salespeople. Since there may be some overlap from list to list when people or groups are in several directories, work out some advance arrangements to handle this to reduce or avoid the conflicts that arise from double contacting. If feasible, go through these lists to eliminate duplications. But if that's not possible, work out procedures to cover what happens when one person contacts someone who has already been contacted. For example, a common pol-icy is to let the person making the initial contact handle any follow-up with that lead, unless there has been a long time lapse after this contact, or it concluded with no sale. Then the person who closes the sale gets the credit, unless the sale seems to be the result of a joint contribution, suggesting that a split of any com-missions would be appropriate.

Once you have these categories and folders set up with the lists of leads, let the people in your group know, and encourage them to use these lists and indicate which ones they are using. If you have already established guidelines for who is working with what type of lead, it may be obvious who can use which category (for example, if someone is contacting women's groups, they would get a list of such groups). You might use a questionnaire to help you determine who is work-ing with or wants to work with certain groups or in certain areas. If you haven't already used such a questionnaire to help you in deciding whom to recruit, you can ask your salespeople to fill it out now. (See Exhibit 12 which we used for such a purpose.) Alternatively, if people are selecting which lists they want to work with themselves, or using parts of different lists, ask them to indicate which leads they are taking by initialing or starring the names of those people or groups they contact. Or, if they use the list in full, they should note this with their name or initials. Then, others will know not to make the contact.

When people do indicate they are using a list, it's important to monitor this to make sure they are actively using these leads, so your leads are worked most efficiently. For example, check with your people from time to time to make sure they are, in fact, contacting the leads they have taken, and if not, indicate in the file that these leads are available again, or reassign them. If there should be any conflicts over who gets what name, speak with the people involved and work out something that seems fair, so each person gets approximately the same number of names, or at least a proportionate number of names if people are working differ-ent amounts of time.

Besides letting your salespeople select their own leads from the leads file, you can make assignments yourself. This approach is especially good if you need some response to a lead quickly, such as might occur if you get some call-ins or write-ins in response to an ad that need to be handled right away, or if you see a current lead in a newspaper or magazine.

When you do make assignments, use the geographic areas and categories of your salespeople as a guide as to which leads to assign to who. Still, stay flexible if you should get a concentration of hot leads in a particular area, so you can spread out the leads you give, so each person gets their fair share in the same number or gets a proportionate share of leads from you.

If you see your salespeople at regular meetings about once a week, you can easily refer these leads by including a copy of the referred names in the salesperson's file folder. Or for more immediate action, especially for an impor-tant lead, call the salesperson and pass on the lead by phone.

Finally, be sure to keep the original lists or a copy of every lead you give out. Invite your salespeople to make copies of the master lists in your files that they want to use—but otherwise advise them not to take any of the master lists out of

Exhibit 12. Travel Associate Questionnaire

This questionnaire is designed to assist us in coordinating a sales network to market the trips currently offered by Creative Travel—to Kenya, China, Egypt, Greece, and Morocco. Also, it is to assist us in assigning leads to you, and in arranging for you to give presentations if you are interested in this. Please fill it out as completely as possible.

NAME _____

ADDRESS _____

CITY, STATE, ZIP _____

PHONE: (Day) _____ (Evening) _____

CURRENT/USUAL OCCUPATION(S) _____

TYPES OF GROUPS YOU CURRENTLY BELONG TO _____

TYPES OF GROUPS YOU WOULD PREFER TO CONTACT _____

BAY AREA CITIES/NEIGHBORHOODS YOU WOULD PREFER TO WORK IN

OTHER AREAS WHERE YOU HAVE OR WOULD LIKE TO DEVELOP CONTACTS _____

NUMBER OF HOURS PER WEEK YOU CAN DEVOTE TO PROGRAM _____

NATURE OF INTEREST: Kenya ___ China ___ Egypt ___ Greece ___ Morocco ___

INTERESTED IN GIVING TALKS/PRESENTATIONS? Yes   No

EXPERIENCE IN SALES _____

OTHER RELEVANT EXPERIENCE _____

the office. This restriction is extremely important, for otherwise, unless you keep your own back-up extra copy, your lists may get lost. Or if a salesperson decides to go on to other things, you may find it difficult to get your list back. Thus, to keep your lists, keep them in your office, and perhaps keep an extra back-up copy just in case.

Developing Sample Telephone Scripts, Letters, and Sales Presentation Guidelines

Even seasoned salespeople may not be sure exactly how to present your product, so your guidance through suggested telephone scripts, letters, and sales presentation guidelines can help them do this effectively.

Ideally, develop these through your own experience—describe what has worked for you. It's ideal if you have already created these scripts, letters, and guidelines in doing your own selling, because you already know what has worked for you. In this case, simply make copies of what you have already done and hand them out to your salespeople. At the same time, since people have different effective selling styles, make it clear that these guidelines are just a suggestion about an approach you have used successfully, but people can adapt it as they wish to suit their own style.

If you previously have done the selling yourself, but haven't recorded how you did it, work on turning your experience into written form. If you don't normally write things down, you can tape some of your phone calls or presentations. Then, get a transcription of these calls or presentations, and edit the copy to highlight the main points you make in your sales call. Afterwards, once this edited transcript is typed, you have a sample script or presentation guideline to hand out as a suggestion.

Should you be introducing a new product or be in a situation where you haven't done any selling yourself, you can handle the development of scripts, letters, and presentation guidelines in two ways:

- Field-test the approach yourself. One method is to draft the guidelines for what to say first, then put them into practice with customers, and afterwards make necessary modifications to improve what you say, and perhaps go through the process again to refine your materials. The other method, if you don't like to write what you plan to say in advance and prefer to improvise on the spontaneity of the moment, is to simply tape your calls and presentations. Then, when you have taped one you feel is good, transcribe the tape and use the transcription to guide your write-up.

- Write up your guidelines based on what you feel someone should say—or what you might say if you were going to be selling. In doing so, highlight the key benefits you feel should be mentioned. This approach is less ideal, since it hasn't been tested in the field for its effectiveness. However, it is still useful for giving your salespeople some general guidelines about what you consider important about your product. They can modify the material in the field, and as they do, ask them to give you feedback on what approach they have found especially effective. Then, you can incorporate their suggestions in subsequent drafts of your guidelines.

When you prepare these materials, consider the major types of customers your salespeople will contact, and, as appropriate, develop separate telephone scripts, introductory or follow-up letters, and sales presentation guidelines for each situation.

Also, keep in mind the basic principles for good sales techniques—attracting attention, maintaining interest, arousing desire, showing conviction, and moving on to an effective close. Whomever the sales materials are directed towards, use a lead-in for your sample script, letter, or presentation guideline to attract attention, and quickly highlight the major benefits to maintain interest. Then, go on in these materials to trigger the emotional impulse of desire, and use a tone of assurance and conviction to be persuasive. Finally, lead up to a strong close, which asks for a specific goal the salesperson wants at this stage of the contact. For instance, a phone script or letter might be designed to build up to a request to set up a meeting, while a guideline for how to do a presentation might be designed to lead up to a tactic to close the sale.

As you prepare more and more of these materials, consider combining them into a small booklet or manual that you provide to your people. Perhaps these might be distributed to new people at your sales orientation, or perhaps you might use your training meetings as a time to go over these materials, too.

Some sample scripts and letters are included (see Exhibits 15 and 16) to show you how these might be prepared to cover different situations and different stages of the sales process:

1. The initial call to find out the correct contact person

2. Introductory phone call scripts

3. Introductory letters

4. Follow-up letters

Then, the presentation manual might be used to guide the presentation itself. Importantly, these scripts and letters share these following characteristics:

1. They're short. The phone call is designed to last about a minute. The letter is only a few paragraphs on a single page.

2. They get quickly to the point in stating the purpose of the phone call or letter.

3. They quickly suggest a benefit targeted to the particular individual or organization being contacted.

4. There's some information about the company to establish credentials.

5. There is a close which asks for action and sets the stage for the next step in the sales process.

In summary, in developing your own sample materials for your salespeople, keep these points in mind:

1. Base them on your own sales experience where you can, and incorporate the main points the person should cover in a call, letter, or presentation.
2. Develop materials for each major type of customer your people will be contacting.
3. Follow the principles for good sales techniques in writing up this material.
4. Provide materials for each step in the sales process—i.e., the initial call to find out who to contact; the introductory phone call; the follow-up phone call; the introductory letter; the presentation.

Providing Tapes or Videos or a Chance to Observe Sample Sales Presentations

Another excellent form of extra support is offering your salespeople a chance to observe or listen to other sales presentations. Inviting newcomers to accompany you or another salesperson is an ideal way to break in a new person. In this case, as previously noted, the newcomer should first go along just as an observer, and then gradually he can assume a greater and greater role, until he can do the presentation himself. Also, additional trips to observe in the field can provide a useful refresher or opportunity to get some new ideas, though generally most salespeople probably prefer to work alone. So, in general you won't be able to use a regular continuing program of in-the-field observations of sales presentations for the bulk of your training and support assistance.

However, you can readily use tapes or videos to provide sales ideas, as well as show these as a basis for discussion about improving sales techniques.

Making the tape is fairly easy. During a telephone sales call, use a phone jack to connect the recorder to the phone, and tape directly from that. Technically, you are not supposed to record a conversation without informing the other person you are doing this, because of invasion of privacy laws. However, since you are primarily interested in recording what you say and not what the other person says, and since you are using the tape for a limited purpose of demonstrating a sales techniques to your own people and not making the tape widely available for commercial sale, you probably can record this without legal problems.

To tape a personal presentation, one approach is to have your tape recorder in your briefcase, and tape without announcing that you are doing this, as you would in a phone call, since again your main interest is recording yourself and your own presentation. However, since this is a live meeting with someone you have already spoken to, it's better, if you have good rapport with this person, to explain that you would like to tape the meeting to help in training your people. Since you have already prepared the way with your call to set up the meeting, the person has already shown some receptivity to what you have to say, then he is apt to be receptive to letting you record your presentation, too. If so, the taping probably will not interfere with his response to your message. Or if he prefers you didn't tape, he can always say no. You can make arrangements to tape in advance, or be more informal and ask when you arrive. If you suggest that this is a common practice in your organization, this may help to smooth the way.

Another way to get a sample sales presentation on tape is to set up a simulated presentation with a friend, associate, or member of your sales group, and record this.

To make a video, you will need one and possibly two other people along. Only one other person is needed if you are using a super-8mm or VHS camcorder, and just about anyone who can aim a camera can do this if you are just making a simple in-house video. However, for more professional quality, go to three-quarter-inch or a digital video recording system, and work with someone experienced in using this kind of camera. A professional or more experienced video person will also probably want to bring along someone to handle sound.

Preferably, arrange permissions to videotape in advance, since the video camera is more intrusive than the tape recorder, and you may be more apt to get a no if you catch a prospective customer unprepared, whereas with an audio tape, a more casual request, is more apt to get a yes. In making these arrangements, explain why you want to tape; make sure the person is completely supportive, since there will be disruptions before you can start your sales presentation to set up lighting and sound. It's important to get this whole-hearted okay; otherwise don't do it, because you want to be sure your videotaping won't interfere with your presentation and cost you a sale.

If you do feel resistance, and you can't find a truly willing customer, use a simulated sales presentation. For this, get a friend, associate, or salesperson to play the customer role.

Once you have these tapes or videotapes, invite your salespeople to listen to or view them at their convenience, or use them as part of your regular training program. If you do, spend about fifteen to thirty minutes listening to or viewing the presentation with your people, and then spend some time discussing it. During this discussion, it's especially effective to call attention to the highlights of the presentation to emphasize the sales techniques that increase effectiveness—such as a good opening to get attention, a successful presentation of benefits, the techniques used to adapt the presentation to a particular customer's interests and needs, and the powerful steps used to close. Afterwards, allow time for comments and feedback, and answer any questions that come up.

Putting on Presentations or Demonstrations for Your Salespeople

Another support strategy, as your sales group grows, is putting on a presentation or demonstration for your salespeople and their prospective customers. These presentations are also a good selling point to attract prospective salespeople to market your product.

To help prepare, preferably go to several presentations of similar or related programs. Notice what information is covered, how presented, and what techniques seem to work especially well. Also notice what questions come up frequently so you can be prepared to answer like questions in your own presentation.

The basic steps to putting on a good presentation include: (1) advance planning, (2) good content and style, and (3) working out the logistics effectively.

Advance Planning

Advance planning helps you determine what to include, and how best to present it and organize the necessary logistics so the presentation goes well. In planning, keep these points in mind.

A good presentation is short and to the point. It should present the essential facts about your products and company in an interesting way, and answer any questions that come up. An effective presentation entertains and involves your audience, as well as informs. As in sales generally, the stress should be on benefits to the customer, (why he should want your product or service) and the presentation should build to a strong close. Your salespeople can then take it from there with the necessary applications or order forms.

As part of your advance planning, determine:

- How long the presentation will be

- What the specific parts of it will be

- Who will present which parts

- What is needed to make each part of the presentation effective (i.e., posters, charts, graphs, dramatizations, slides, overhead projections, videos, etc.)

- Where the presentation will be and what needs to be done to arrange for the site

- Whether there will be refreshments, and if so, what ones and who will make arrangements to have them there and/or serve them

- What kind of product samples, company brochures, handouts, etc. will be necessary, and what is necessary to have the required amount available

- What kind of arrangements will be necessary to invite prospective customers, salespeople, etc., and who will make these

- Any other elements needed to make your presentation a success

Since the average person only remembers about 10 to 20 percent of what he or she hears, you should emphasize and repeat key points. Use illustrations and demonstrations where you can, since a person remembers more—about 30 percent—if he sees something. Plus, visuals have immediate impact. Also, to make your presentation more entertaining and involving, include a few anecdotes or personal experiences. Use these to highlight key points and add color.

If this is new to you, don't worry about being nervous. As you get used to speaking and doing group presentations, your nervousness will subside. In fact, many of the most talented, well-paid speakers have a twinge of nervousness before they go in front of an audience. And they tend to perform better as a result of that tension, because they put that nervous energy into their performance.

The best way to reduce any anxious feelings is to be effectively prepared by knowing exactly what you want to say. Then, you'll be more confident when you start. Once you begin, relate to your audience and concentrate on your material—not on yourself—and soon you'll be totally involved in your presentation, and won't have a chance to feel nervous.

Having Good Content and Style

Organize your presentation or demonstration to last about forty-five minutes to an hour, including about fifteen minutes for arrivals. Plan on about fifteen minutes at the end for your salespeople to do a wind-up leading up to either (1) an immediate close, or (2) setting up a time for further discussion—such as going out for coffee after the meeting or meeting for lunch the following day.

This time format, about one to one and a half hours, can work for just about any presentation—beauty shows, cooking demonstrations, health and exercise programs, prepaid legal plans, accounting services—whatever your company sells.

The key is to start with a good opener to attract attention (such as a product demonstration, presentation of startling statistics to show why your program is needed, or slides of people using your product), and keep your following program tightly organized and compact. Preferably, ask listeners not to interrupt with questions, but to save them for the question period at the end. Allow about ten minutes for questions—but not much longer, because then people have a chance to bring up all sorts of trivia. It's better to invite those who still have questions to wait until the formal meeting breaks up. Finally, conclude with a close and wind up the meeting. Afterward, you'll be amazed at how many of those seemingly burning questions disappear.

Expect to include most of the same basic information as you would in a good one-on-one presentation (see Chapter 4). But add a little bit more "sizzle" to give your presentation added impact. Some possible ways to do this include:

- Start with or include a slide-sound presentation or film about how your product or service works
- Use a flip chart with pictures, graphs, and other visuals
- Have different salespeople present different parts of the program

As in a one-on-one presentation, have informative handouts or brochures about your company and what you offer, which people can take home with them if they are not ready to make a commitment now. Depending on your meeting format, these might be handed out or available on tables as people arrive, to give them something to glance at while they are waiting for the program to begin. Or if most or all prospective customers will be coming with the salesperson who invited them, it may be better to distribute these materials after the meeting, or let the salesperson hand out any materials. This way, the salesperson stays more in control of his or her prospects.

In organizing your presentation, use the same basic categories as in putting on an effective one-on-one presentation, and select those categories appropriate to your product line. These include the following:

- Introduction

- Information on the product or service

- Background information on your company

- Description of any back-up support your company provides in using the product or service

- A brief question-and-answer period

- A close that asks for some action or the order, and turns further follow-up over to your salespeople

If several people are able to do different parts of the presentation, so much the better. Having more than one presenter adds strength and substance to what you are saying; also, the variety in personalities and style can increase interest in what is being presented. Then, too, these different styles may find a resonance with different customers, increasing the chances of tapping someone's hot button to respond. Should you have someone in your organization who is an especially good motivator, have that person lead off the meeting to get everyone's attention and increase the excitement and interest level. Also, use your especially powerful motivators to handle the close, to better motivate everyone to act now.

Working out the Logistics

To make sure your meeting flows smoothly and professionally, work out the logistics in advance. Even if this will be a fairly small meeting in your home or office, with a handful of people, plan ahead so everything works well.

For a Smaller Meeting. For example, if this is a small meeting in your home or office, the following key points will contribute to an effective meeting:

Keep the tone of a small meeting friendly and informal. For example, have coffee or light refreshments on hand and invite people to help themselves before the presentation starts. This way people can mix and mingle, and feel good about being there when the meeting starts. Also, it's preferable to keep the chairs in a circle or semicircle, which creates a warmer, more personal atmosphere, so people feel more comfortable, not like they are being talked at in a classroom or theater.

Dress comfortably but well. If the meeting is in your office, you'll be dressed for business. If it's a home meeting, dress a little more nicely than you might normally do, to present a good, serious, professional impression. But don't overdo it, because if you dress much more formally than everyone else, others may feel uncomfortable. Essentially, dress just a notch above everyone else, but not much more.

If guests are late or don't show, start the meeting anyway, no later than fifteen minutes after it was scheduled to begin. You want to press ahead, because often people don't show up at these group presentations, so there's no need to worry about this or express concern to others. Also, it's not fair to the people already there to delay the meeting for latecomers. These people have shown enough interest to come, so orient your meeting to them and their needs. Should latecomers appear, invite them to quietly join the meeting, and indicate you will be glad to answer their questions about what they may have missed later. But *don't* try to start the meeting over for them—a sure way to antagonize the people who arrived on time.

Start with appropriate introductions to make everyone feel comfortable. In some smaller meetings, it makes sense to start with brief introductions (such as when you're marketing memberships in a social club, because people will want to know a little about the other people who may join with them). In other cases, where the product being sold is less personal, names are enough. Also, local customs may affect what people prefer, so use your own judgment in deciding how far to go in making introductions. However, generally, in a small meeting setting, introductions are appropriate, since everyone is sitting in a small area, and usually in a semicircle or circle. But then, if everyone knows everyone else, you can, of course, dispense with this.

Besides asking for introductions from others, say a little bit about yourself and any others making the presentation. Some things to note might be how you got involved with this company, product, or service, and your past experience with other companies and sales programs. Then go into the presentation, using the format already prepared.

For a Larger Meeting. To organize a larger meeting, expect to do additional groundwork to coordinate arrangements. Also work on building up some advance excitement to encourage a good showing. Some ways to prepare include:

Encourage your salespeople to make calls and invite guests. Stay in touch with them to keep them motivated, and find out how many people they are bringing. If they are having trouble getting prospects to attend, give them suggestions on what to do.

Give your salespeople plenty of advance notice and make the event seem special. As one approach, put on a special meeting each month, besides any regular small presentations you hold, and build this up as a special rally or presentation. Perhaps even invite a special motivational speaker.

Work out the program details in advance. Big sales presentations are not a time to improvise, though you want to leave room for spontaneity. So decide in advance who will participate and who will say what. If your salespeople are fairly new at giving presentations, rehearse a few times. Make sure everyone knows his or her part, and work out smooth transitions from one person to another. Also, plan a rough timetable for each part of the presentation, and remind everyone to stick to this.

Determine in advance what product samples, handouts, and audiovisual or other equipment are necessary. This way, you won't start your presentation, only to discover something you need isn't there. Also, determine who is responsible for preparing what, and provide plenty of time to prepare what you need. Use the Group Presentation Checklist, Exhibit 13, to help you prepare.

Find out in advance how many people are coming. Ask your salespeople to let you know if they are coming and how many guests they expect to bring, so you can properly prepare to have enough literature, refreshments, product samples, chairs, and other items on hand. Not all of your salespeople and their guests will let you know, and inevitably people will say they are coming but won't, while others will show up unannounced. But at least advance estimates will give you some rough guidelines to use in deciding how much of everything to prepare.

Dress to make a good impression. The usual rule here is to dress a little more formally than you might at a small informal presentation. This helps to give you a success image, which rubs off on your product or service and which contributes to making sales. Generally, men should wear a conservative suit or good sports jacket and slacks. Women should wear a dress, business suit, or fashionable pantsuit.

Set up everything properly in advance. Plan to arrive early before the meeting with everything you need, and give yourself plenty of time to set up. Then, check everything! If you're going to do a food demonstration, be sure the stove or hot plate works, and know how long it will take to prepare the food to serve it. You don't want to end up waiting an extra half-hour while everything heats up. Likewise, if you're showing slides or a video, check the projector and the video—TV connection. You don't want to find when you start your talk that a bulb is out, that the connection doesn't work when you're ready to start, or that your slides are missing or your video isn't rewound.

Get started on time. As in the informal setting, getting off to a timely start is critical to keep your audience with you. So allow about fifteen minutes to a half-hour for arrivals and socializing (perhaps even state this in your invitation). Then start on time, or at most ten to fifteen minutes late. People can get very impatient if they have to wait, and some may have plans for after the meeting. So let the

Exhibit 13.   Group Presentation Checklist

Date of Meeting _____   Speakers/Participants: _____
Location of Meeting _____   _____

Types of Materials Needed	Items Needed	Who Is Getting Needed Items

Equipment:

Literature:

Refreshments:

Other:

Topics Covered in Presentation	Speaker(s) Handling That Part of Meeting	Items Used in That Part of Meeting	Person Getting Item
1.			
2.			
3.			
4.			
5.			
6.			
7.			
8.			

latecomers miss whatever they miss, and fill them in later. This way you show you care about the people who have come on time.

Choose a good meeting location. Once your meetings grow beyond a size you can accommodate in an office or private home setting, find a larger public or commercial site. When you do, besides taking into account size considerations, choose a location that contributes to your professional image, and is in keeping with the image of your product and your selected target market. For instance, if you're selling a high-cost product to a business and professional market, use a nice hotel or restaurant for your meeting. If you have a product targeted to a lower-income, blue-collar market, perhaps use a church, bank meeting room, or your local YMCA. Other possible sites include large apartment complexes with conference rooms, lodges and other public buildings. The key is suitability for your selected audience. Also, choose a site centrally located to your market and easy to get to by the expected methods of travel (i.e., if people will be coming by public transportation as well as by car, choose a site accessible to both).

A good source of recommendations for sites is someone who puts on a lot of parties and events. Ask for suggestions. Also, should you go to a place that looks suitable (such as a restaurant where you happen to go for dinner), ask to see the manager about using it for your meetings.

In order better to choose a location to accomodate your meeting, estimate how large a space you will need in advance. To do so, ask your salespeople how many people they think they can recruit, and estimate how many people any ads or notices you are using are likely to pull. If possible, ask people planning to come to RSVP, so you can plan accordingly. Then, if you seem to be attracting a big response, consider organizing a second meeting for the overflow, or quickly arrange for a larger room. Alternatively, if the response is low, move to a smaller room, at the same location if you can. In fact, when you book the room in the first place, check in advance to see if such changes based on the expected response are possible. If so, that could be a good reason to make these arrangements. If not, consider how certain the expected attendance may be, and decide if you want to take the chance, or find another place allowing this greater flexibility.

Work out any room arrangements in advance. When using a commercial meeting space, the standard theater or classroom arrangement with a podium, blackboard, flip charts, and/or audiovisual equipment usually works best. It looks professional, and focuses attention on the speaker. But if the turnout is small, consider using a more informal arrangement.

Check in advance to see what equipment the management has, and arrange to supply the rest yourself. Find out, too, if the management will arrange the room the way you want before the meeting, and if so, give the manager the necessary instructions. If not, allow extra time before the meeting to set up. Afterwards, if you need to return the room to its original arrangement after the meeting, allow time for that, too.

Creating Sales Presentation Books

Another sales support is the presentation book. If you have been using your own book on presentations (see Chapter 8, on Creating Your Materials to Sell), show your people how you have done it. When you do, point out that this is just a model, and people can follow your example, or modify what they include and how they arrange it to suit their own style.

To sell your salespeople on using such a book (if they are not already sold on it), point out some of its advantages. These are:

- An attractive, well organized book helps to impress a prospective customer because it looks professional.

- It helps to create a stronger, more dynamic presentation; it organizes the information on your product in a systematic, attractively presented way.

- It gives whatever you are selling a greater feeling of solidity and style.

If your salespeople want to organize their own book, point out that it should be designed to highlight the most important benefits, and it should be arranged to follow whatever presentation format your salespeople use. If they use a different presentation with different customers, it is best to arrange their book accordingly, so they don't have to flip back and forth in the book to illustrate their points, which can look unprofessional if it happens a great deal. So that they can obtain this flexibility, recommend they get a looseleaf binder. Then, before a presentation, the salesperson can easily change the order to match what he plans to say. For the same reason, you might recommend they use clear plastic sleeves that slip into a notebook, since the contents can easily be changed by removing one sheet of paper and putting in another. Also, such plastic coverings provide a high-quality, professional touch.

As for what to include in the binder, suggest that your salespeople include:

1. The various promotional materials you have developed, such as flyers, brochures, questions and answers about your product or service, testimonial letters, and the like;

2. Any of their own materials they have developed (such as letters of appreciation and support from customers, price comparisons with competing projects, informational brochures on the field, etc.).

You can also help them decide what to include and how by providing a list of suggested items to include, with a suggested order. Preferably, base this on a sales approach that has worked for you; otherwise just recommend a format that seems to make sense, and later test and get feedback on this if you can. An example of one way to arrange a book to accompany a presentation might be something like this:

1. Flyers highlighting the products or services your company offers;

2. Detailed brochures describing each product or service in depth;

3. Any customized features your company offers to adapt your product or service to the customer;

4. Any special meetings or demonstrations you offer to explain your product or service in more detail (i.e., films on health and nutrition to market a health product or weight loss program; videos on travel destinations to market travel);

5. Background information on your company and on the development of your product;

6. Any articles that have appeared about your product or your field generally;

7. Any ads you have run in national or local publications;

8. A listing of common questions and answers about your product;

9. Sample price comparisions with the competition;

10. Testimonial letters from past customers;

11. Examples of awards or recognition you have received;

12. Photographs of people using your product;

13. Price breakdowns, discount rates, purchase policies, and procedures;

14. Application forms, order forms, and registration forms.

Note that in a presentation book, as in your presentation, the information highlighting the benefits of the product should come first, to create value and spur customer desire. The information on price and getting the product should come after this, since the customer must first feel he wants the product before he is interested in the price or how to get it. It's at the close that this information on pricing and how to order or sign up becomes relevant.

Besides describing how to make one of these books, give some suggestions on how to use it, too. For example, one common approach is to sit down with the customer with the book open. Then, as the salesperson brings up different topics, he flips through the book to show an example that illustrates his point; so, the presentation book becomes a way to reinforce the sales message to the customer.

When people are just getting started, perhaps supply them with a presentation book you have organized yourself (though preferably with the understanding that this goes back to you should the salesperson leave the company). This pre-organized book can be helpful, since newcomers may not be sure what to do in making their presentation, as they are unfamiliar with the product, company, and desired approach. With a book supplied by you, they can readily use the book to help them organize their presentation; as they flip through the pages in sequence, they can cover each topic illustrated.

As soon as possible, however, encourage people to create their own presentation books. This way, they can organize it based on how they prefer to make their own presentation, using their own personal style. The advantage is that by doing this, their message will carry more conviction, since it will come from them, and the presentation book they use will serve to reinforce the message that expresses them.

Getting Regular Feedback

Finally, get regular feedback from your people on the kind of support and assistance they need from you. This way, you can be reassured that you're on target in what you're doing.

One way to get feedback is to ask for it at your regular sales meetings. Ask what kind of support people would like from you; ask them if there is anything they want that you aren't doing now. Also, invite people to contact you personally if they like, and emphasize that you are always open to listen. Stress that you want to provide the support and assistance people need, and you need their input to be able to know what they want so you can provide this. Sometimes people may resist giving you negative or critical feedback, because of the common ethos in selling to be positive and upbeat, or they may want to avoid hurting feelings, or perhaps fear negative repercussions themselves for truly saying what they think. Thus, you may find that people seem to be holding something back at meetings when you ask for feedback, and they won't come to see you alone. If this happens, try to be supportive and encourage people to speak with you personally, or, if your sales group is large enough to offer some anonymity, perhaps hand out a questionnaire every few weeks to find out what people want or would like to change.

In using a questionnaire, explain why you are using it (i.e., to get information about what people need and want from you), and stress that everyone's comments will be anonymous. Therefore, people can feel free to say whatever they want, even if it is critical. Encourage everyone to be really open and honest on these questionnaires—you want to hear exactly what they think, both the good and the bad.

The best way to make sure these questionnaires are completed is to set aside some time during a regular sales meeting for people to fill them out. If you ask people to take them home and bring them back, you're likely to get few returns, since people forget, get involved in other things, or can't be bothered. Thus, request that people complete them on the spot.

Ideally, keep these questionnaires short—one page, or at most, two. Use closed, multiple-choice questions to get a general response (such as how do people feel about your support generally). But to get specifics, particularly when you aren't certain yourself about the range of possible responses, use an open-ended question, and ask people to be specific.

When you review these questionnaires, it's easier to find out what everyone thinks about different topics by looking at the answers to each question individually. With multiple-choice questions, do a tally. As you look at each questionnaire, make a tally mark for each person checking (a), each person checking (b), and so forth. Then, add up the tallies for each category to give you a picture of how people respond.

When you have open-ended questions, start by reading over all of the answers to one question first. Notice the general flavor of the responses, and that may give you enough information without doing a more formal analysis. However, if people have raised several different points, note each theme or category that comes up, and make a tally mark each time it does. That way you can tell what concerns are most important—those with the most marks.

Do this for every question, and when finished, you will have an overall picture of what your people would like from you. Then, act accordingly to provide this support if you want to do so and can.

It's also a good idea to report back on the results of your survey to your group. This way group members know what the general concerns are and can see how their own concerns relate to what others want. Then, too, your report shows that you are seeking to respond to the concerns they have expressed. If you plan to do something that some have requested, indicate this and explain what you will do and when. If some other concern has come up several times, but you can't or don't want to do anything about it now for whatever reason, mention this concern and explain why you can't or don't want to deal with it at this time. (For instance, maybe several people have suggested putting in a computerized system for your leads, but it's just too expensive or you don't have the personnel to do this right now.) One advantage of mentioning something that has come up for several people, even though you can't respond to it now, is that maybe someone will have another viable suggestion for dealing with the problem (such as a friend with a computer service that manages mailing lists). On the other hand, if only one person mentions something, and you think this is an inappropriate, unfeasible request that you don't want to meet, skip it at the meeting. It's probably not a concern for most other people, since they haven't mentioned it, and you don't want to make this change anyway. So just drop it though you may want to mention that you have reviewed this to the person making the suggestion, just so he feels heard. Later, if this subject becomes important for other people, they can always bring it up on a subsequent questionnaire, and you can deal with the issue then.

The questionnaire, Exhibit 14, provides a sample you can use for feedback. Feel free to add to it or adapt it to your own situation, so you get the information you need about your group.

Exhibit 14.   Questionnaire on Group Needs

This questionnaire is designed to find out what kind of assistance and support you would like from me, and how you feel about what I am already doing. Please answer as openly and honestly as you can. Don't sign your name, since the questionnaire is designed to be anonymous. I will try to institute as many of the changes you suggest as I can.

1. How do you feel generally about the kind of support and assistance I am providing? (please check one)

    ____   Excellent
    ____   Good
    ____   Average
    ____   Fair
    ____   Poor

2. Why do you feel the way you do?   _____
    _____

3. What types of assistance and support do you consider the most helpful to you? (please be specific)
    _____
    _____
    _____

4. What don't you like, if anything, about the type of assistance and support you are getting? What would you like to see changed? (please be specific)
    _____
    _____
    _____

5. What other kinds of assistance and support would you like to see added? What other ways can I help you with your sales?
    _____
    _____
    _____

Exhibit 15.   Sample Phone Script for Calling Groups and Organizations

Plan to adapt the following sample phone script to suit your own style and who you're calling. Use it for ideas on what to say. Note that there is a slightly different way of sharing much the same information with the leaders of different groups in order to emphasize the benefits and selling points that would be of particular interest to that group's membership. I have boldfaced the key principles applicable to other sales programs.

To Find Out Person to Contact

Hello, I'm _____ with Creative Travel and Metco Tours. **Who's the person I would speak to about this in your organization (group/company/etc.)? We have a travel program to Egypt and Kenya that would be of special interest to your group, and I'd like to talk to this person briefly, and then send information.**
(RECEPTIONIST GIVES YOU NAME). **Thanks. Now before you switch me to that person, can you just tell me how you spell that name . . . And what's this person's title? . . .** Thanks. Now go ahead and switch me.

INTRODUCTORY PHONE CONVERSATION

To a Membership Director/President of a Social Organization:

Hello. I'm _____ with Creative Travel and Metco Tours. We've organized some special trips to Egypt and Kenya **that might be especially interesting to your group.** The trip to Egypt features a cruise down the Nile in a luxury liner with stops along the way to visit temples, pyramids, and cities and villages. And the trip to Kenya features a safari to game preserves with side trips to visit tribal villages.

We can adapt the trip **to include activities your group would be especially interested in.** For example, we can add (special parties and mixers for singles; seminars and workshops for business people and educators; visits with religious leaders for church groups; visits to archaeological sites for outdoors groups; etc.—tailor your suggestions to the particular group you are contacting).

Also, if enough people are interested, **you may want to use this** trip **as a fundraiser,** and we can offer a free trip for you or someone else who wants to lead your group.

The company we're working with has already taken several hundred people to Kenya and Egypt over the last three years and has an excellent reputation with the Kenya and Egypt tourist agencies and British Airways. We have a network of resource people we work with in both countries, and we'll be meeting with experts from various fields. Also, these trips are several hundred

Exhibit 15.   (continued)

dollars less than comparable trips by other highly reputed companies I'm sure you're familiar with, like Linblad and Maupitour. The trip to Egypt is around $2,400; the Kenya trip about $2,900.

So, what do you think? . . . If **you're interested, I'd like to send you information or set up an appointment, so we can talk about this more.**

To a Company President, Personnel Director, Company Activities Director

Hello. I'm _____ with Creative Travel and Metco Tours. We've been working with a number of companies on arranging special trips to Egypt and Kenya, and we **thought these might be of special interest to your (employees; sales people; managers).** These could be (a great vacation trip for your employees; an excellent incentive award trip for your sales people; an opportunity to combine a seminar with a vacation for your managers).

The trip to Egypt features a cruise down the Nile in a luxury liner with stops along the way to visit temples, pyramids, and cities, and villages. It's like traveling in a hotel, and there are seminar rooms on the boat you can use for meetings. The Kenya trip features game preserves.

We can also offer you a free trip for yourself or someone else in your company if enough people are interested.

The company we're working with has an excellent reputation in the field. It has already taken several hundred people to Kenya and Egypt over the last three years, and you're welcome to check out its reputation with the Kenya and Egypt tourist agencies and British Airways. The trip is fully escorted by expert tour guides, and we've arranged special meetings with noted experts from various fields. We can also set up additional activities that members of your company might be especially interested in (i.e., visits to see agricultural sites and factories).

Another advantage is these trips are several hundred dollars less that you'd spend with other highly reputed companies like Linblad and Maupitour. The trip to Egypt is around $2,400; the Kenya trip about $2,900.

So, **would you like to hear more about these** trips for your company? If so, **I'd like to send you some information and set up an appointment, so we can work out arrangements.**

To a Minister, Church Membership Director, etc.

Hello. I'm _____ with Creative Travel and Metco Tours. I'm calling to let you know about a travel program to (Egypt and/or Kenya) that **might be of special interest to the members of your congregation, and a fundraiser for your church.**

Exhibit 15.   (continued)

The trip to Egypt features a cruise down the Nile in a luxury liner that stops along the way to visit temples, pyramids, cities, and villages. It's like traveling in a hotel, and there are large rooms on the boat you can use for meetings or services.

The trip to Kenya features a safari to game preserves with side trips to visit tribal villages. We can also arrange special meetings with African healers and religious leaders for your group.

You can use this trip as a fundraiser, since the company offers you a bonus for everyone who signs up in your organization, and if there is enough interest, we can offer a free trip for yourself or someone else who wants to lead your group.

The company we're working with has already taken several hundred people to Kenya and Egypt over the last three years, and **has an excellent reputation** with the Kenya and Egypt tourist agencies and British Airways. We also meet with special resource people and experts in various fields, and these trips are several hundred dollars less than comparable trips from other major travel organizations, like Linblad and Maupitour. The trip to Egypt is around $2,400; the Kenya trip about $2,900.

If you think this might be of interest for your church, I'd like to send you more information or set up an appointment, so we can talk about this more.

SAMPLE LETTERS TO GROUPS AND ORGANIZATIONS

Again plan to adapt the sample letter to suit your own style and the person to whom you are writing. Notice again there is a slightly different way of stating similar information to different types of group leaders to emphasize different benefits.

Again, I have boldfaced key principles applicable to other sales programs.

To a Membership Director or President of a Social Organization
(adapt or print out on your own or the company's letterhead)

I'm pleased to hear of your possible interest in a trip to Kenya or Egypt **for your organization, and accordingly, I'm sending you some material** on the trip. **I'm enclosing some flyers, brochures, and other information.**

Please note that besides the basic features of the trip **described in this material, we can adapt** any trip **to include activities your group would be especially interested in,** such as special meetings, seminars, parties, or visits to sites of special interest.

Also, we have a program so that your group can use this trip **as a fundraiser,** and if enough of your members want to go, we can offer a free trip for you or for someone else who wants to lead your group.

Exhibit 15.   (continued)

As **you'll see in the enclosed material, the program coordinators** who have organized these trips are **experts in the field,** with over ten years of experience in the travel industry. The coordinator of the Kenya-Egypt program has been to these countries over twenty-five times, and as a result has put together a program with experts and resource people not available on trips by other travel companies. Also, you'll find these trips are several hundred dollars less than comparable top-of-the-line trips by other highly reputed companies, like Linblad and Maupitour.

I hope you and your group will be as enthusiastic about these trips as **I am, and I will be in touch with you in a few days to discuss setting up a meeting to work out arrangements with you.**
Sincerely,

To a Company President, Personnel Director, Company Activities Director
(adapt or print out on your own or company's letterhead)

I'm pleased to hear of your possible interest in a trip to Kenya or Egypt **for your company, and accordingly, I'm sending you some material** on the trip. **I'm enclosing some flyers, brochures, and other information.**

As discussed, you can use these trips for **many purposes in your company**—a vacation trip for employees, an incentive program for sales people and managers, or a chance to combine a seminar with a vacation. Besides the basic features of the trip described in this material, **we can adapt** any trip **to include activities your company would be especially interested in,** such as special meetings, seminars, parties, or visits to sites of special interest.

As you'll see in the enclosed material, these trips feature the finest accommodations available, are led by travel experts, and include visits with resource people and experts in the field, not available on comparable top-of-the-line trips. We can also offer you a free trip for you or for others in your company who will be leading your group.

Please note, too, that the company we are working with, Metco Tours, has a long track record and excellent reputation in the field. It is well known by the Kenya and Egypt tourist agencies and British Airways. You'll also find these trips are several hundred dollars less than you would spend with other highly reputed companies like Linblad and Maupitour.

I hope you and your company will be as enthusiastic about these trips as I am, and I will be in touch with you in a few days to discuss setting up a meeting to work out arrangements with you.
Sincerely,

Exhibit 15.   (continued)

To a Minister, Church Membership Director, Etc.
(adapt or print out on your own or company's letterhead)

I'm pleased to hear of your possible interest in a trip to Kenya or Egypt for your church, and accordingly, I'm sending you some material on the trip. I'm enclosing some flyers, brochures, and other information.

Please note that besides the basic features of the trip described in this material, we can adapt any trip to include activities your group would be especially interested in, such as special meetings, seminars, workshops, talks with religious leaders, or visits to sites of special interest.

Also, we have a program so that your group can use this trip as a fundraiser, and if enough of your members want to go, we can offer a free trip for you or for someone else who wants to lead your group.

As you'll see in the enclosed material, the program coordinators who have organized these trips are experts in the field, with over ten years of experience in the travel industry. The coordinator of the Kenya-Egypt program has been to these countries over twenty-five times, and as a result has put together a program with experts and resource people not available on trips by other travel companies. Also, you'll find these trips are several hundred dollars less than comparable top-of-the-line trips by other highly reputed companies, like Linblad and Maupitour.

I hope you and your church will be as enthusiastic about these trips as I am, and I will be in touch with you in a few days to discuss setting up a meeting to work out arrangements with you.

Sincerely,

Exhibit 16.   Guidelines for Follow-Up on a Trade Show

Leads Sheets

Along with these guidelines, you are getting a list of the people you contacted at the Whole-Life Expo or who have been assigned to you based on the area where you live. Also, as ads appear in other publications, I will be assigning additional leads to you, based primarily on geographical area. Bill Krick, who has a word processing service, put this list together.

The leads assigned to you have your initials by them. In the event you have a lead outside of your area, it may make sense to switch with another Travel Associate in that area, or simply assign the lead to them. Also, some people who have many more leads than others from the Expo since they were there much longer may have too many leads to handle themselves, and it may be better to assign these to someone else, too.

Please work out these arrangements among yourselves. I am enclosing a list of all the Travel Associates, indicating the geographic areas each person is covering. I would recommend on any assignments that you simply split any commissions and trip credits on a 50-50 basis, and switch names on a one-for-one basis. Just let me know if someone should sign up what you have decided to do.

In any event, please arrange to follow up on these leads within 2 weeks, either by yourself, through an assistant you are working with. or by assignment to another Travel Associate. Also, please let me know about the results, so I can help you with follow-up as necessary. You can easily note the response next to the person's name on the leads sheet, and send me a copy of a sheet with all these comments.

This quick follow-up is extremely important!!! If you are unable to do it yourself within 2 weeks or make alternate arrangements, please call me and I will reassign your leads to someone else.

How to Follow Up

Do your follow-up by phone where possible. If there's no phone number listed, see if you can get a number from the phone book or directory assistance. If you can't get a number or the person is out of town, then write a brief personal note and send any information as appropriate.

When you call, if the person isn't there, preferably try to find out when the person is there and call again. If you do have to leave a message, I would suggest something like: "I'm calling to invite you to an exciting event," so you don't sound like just another salesperson. If the person doesn't call back in a few days, try again yourself.

Each time you call, keep notes of what happens (possibly on the print-out). Note when you called, the response if any, and what you need to do now or in the future (i.e., call again and when, send literature, etc.).

Exhibit 16.   (continued)

What to Say

When you call, sound enthusiastic, upbeat, like you have some exciting, important news to share.

Then, introduce yourself as being with Creative Travel, and say something like:

Hi . . . I'm calling because you indicated you were interested in going to Kenya or Egypt (and several other destinations), and we're having a get-to-gether for people who would like to find out more about these countries and our trips. The evening will include some films and a slide-sound presentation, plus some discussion, and there's a potluck, too. Our first event is May 14th at a mansion in San Francisco, and then we'll be having another get-together later in June.

Are you still interested in going to Kenya (or Egypt or both)? When are you interested in going? (This year? Next year?) Would you like to come to our get-together in May? (If not, would they like to come in June? July? In the fall?) (IF THE PERSON DOES WANT TO GO, GIVE THEM COMPLETE DIRECTIONS; IF THEY WANT TO GO TO THE POTLUCK, FIND OUT WHAT THEY WOULD LIKE TO BRING SO WE CAN PLAN BETTER; AND PLAN TO CALL THEM A DAY OR SO BEFORE THE EVENT TO RECONFIRM— MAYBE EVEN ARRANGE TO PICK THEM UP IF THEY LIVE CLOSE ENOUGH TO YOU).

(IF THE PERSON CAN'T OR DOESN'T WANT TO GO, ASK: Would you like me to send you additional literature? Would you like me to let you know about our other events on our new destinations: China? Morocco? India/Nepal? Australia? Greece?)

In short, the purpose of this call is to establish if the person is seriously interested in going to these destinations and wants to find out more—either by coming to an event or getting literature from you.

Also, realize that your approach can make a difference in what people say. Some people will already be interested; some people won't be interested; and some people can go either way depending on what you say.

Be ready to come up with solutions to obstacles too if people indicate an interest, but give a reason why they can't do it now.

Overcoming Obstacles Where the Person Has Some Interest

As long as the person seems interested, suggest some ways they might be able to overcome an obstacle they present. Some likely obstacles and responses:

I CAN'T GO NOW . . . You can go in 1986.

I CAN'T GO ON THE DATES SCHEDULED . . . We can arrange other dates for you if you go with a group . . . We have a 12-day tour that leaves on a regular basis.

I CAN'T AFFORD THE TRIP . . . You can go on our shorter 12-day package which costs less . . . You can help to pay for your trip or even go for free if you get others to go on a trip.

CHAPTER 8

Creating Your Materials to Sell

In today's media-conscious world, packaging has become a crucial part of selling, since it is used to create an image for the product, position it, and enhance its value to the consumer. In turn, when most people go to buy something, they already have an idea of what they want, formed in part by the advertising and publicity they have already seen. Likewise, retailers and wholesalers are impressed by advertising and sales materials that position and present the product—such as a brochure, flyer, catalog sheet, or ad. And with some products, even films, slide presentations, and videotapes are expected.

That's why you and your salespeople need such materials to sell, while prospective salespeople will want to see and evaluate the effectiveness of your sales tools, including instructional and training materials, in considering whether they want to sell your product.

Thus, a first step in creating a sales organization is preparing the materials you need to (1) sell your product (such as flyers and catalog sheets), and (2) sell your sales people on selling your product (such as sales training material, plus product sales literature).

Your sales literature really makes a difference, even if you are selling the same product as someone else. People see the quality of your materials as representative of your reputation and ability as a company.

I experienced this myself when I was a distributor for a consumer savings club. Some materials were prepared for us by the company, but a number of distributors, including myself, started creating our own sales materials, too, such as attractive posters and charts for presentations, and short slide presentations. I also made a sales manual with techniques I found effective, such as telephone sales scripts I used, and samples of flyers and newspaper ads. The result was that those of us who did this little bit extra had people flocking to join our companies, even though many other people were selling the same consumer savings program through their companies. However, since we offered a little bit more, people preferred to join our sales team. In fact, several distributors in another sales organization told me they wanted to switch over to mine, because they were impressed by my sales manual. It gave them more confidence than working under their present sales group leader.

In making a buying decision myself, I reacted similarly when I recently attended a gift industry trade show. I was looking for some new telephones for a new office and saw several companies with telephones. But one had a slick, glossy color brochure that illustrated the phones, while the others with the same phones only had xerox copies of a catalog sheet with black and white photos and a price list. Though the phones I wanted were carried by all three wholesalers, and the one with the glossy color brochure was charging about $2 more per phone, I decided to get my phones from them. Why? Because the attractive catalog sheet made me feel more confident in the company's ability to deliver what I wanted. The catalog sheet made them seem like a more solid, substantial company, because it looked better. Since it had more quality, this suggested the company would be like that, too.

What Do You Need? The Basics

The type of materials you need depends on the type of products you offer, how many, how complex they are to explain, and other factors. You can also evolve materials as you develop your program and discover more about what your customers and salespeople need. The more complete your materials, the better, although in the early stages of company and sales group development, you may find it best to develop your materials as you go, so you can test out what works and what doesn't. For example, I did this when I began working with a travel company to develop a network of salespeople to sell their trips. At first, the company supplied me with some masters to make flyers describing trip highlights, as well colored brochures with trip details, informational booklets on the countries to be visited, and sample press releases to send to local newspapers about the trips. This was enough to sell the trips on my own, but not enough to recruit a network of salespeople to sell for the company.

Thus, I gradually developed the additional materials I found necessary to attract salespeople to become part of a sales team selling the program. For example, some of these additional materials included:

- *A flyer describing the income opportunity involved in marketing the trips*, which began "Travel—Earn Money—Free Trips," and briefly described the types of trips, what was involved in selling them, and how much could be earned. The flyer was an ideal initial recruiting tool, since it was something I could hand out at introductory orientation meetings, as well as pass out at events I attended if I encountered a prospective salesperson.

- *A list of "Common Questions and Answers"* that dealt with the various questions I had encountered in the course of selling the trips myself. It was designed to help prospective salespeople know what to say when such questions came up for them.

- *A short questionnaire for prospective salespeople to fill out* on their background, to help me assess each person's abilities and interests, and to show I was being selective in choosing salespeople to sell the program.

- *A list of the types of groups people wanted to contact first* in selling the program, designed to help new salespeople start thinking about potential leads and prospects right away.

This preliminary material was a key factor in building a small sales organization, since it helped provide the necessary support and credibility to motivate new salespeople to get involved in what was then an unknown venture for several reasons. The company was new in the area where I introduced it; I had never been on a trip with the company myself; and none of the company principals from the East Coast were at these first meetings in the San Francisco Bay Area. But the literature I developed provided the credibility needed to recruit as salespeople a half-dozen of the thirty-odd people who responded to ads and attended the introductory meetings I organized—a response rate of about 20 percent.

Then, working with this group, I gradually created or acquired other sales materials, as I got feedback on what people still wanted—such as a price comparison list to show what the competition was doing, sample letters and phone scripts to suggest effective selling approaches, a newsletter to keep people informed of new developments, a marketing manual with miscellaneous ideas and sales techniques, plus videos and slide shows of our destinations from a local tourist office and from a man who went on one of our trips.

In turn, this additional material contributed to an even higher response rate to selling the program. A year later, when I advertised again for new salespeople and got about the same response rate to the ad as before, I had a much higher percentage of attendees at an introductory meeting who wanted to sell the program—about 60 percent, compared to 30 percent the previous year. A key reason was the additional materials, because these gave them more confidence that the program would be a success and that they could sell it. They had more tools.

Thus, in deciding on the particular materials you need, keep these key points in mind:

1. Have as much appropriate material available as you can when you start creating your sales organization. This material will help to give your program credibility, particularly if it is new, as well as help give your prospective salespeople tools with which to sell.

2. Be responsive to your salespeople and develop or acquire the materials they need as you go along; you'll find your people appreciate your flexibility, in addition to being better able to sell.

3. As your material improves, consider recruiting new salespeople. There's a great deal of turnover in sales anyway, and as you get better material, the

quality of the salespeople you attract will go up too, because you have more experience and have a more developed track record. In turn, your sales literature will convey this; it represents you.

A Checklist of the Material You Need

The following section lists the types of material you may need. Choose what's most appropriate for you. The list is organized into two categories: (1) customer-oriented materials, which are designed to be shown to the customer, and are also useful for recruiting salespeople and for sales training; and (2) sales and training materials, designed primarily for your salespeople, although in some cases these may be shown to customers, too. The materials I consider most important are listed first, although the relative importance of different materials for you will depend on the type of product you sell. There are checklists to help you determine what you need at the end of the chapter (see pages 163 and 164).

Promotional Materials for Your Customer

These can be used in several ways:

- *To attract a customer* (for example, you can post flyers or brochures around town, leave them at meetings with your target market, or include them in a mailing to get a customer to call for information or place an order);

- *To go over product benefits with a customer* (for example, a salesperson at a presentation can use a brochure, information sheet, or presentation booklet to explain the benefits and features of the product, and using the materials will help him gain credibility, because the message is not just spoken . . . it's written down—or on tape);

- *To give the prospect something to review or to provide a reminder after your presentation* (such materials are especially useful if the customer isn't ready to make a purchase on the spot, because he can take them home to help him to think about the product, discuss it with significant others, or reassure himself that he really does want or need this. Having a promotional brochure and order form can help to make the sale).

The key promotional materials you may want to develop include the following, roughly in their order of relative importance:

A Brochure or Catalog Sheet. While some new companies just use flyers and order forms to keep costs down, a professional-looking brochure or catalog can make a big difference in increasing sales. Although there may be some notable instances in which these are unneeded (such as an impulse product that immediately sells itself, or a person offering services who already has an established name), a good brochure or catalog helps to increase credibility, reputation, and product appeal. They're like a calling card for you and your company.

Thus, it's important to make these as good as you can. Put a lot of thought into what you want to say and how to say it. Take into consideration your primary target market, and design your brochure or catalog to appeal to this group. If selling to the ultimate customer, ask yourself who is most likely to buy. Women or men? Upscale or downscale? Urban sophisticates? Suburban couples? Older people? Middle-aged? Young adults? Or, if selling to a wholesaler or retailer, design your brochure or catalog sheet accordingly, so it's similar to or more appealing than those he usually gets.

In designing your material, look at what others marketing to a similar audience are already doing to get an idea of the type of look or style that might be appropriate for your material. Don't copy—you want your material to be distinctive and to stand out—but draw on the ideas you like to help shape your own material. Also, consider going to a professional unless you or someone in your company has a good design sense. In that case, you may be able to develop the brochure or catalog internally, by coming up with the layout and then going directly to a printer and choosing the type and paper stock you want. A printer also can work with any photographs you have if you indicate cropping and layout placement. But if you're uncertain about what to do, it is better to pay a pro, since pros know what they are doing, and they will save you time and money in the long run. Your brochure or catalog sheet is such an important selling tool, it pays to do it right. The cost of it will be more than paid off in greatly increased sales.

A Price List and Order Form (or a Sign-Up Form or Application). These items might be included in your brochure or catalog if you have determined your prices for the life of this material or only expect this material to be out for a short period before you bring out an updated brochure or catalog. But many companies do better with a separate price list and order or sign-up/application form, which can be printed easily on an as-needed basis. The advantage of this is that prices or terms can readily be changed as needed, because they are printed separately from the regular catalog or brochure. Thus, they can be duplicated readily in needed quantities, whereas a change in the catalog or brochure requires a new print run and new plates.

Also, consider carefully how you design your order form, since a well designed form helps you increase your orders, and can be used as well to market research your customers, so you can better target your marketing to them. In fact, order forms can be so important that there are some seminars and workshops devoted to them alone. Briefly, here are some key points to keep in mind in designing a good order form:

- Be sure your order form has sufficient space for the person's name, address, and zip (and if you permit credit purchases, include an MC/Visa/American Express check-off with a space for the card number, expiration date, and phone number).

- Make it easy for the person to order, by listing your products with their prices and a space to check off the quantity ordered, followed by a space to write in the total price. Or leave spaces so the person can write in product names.

- Provide the necessary spaces so a person can easily add up any subtotals, subtract any discounts for quantity purchases, record any subtotals, add tax (if applicable), and add any freight and handling.

To obtain any information about your customers, add a few brief questions for them to fill in or check off. For instance, one woman with a small catalog featuring products for cat lovers asked questions like: "Do you have a cat?" and "About how much do you spend on products with cats on them each year?"

If you accept CODs or after-delivery payments, include some space to ask for credit information if you want this (best with big orders, except for customers with A-1 reputations, such as schools and the U.N.). The type of credit information to ask for includes references about previous purchases or a bank name or a credit card number (though you can't charge to a credit card if the person doesn't agree to this and hasn't paid the bill).

Sign-up or registration forms or applications are also both sales and information tools. These are usually most appropriate when you're selling a program service or customized product. Ask what you need to know about your customer to provide the best possible product or service. For example, in the travel program registration form we asked about the registrant's age, sex, marital status, purpose for the trip, and special interests, to better match travelers with others of like background and interests.

There are some sample order forms and sign-up forms at the end of this chapter. Also, check over the kind of lists and forms used by companies in your field for ideas on how to prepare this material.

Flyers. These are ideal for drawing attention to your product and highlighting benefits. But usually flyers are not enough for making the final sale, since people will want more information and reassurance about the qualities and advantages of your product than are offered in a typical flyer.

However, flyers are a good introduction, and it is more economical to use a flyer first, so you can save your more expensive catalog sheets or brochures for more serious prospects.

Some companies provide their salespeople with all the flyers they need, particularly when their salesforce is on salary or a draw-commission basis, so there is more company control. But if you have reps working for you on commission basis, or independent distributors, consider having your salespeople share the costs of making flyers themselves, a common approach. In this case, you supply each person with a printed master on white for making copies (a velox if you are having these made by a printer, though a good copy of a black and white master will usually be fine). Then, the salesperson inserts his or her own name, address, and phone number on the master and copies as many as needed.

If you have a limited budget, you can make your own flyers fairly inexpensively—for less than $25, by working with some graphic aids, tools anyone can use. Some of these aids include:

- Rub-on letters and a burnisher, available in any art store, to create good-looking headlines (or if you have access to a computer with a laser printer and large type sizes, you can use this even more easily, though the type styles you can choose are more limited);

- A rubber stamp catalog or book of clip art to liven up your layout;

- A light blue pencil and ruler to rule your lines for headlines;

- Scissors and spray glue to cut up headlines, artwork, and typed copy, and paste it on a sheet of white paper;

- White artists' tape or correction fluid to clean up your final layout.

Now you're ready to make copies, preferably on colored paper to add eye appeal. Choose colors to support your company image or message (i.e., green paper to promote environmental products or a company involved in environmental activities; blue to promote products related to water). You can find all types of papers in different colors in a paper supply store.

In writing your message, keep it simple. View your flyer as if you were writing an ad. Focus on a few key points, and use a larger size or special type of letter to highlight major ideas. Leave plenty of blank space around your copy, so it is easy to read. Break up your copy into a few brief paragraphs to encourage readability. And ask for some action, such as inviting people to come to a particular event, call for more details, or ask for a product presentation in their home.

Some common types of flyers include flyers to:

- Promote a customized service;

- Describe a money-making opportunity;

- Show how the customer can save money;

- Invite people to a product demonstration;

- Highlight the benefits of a product and offer more information on the product.

Advertising Copies. Reprints of your ads are ideal to show the customer that your company is providing advertising support for the product. Today, given the plethora of advertising, customers often view advertising as a kind of reassurance that the product is okay. Thus, even if they don't see your ad themselves, if you can show them your product has been advertised, this adds to your credibility in a product presentation.

Ad reprints can be used in a number of ways:

- Use the original or a copy in a presentation book to show the customer;

- Turn the ad into a flyer, if it's a strong, visual one, and distribute it or post it just like a flyer;

- Combine a copy of the ad with a letter and use it in an introductory mailing.

Besides attracting customers, advertising can also attract salespeople. They know the power of advertising, and they know it will help them make sales if customers have seen the ads or if they can show customers the ads as part of a presentation.

Use an ad agency if you have the budget to do so. If you are doing a substantial amount of advertising, the agency will take its 15 percent commission from the regular cost of the advertising from the publication or other media running the ad, and you won't have to pay anything more. Even if you are doing only a small amount of advertising, it may still be worth the small fee for copy work and art. Having a good ad will more than pay for itself in the long run through better sales—and it will help to attract good salespeople to your company by further enhancing your image.

Coupon Offers. These are ideal to supplement your brochure, price list, sign-up sheet, or flyers. They give customers a bonus for acting now or before a certain date, or they offer a better price if the customer buys a certain package of services or products. They encourage action, and both customers and potential salespeople like them, since they are an incentive to buy more or to buy now.

As with flyers, you can create your own coupon offers by typing up the offer and embellishing the coupon with some attractive graphics and headliner type. Then, print up multiple copies on a page and cut them up.

Posters. These are good for certain kinds of products or services, where there is potentially broad appeal and you can dramatically highlight a special event or product benefit. Make the look of your poster consistent with the product or service you are advertising, and if you are not artistically talented, work with a local printer or artist. Another possibility, if you are making a few posters with a limited amount of copy, is hiring some student artists at about $5 to $8 per hour. They can create from one to two posters an hour. Call your local college or university part-time employment office to list your opportunity.

As for distributing your posters, good possibilities are the various stores that are receptive to putting up posters, and local bulletin boards. Pick out the locales likely to attract your target customer. For instance, if you have got a sports-related service, a sports shop would be ideal; for a travel product, perhaps contact a camera shop or luggage store.

While you or your salespeople can make these contacts to distribute posters (or perhaps hire students or part-time help to do this), it is often more efficient to use a special postering service, which operates in some cities and towns. These services have people who go around regularly with several posters and flyers and hit all the major stores and bulletin boards that accept posters. The services cut down costs because they put up several posters at once. Check in your local telephone directory or business newspaper for such services.

In-Store Display Coupons. These are designed to appeal to the ultimate customers, and are displayed in stores. To use these, work out a system to give the store owners credit for any leads they refer to you or for any orders from the coupons they hand out. Have your salespeople put their own addresses or coding on these coupons, so they can follow up on the leads from these coupons.

Promotional Letters. These work well when combined with an initial or follow-up phone call to establish interest. Use the letter to accompany sales material sent to the customer, and then follow up with a phone call to get the order or to set up an appointment for a presentation.

If you use these, it's good to send out a few yourself to test the letter. Then, if it seems effective, give copies to your salespeople, so they can use it or adapt it as they want. If you don't get a good response, consider why, and adapt the letter accordingly. In many companies salespeople write their own letters, but they also appreciate having some sample formats to use as is or as guidelines to help them know what to do.

Common Questions-and-Answers Sheet. Sometimes certain questions may come up again and again, even if your brochure covers many of these points. This is because people don't always remember everything they read, or they want further clarification. Then, too, certain topics can't be covered fully in a brochure, so some people may want to see a more detailed explanation sheet describing specifics, such as how exactly this health product works, and what is in it.

In such cases, create a questions-and-answers sheet to cover these topics. The sheet will not only give your customers the answers directly, but will also help your salespeople know how to answer common questions, and reassure them about your support in the field.

To make up such a sheet, keep track of the questions people ask you, and ask your salespeople to do the same. Then, take the questions that keep reoccurring and write up the answers.

Publicity Materials. As you get publicity for your product or company, collect reprints or tapes and use these to impress customers. For example, paste up newspaper articles or photos, and make copies of them to send out with promotional letters or put in a presentation book. Also, make sure your paste-up looks good. Include the full name of the publication in which the item appeared and the date, and, ideally, clip that information out of the publication, rather than typing it in, to make the clipping look more official.

When you have only a few clippings, it's fine to put each one on a single page. But as the clips accumulate, perhaps make a collage of articles to show your successful expansion. Or cull out the best ones to feature, and perhaps just include a list of the rest.

Miscellaneous Articles and Information About Your Product. Besides publicity about yourself, collect relevant articles about your field that may help promote your product line or type of company generally. Of course, the closer the article comes to mentioning your type of product, the better. Then, you can use copies of this material in your own press kits or presentation books.

For example, when I was organizing a presentation book for a travel company, I used some articles by a local columnist who described taking a trip on the same cruise liner our company used for its tours. Also, since we offered some trips to Africa, I made copies of these articles for handouts our salespeople could use.

When you prepare such materials for handouts, you might also leave some room for the salesperson to stamp in his or her own name and address, which is sometimes easier than attaching a card, unless this handout is designed to be given out with other material that will have an address. For example, we did this when we used some articles on Africa as a handout; these were used to interest a potential traveler in going to Africa through a general article on the topic. Then, when the person called to learn more about going there, the salesperson would describe the company's various trips.

The same approach can be used with any kind of product. For example, if you're marketing a financial planning service, a handout on how people save money through financial planning might help. If you're selling computer consulting services, an article on the latest in computers might stimulate customer interest.

Special Letters and Testimonials. If you get any letters praising your products or activities, or have favorable testimonial statements, these can be included in your presentation materials, too. They can help impress customers, and establish credibility and support for whatever you're selling.

For example, when our organization received a letter of support from the Mayor of San Francisco for a promotional event we were staging, we made copies of this for both customers and salespeople. Similarly, I used a list of comments from various people in a promotional flyer to help sell a game—*Glasnost: The Game of Soviet-American Peace and Diplomacy*—in a direct mail promotion to prospective customers. To get such letters and testimonials, simply write some letters asking for what you want. For example, when we put on the promotional event, I sent a letter to the Mayor describing what we were doing and asked for a special letter or proclamation we could read at the event. When seeking support for the game I contacted some people who had already bought it and asked for a statement to use in our publicity. Also, I staged some events at which people played the game, including in the Soviet Union, and then obtained their comments.

Occasionally, when you are seeking such comments you may find that people ask you to write them yourself and then check the statements with them for approval. If so, by all means do, and if someone seems hesitant to write something because of time pressures, perhaps take the initiative and offer to write the comment for them. You'll find such helpfulness will get you some comments you might not get otherwise. And writing the comments yourself is an ideal way to get someone to say exactly what you want to promote your product in your PR.

Tapes. These are useful to give a prospective customer a more direct experience of the testimonials supporting your product, or to impress with the words of an expert. However, make sure any taped material is short, no more than about fifteen minutes, since people's attention spans are limited.

If you are setting up a sales organization for a large company, you may be able to obtain tapes with testimonials or comments from the company's president or founder. It's also easy to make your own tapes for your company or sales group.

For example, to get testimonials, you can do a series of mini-interviews, even by phone with the appropriate recording device (though be sure to say you are recording to avoid any legal problems if you do tape over the phone). In these interviews, ask perhaps a half-dozen or so people who have used your product and were satisfied to say what they liked. To get comments from an expert, you can take comments from a talk this person gives—and perhaps string together the remarks of a few experts to prove your point (as a courtesy, ask for permission).

Slide Shows and Videos. Increasingly, slide shows and videos are being used in presentations to give the customer a more immediate view of how a product is used, so the prospect can better imagine himself as a customer. These presentations can also help explain and reinforce visually your key points. Again, you may be able to obtain these if you are working with a large company, or organize your own. When you do create your own presentations, you can use two approaches, depending on your budget and skill. If you can and want to, go top-drawer, with a slick professional presentation. Or alternatively, use a more personal, less professional approach. You can get away with a more home-grown look when you emphasize the personal touch. For example, when I coordinated the travel sales group, several salespeople put together their own slide shows from slides they took on their own trips, and we used a homemade video from a man who went on one trip with his video camera. The films from the tourist offices were much better in quality, but these home-grown efforts still worked well because they offered that personal touch. In fact, sometimes they packed even more appeal for some people, because they showed that someone had gone on one of our trips and had returned a real enthusiast. His film had a number of flaws any professional could spot (i.e., weakness in cutting, dialogue, and editing), but what was most important to prospects was that they could identify with his tourist point of view—they could see themselves going on a similar trip.

More specifically, some of the ways you might use slides or videos with your people include the following:

1. Organize a master slide show or obtain the original videotape; then loan it out;

2. Make duplicates of any slide shows or videos for salespeople who want these (and perhaps provide these at cost);

3. Ask if any salespeople have or would like to create their own slide or video programs; then, make copies of these to loan out to others;

4. Photograph or make a video of demonstrations of your product or sales activities, and use these to make a slide show or video tape. Later, as your

sales program changes, make the appropriate changes in your slide show or videotape to reflect these.

Since videos are more dramatic than slide presentations, and it is actually easier and less expensive to make copies of videos, use this format wherever you can. And if you have slides or film presentations, consider having them transferred onto video so you can readily make copies for your salespeople. For example, you can have slides and films transferred onto video for about $.75 a minute. Once you have your video master, copying it will cost about $10 to $20 per copy if done commercially. Or, if you can hook up two VCRs yourself, it will cost just the price of the video tape—about $5 to $8 per reel. If you plan to loan out the masters or dubs, you can absorb this cost yourself. Another possibility might be to give your salespeople an option of getting the tapes done by you at cost, or they can arrange to make their own if they plan to use these tapes regularly, and find it inconvenient regularly to return the loaner to you.

Presentation Book. If you are marketing an expensive product or a variety of products, a presentation booklet can be an excellent and impressive way to systematically present your various promotional materials to your customer by combining them together in an attractive book.

A good way to do this is to put these materials together in such a way that you or your salespeople can easily move them around to suit a presentation or your personal style. A looseleaf book works well for this purpose. Also, you might find transparent binders especially useful for their flexibility, since you can readily slip in and out different title pages for the cover. Alternatively, leather and vinyl covers may be ideal for expensive or customized products. To move things easily around during your presentation, you can use plastic sleeves with three holes. These enable you to rearrange your materials easily, since you can add or drop items at will by simply putting them in or pulling them out of the plastic sleeve.

Sales and Training Materials for Your Salespeople

Besides having promotional materials for you or your salespeople to sell to customers, develop sales and training materials to help your salespeople sell.

These can be developed in a number of ways, depending on your own style.

1. Do some selling yourself first, to find out what works and what doesn't for your product. Then, turn your knowledge into policies, procedures, and suggested marketing techniques for your sales people.

2. If you are doing some selling yourself, invite your new salespeople to accompany you and watch you do it. Then, use any policies, procedures, and marketing guidelines to supplement your own field demonstrations.

3. If you don't do the selling yourself, get feedback from someone who does to help you develop the necessary sales materials.

4. Ask your sales manager to develop the material needed, and hire someone
    who can do this.

The amount and type of material you need depends on a number of factors,
including the type of product, the target market, the sales approaches used to
reach this market, the complexity of the product, the sales experience of your
salespeople, and the size of the sales group. Another key factor is whether you
are using outside sales reps who already have their own sales methods and
connections, and only need your catalog sheets, price lists, order forms, and any
publicity materials, or whether you are setting up your own sales force, which
will need more assistance and material.

Having good sales and training materials is extremely important because these
materials not only help your salespeople sell, but they also impress prospective
salespeople, increasing their interest in selling your line.

In working with in-house salespeople, start with the basic material needed for
people to start selling and for any introductory training. Then, pay attention to
what your people are doing and be open to feedback to develop additional sales
aids and training materials as you go along. Also, be receptive to change, so if
something doesn't work, you can change it or drop it. This way, you better help
your salespeople sell your product.

The following are some suggested materials, listed roughly in the order of
importance.

A Sales Associate or Representative Questionnaire. Skip this if you're hiring a
sales rep with his own business, since the product lines he currently represents
will tell you about his track record. But if you're recruiting your own sales group,
a questionnaire or interview guide can help you find out about who you're hiring, as well as provide some details about where, when, and how this person
wants to sell. A good time to use this is at your initial individual or group
interview, when deciding who to recruit.

A sample questionnaire that I have used is provided at the end of this chapter.
Some of the basic information to include on such a questionnaire is the following:

*   Name, address, day and evening phone numbers
*   Current or usual occupation
*   Past experience in sales
*   Past experience in fields related to your product line
*   How many hours the person wants to work each week (if you are looking
    for part-time people)
*   Relevant interests and skills (such as what kind of groups he belongs to or
    would like to contact, if the salesperson will be contacting groups)
*   Preferred geographic areas for selling

- Any background or interest in giving talks or presentations (if your product lends itself to giving these)

- Any background or interest in doing publicity (a useful skill if you are planning a PR campaign)

Such information will help you decide who to hire and how best to use these people.

A List of Ideas on Who to Contact. Some prospective salespeople will already have ideas about who to contact or may already have connections. Others will welcome suggestions.

Masters or Copies of All Your Promotional Materials. While some companies supply their salespeople with materials to show or give to prospects, such as brochures and catalog sheets, others give salespeople enough to get them started. These salespeople are then expected to make their own copies from a master supplied by the company, or, in the case of independent distributors, purchase their sales materials at cost from the company.

Some considerations in deciding what approach to use include: the cost of sales material, the number of salespeople working for you, and how independent and committed they are to your company. For example, if you are working with people who are working for you part-time and are fairly independent, then it may be better to let them be responsible for their own materials, and perhaps give a larger commission to compensate for this. Conversely, if you have a few committed salespeople on a draw-commission basis, providing the materials yourself may make more sense. In either case, limit what you hand out *gratis* in the beginning since there's often a high turnover with new salespeople—keep your costs down in what you hand out until you are sure the person will stick with your company.

The approach I have used is to provide new salespeople with single copies of the more detailed materials to show prospects, along with a small supply of brochures to hand out only to serious prospects. Then, I have given them a master on which they can insert their own address and number to make additional handouts.

Another approach some companies use is to figure out the cost of the materials provided in a sales kit and ask the salesperson to cover that cost. Should the salesperson stop selling for the company, he can always return any materials and be reimbursed accordingly. If he drops out, at least the company hasn't fronted the cost, which can add up with new recruits, since perhaps 50 to 90 percent eventually drop out.

Alternatively, you might provide the new salesperson with a basic kit of promotional materials to get started. Then, if he seems serious, give out additional materials, as appropriate, depending on the types of approaches he is using and the kinds of customers he expects to contact.

Marketing or Commission Plan. Since one of the first things every salesperson wants to know is how much will he make, have a clear statement of this. This statement should indicate the commission you are offering, and any increase or bonuses for higher sales volumes. Also, if you have an override or network marketing plan, whereby salespeople can earn more by working with or supervising others, describe how this plan works. You might also make some limited projections of what earnings will be on a typical level of sales, although if you have an override or network marketing plan, be sure to go only a few levels, and keep any projections geared to what the average distributor or salesperson makes, to avoid legal problems that could arise if you seem to be promoting a pyramid sales plan.[1] Additionally, if you know how much sales volume is likely for a given amount of time spent in sales, based on your experience or the experience of other salespeople, explain that, too, since salespeople will want to know this.

If your company or sales program is new and you don't have a track record, use what you know about the sales of similar products for comparison. As much as possible, you want to suggest realistically what the salesperson is likely to make, so he can feel comfortable that a given time commitment to selling your product will be worth the effort.

Product Information. While your brochures may provide enough product information on certain products, sometimes your salespeople will need more detail than the customer normally receives. If so, have a detailed write-up on your product, and any relevant information on your related policies or procedures. In some cases, your salespeople may also want to give this detailed material to customers who show serious interest.

Such information may include instructions for use, details on product manufacture, background information on the product developers or management, a description of the competition, etc.

Sample Price Comparison. At times, you may want to prepare price comparison sheets to be given out or shown to customers. In other cases, you might simply want to prepare these for your salespeople, so if a customer asks about the cost of your product relative to the competition, the salesperson can quickly respond. These price comparison sheets also can be useful for making the salesperson aware of what else is offered on the market, so he can better discuss the benefits of what he is selling.

Guidelines for Selling; Policies and Procedures

If you have found that a certain kind of approach works best, or believe certain techniques will be best, by all means, suggest these to help prepare your salesper-

---

1. If you are working with a multi-level or network marketing company that already has a commission structure worked out, it's fine to provide people with a general idea of possible earnings. But avoid unrealistic projections of fantastic earnings from huge marketing organizations. It's illegal to distribute material like this, and most people don't make such huge sums. Instead, stick to some basic examples to illustrate how the multi-level/override system works, and some examples of typical earnings for most distributors.

son to sell. Besides giving verbal suggestions, written guidelines can be very helpful to reinforce your message and serve as a future reminder.

For example, in the travel program, since we were encouraging salespeople to sell in bulk to organizations rather than individuals, I wrote up several pages of guidelines on the types of groups to contact, whom to speak to, what to say, and how to follow through. Certainly, experienced salespeople may already know this, but they will appreciate your efforts, while new salespeople will generally find such guidelines vital to give them direction.

Sample Phone Scripts and Letters

Many salespeople will appreciate some direction in what to say on the phone or what to write in a letter; thus, sample phone scripts and letters can be quite helpful. The person can use them as a guideline and can also adapt them to put the message into her own words.

To write effective scripts or letters, draw on your own experience of selling to customers or work closely with your key salespeople to develop this material. Notice what phone approaches or letters are most effective, and as you find ones that get a good response, share them with your salespeople.

For example, when we found that a three-step sales approach worked well in marketing our travel program, I incorporated guidelines on what to say in each phase in the materials I prepared. Specifically, the three steps were these: (1) making a call to find out the leader or program director, (2) calling that person to set up a meeting or to send a cover letter and information, and (3) following up with those people who received information to arrange a meeting. Accordingly, with these phases in mind, I developed a series of scripts to cover the types of phone call situations salespeople might encounter in dealing with different types of individuals in different types of organizations (i.e., membership directors or presidents of social organizations; company presidents, personnel directors, or employee activities directors; academic department chairs, alumni directors, and museum directors; and ministers and church membership directors). Also, since different follow-up letters would be needed in each case, I prepared several versions of a follow-up letter.

While salespeople in many companies may be expected to create these kinds of letters and phone approaches themselves as needed, many salespeople will find these materials very useful if you can provide them. I found these worked very well with the sales groups I organized; whether the salespeople used the materials as is or adapted them to their own style, they all found these materials gave them a clearer picture of what to say and how to do it.

Sample Ads

In some sales programs, salespeople can place their own ads; if this is the case, sample ads that you supply are helpful, especially if you've already run and tested those ads. With such samples, salespeople are more likely to advertise and do so effectively, and they will be impressed by your efforts in supplying these.

The two types of ads are classified and display. With classified ads, typed write-ups are fine. With display ads, get some veloxes or good photocopies made in different sizes. Then, if your sales people want to use an ad, they send in the copy, after inserting their own phone number, address, or coding for a reply.

Suggested Marketing Ideas

Write down any suggestions you have about approaches that work cr new ideas to try. These can either be general marketing tips or guidelines for contacting specific groups. You may wish to organize these by topic—for instance, "techniques for contacting groups and organizations," "recommendations for getting leads," or "what to say when you make your presentation." Or, perhaps make lists of tips by specific target market, such as what to say in contacting a given market (i.e., senior citizens, business professionals, nature and environmental groups, singles, the gay community, etc.). When you do focus on target groups, make your recommendations as specific as possible, and if you know them, even suggest specific organizations, stores, associations, etc., to contact by name. Also, if your product might tie in with certain upcoming events (i.e., fairs, festivals, performances, etc.), mention these by name.

To develop ideas for these lists of marketing tips, think of all the ways you might market your product yourself, and perhaps have a brainstorming session with your salespeople. Then, create a list. The list-making process will help you organize your ideas, and the list will serve as an excellent reminder for your people on what to do.

Letterhead, Business Cards

Often, salespeople working with small companies, on a part-time basis or as an independent distributor, will use their own name in selling your product. This approach can work fine, and it may be a way to get some people who want to keep their own company identity to work for you. On the other hard, to reinforce your own identity, ask your salespeople to use your own letterhead and business cards when they're selling your product, or give them the option of using their company identity or yours.

Another area of choice is in who pays for the salesperson's letterhead and business cards, which again depends on your company structure and how independent your salespeople are. Some companies print up their letterhead and business cards for their salespeople, and they foot the bill. But if you're on a tight budget, one way to keep down expenses, particularly when you're not sure whether a new person will stay, is to give your salespeople a master of your letterhead and business card. They can then print up their own materials on an as-needed basis.

Sample Publicity Releases

If you are doing any publicity, copies of your releases will keep your salespeople informed. Once your publicity starts appearing, you can add promotional clips to your arsenal of sales and training materials. Again, this material will give your people more confidence in your own efforts—and they may be able to use this information in talking to potential customers, too.

Updates and Newsletters

These are good for keeping your people posted on recent changes in policies and procedures, on special sales meetings and events, and on information about your field generally. Also, they can be a good tool for motivating salespeople, if you include sales ideas, recognize the accomplishments of people in the group, offer sales bonuses, and the like. You can also use newsletters and updates to coordinate your sales efforts by describing overall sales plans and indicating who is doing what in what area.

Such updates can be as simple as a sheet of paper or copy of your letterhead with the title, UPDATE, and the date you have written or released it. What's especially important is getting them out with some degree of regularity—perhaps every week, biweekly, or once a month. (See Exhibits 9 and 10 in Chapter 6.)

List of Current Sales Reps or Associates

These can help salespeople coordinate their efforts and work together where appropriate. To this end, list the types of markets or the geographic areas where different sales people plan to concentrate their efforts (such as business groups, civic groups, schools, universities, church groups, singles).

Some people will find such a list useful for contacting others working in the same area to see how they might work together.

However, keep in mind one caution in providing people with lists when they first join your organization. An unethical person might use your list to find recruits for his own project, and then leave your company with some of your people. But generally, the people who are successful and happy in your organization won't do this, while those who leave are probably not working out anyway. For example, this happened when I was first setting up a sales group. One man who seemed especially eager but had limited experience suddenly decided after several sales meetings and training sessions that he could make more working on his own. He used my list of salespeople to meet someone to whom he proposed a partnership, and both of them left the group. However, they soon floundered on their own, because neither really knew what to do without professional support. So, their departure was no real loss.

Thus, try to assess your people carefully before giving out any lists. It's best if you feel confident, trust the person, and feel he is really going to stay with your group before you reveal all your key people to that person.

List of Resource Materials

As you accumulate useful resource materials or have suggestions on what people might do to improve their sales, make a list of what is available to let your people know this. For instance, you might list useful videotapes on your type of product, or recommended books and tapes on sales techniques. As an example, in marketing the travel program, our resource list included books and videotapes on different travel destinations; I used some of these in our own training program, and others I just liked.

Marketing Techniques Manual

Such a manual can be a good way of combining your various sales and training materials together in one place. It's convenient, handy, and looks impressive. Also, the manual can be one more tool in helping you recruit good salespeople, because it can help to convince them that they are going to get good training, as well as have a good product to represent.

You can start a manual quite easily, with the materials you plan to hand out anyway. It can then be expanded as you develop more material.

To do this, all you need is a cover page that says something like: "[Your Company Name]—Marketing Techniques Manual." Then, add a Table of Contents, listing the types of materials in the book and the page numbers where they can be found, and add a back cover. If the manual is short, you can staple the pages together, or perhaps dress it up with a vinyl cover. For example, I started off with a book with sixteen pages and four sections: "Guidelines for Contacting Groups and Organizations," "Sample Phone Scripts for Calling Groups and Organizations," "Sample Letters," and "Marketing Policies and Procedures." The total cost of each book came to about $1.

As for when to give such material out, it may be best to hold off for a little while when you first recruit someone, to be sure the person will really stick with your company—perhaps just show it at your initial orientation, then hand it out to those who return for a regular meeting or training session. This is what I did to make sure the person was seriously interested in getting involved. Otherwise, I felt the costs of these books would be too high, and I felt I would be giving away my sales secrets to people who were still deciding whether to sell the program.

Still another possibility for giving out these manuals might be to ask your new people to put up a few dollars in advance for a sales kit. Then, they can always get that money back by returning the kit. This approach will also help to screen out people who aren't serious, since they may decide not to put up the money.

Sales Training Tapes, Books

If you offer a sales training program, you may want to include some commercial sales training tapes and books in your own training, or at least recommend them for outside reading and listening. These materials are available at your local bookstore or by direct mail through the several dozen sales trainers who offer them. If you include these in your training meetings, perhaps set aside twenty to thirty minutes to listen to tapes or review the highlights of books you like. Or, invite your salespeople to come to the meetings with summaries or tips based on their own reading or listening, perhaps having people take turns doing this or having a few participate in each meeting.

Deciding What You Need

The foregoing list has provided a broad overview of the types of materials you might use in setting up a comprehensive sales program and getting salespeople to sell for you effectively. You still have to decide what you actually need for yourself.

If you're just getting your company started, begin with what you consider the most important essentials, then gradually build up your promotional and sales materials as you go along.

Exhibits 17 and 18 give two checklists to help you do this. One lists possible promotional materials to sell to the customer or client. The other lists possible sales items for your salespeople to help them sell. After you assess what you need now, review these lists from time to time to see if you need anything else.

When new recruits, who will be working independently and generating their own leads, are just starting, it helps to give them some guidelines so they can get started right away. Some of the things to tell them include the following, which I have used as a handout for people in various sales programs. You may wish simply to extract what you find useful to tell your people or use in your own handout.

Some Easy Ways To Get Started

After targeting your potential market and thinking about leads, the next step is contacting potential consumers or clients. An easy way to get started is to do things close to home and talk to others about the program as you go about your everyday business. Then, as you acquire experience, gradually expand your efforts through techniques such as advertising and contacting group leaders.

Here are some things you can do with little or no effort or expense:

Invite a few friends, business associates, or neighbors to a presentation at your home or office. People in small businesses do this all the time. For example, some women who run a small customized dress business from their home regularly put on sales presentations in which they invite women they meet at business groups or at other activities. They may also invite the neighbors on their street.

Tell the group leader or program chairman of an organization you belong to about your product, and offer to put on a free event for the group. For instance, they might be interested in a lecture on a topic related to your business (i.e., on image if you're marketing beauty products or clothes; exercise techniques if you're selling a sports or health product).

Exhibit 17. The Promotional Materials for My Customer/Client

Check the items you need for your customer. Indicate what you have and what you plan to get when.

			I Plan to Get		
Possible Items Needed	I Need	I Have	Now	1-3 Mo.	Later
Brochure					
Catalog Sheet					
Price List					
Order Form					
Sign-Up Form/Registration Form/Application					
Flyers (fill in name or subject					
Advertising Copies (fill in)					
Coupon Offers					
Posters					
In-Store Display Coupons					
Promotional Letters					
Common Q&A Sheet					
Publicity Materials					
Articles & Product Info					
Letters and Testimonials					
Tapes					
Slide Shows					
Videos					
Presentation Book					

Exhibit 18. Sales and Training Materials for My Customer/Client

Check the items you need for your customer. Indicate what you have and what you plan to get when.

Possible Items Needed	I Need	I Have	I Plan to Get		
			Now	1-3 Mo.	Later
Sales Associate or Representative Questionnaire					
List of Ideas on Who to Contact					
Masters or Copies of Promotional Materials (fill in items to supply)					
Marketing or Commission Plan					
Product Information					
Sample Price Comparison					
Guidelines for Selling; Policies and Procedures					
Sample Phone Scripts					
Sample Letters					
Sample Ads					
Suggested Marketing Ideas					
Letterhead, Business Cards					
Sample Publicity Releases					
Updates and Newsletters					
List of Current Sales Reps or Associates					
List of Resource Materials					
Marketing Techniques Manual					
Sales Training Tapes, Books					
Marketing Techniques Manual					
Sales Training Tapes, Books					

Carry little packets of literature with you. These might include an introductory flyer or brochure on the program; a list of any presentations you are giving and locations; and a small sample of the product, if feasible. Hand these packets out to the people you meet, suggesting they might like to try the product or use your service.

As appropriate, hand these materials out to almost any potential customer. Some possibilities include:

- The tolltaker where you pay your toll
- The gas station attendant who sells you gas
- The waitress in a restaurant who serves you
- The bartender who sells you a drink
- The store clerk who sells you merchandise
- The teller at your bank
- A person you sit next to on a bus, train, or plane
- A person you meet at a party or meeting
- Customers or exhibitors at trade shows and fairs
- People waiting in line with you
- People leaving an event related to your type of product, since this suggests they may have a special interest in your product (such as people at a health fair if you have a health product)
- Anybody else you happen to meet

Put up posters or flyers at places you go to, such as campus buildings and bulletin boards, churches and community centers, supermarkets, coin-op laundries, and stores or restaurants that display posters and flyers.

Leave flyers for display at parties, meetings, and conferences, and at your school or office. If possible, also make an announcement about your product or company at an event, before you pass out flyers or leave them somewhere. The announcement provides added impact, since it will focus attention on your message and give you more credibility. It also suggests you have the support of the leader of the group.

Start talking about your product wherever you are. You can easily promote your product or business, whatever it is you do—just bring it up casually in conversation when you talk to friends, business associates, or whomever you meet. Emphasize the benefits of the product as appropriate. For example, if someone mentions having trouble losing weight and you are promoting a health product, that's a perfect opener to describe your products.

Tailor Your Approach to Your Target Market

Since everyone has different wants and needs, and certain groups or individuals have special interests, think how you can slant your approach to appeal to different markets. This way, you emphasize the features of your product or program that are likely to be of special interest to the individual or group you are contacting.

Many salespeople vary their approach on an ad hoc basis as they contact people, but it helps to think about what you intend to do in advance. Then, you more systematically and efficiently plan advertising, create flyers, send out letters, or otherwise take steps to contact people.

The Target Market—Product Benefits form, Exhibit 18, will help you adapt your approach to your target, by helping you think about what features or benefits might be best promoted to each group.

Use the matrix in this way:

1. List the key features or benefits of your product or service in Column 1.

2. List the types of individuals or groups you think might be most interested across the top.

3. Go down each column, and for each individual or group, place an X in the box if you think they might be especially interested in that product feature or benefit.

4. Indicate how important you think each feature or benefit might be to those contacted by rating it from one (least important) to five (most important).

5. Tailor your advertising, flyers, letters, or other promotional efforts to emphasize these features and benefits with special appeal to this group.

CHAPTER 9

Organizing Effective Sales Meetings

Once new salespeople are oriented and make a commitment to come aboard, it is critical to have regular sales meetings. Even if you only have one or two people working with you, plan a regular time to meet, or at minimum have a long conversation by phone if the person is working in a distant area. Preferably, schedule this once a week—at a minimum every two weeks.

Also, clearly indicate that people need to stay in touch at least this often. Otherwise, people are apt to start drifting away, and once they do, it is hard to get back that initial enthusiasm and commitment.

In turn, so people will want to attend these meetings and find them valuable, you need to plan for an effective meeting.

Purposes of the Meeting

Sales meetings have a number of functions. At times, you will focus more on one purpose than another, but all these functions play a part in keeping people involved and motivated.

The major purposes of a sales meeting include social networking; giving information and getting feedback; planning, coordinating, and organizing; developing sales strategies and training; providing motivation and inspiration; offering recognition; and planning the next meeting. More graphically, the major functions of a meeting can include any or all of these:

- Social Networking
- Information and Feedback
  - Providing new company and product information

- • Reviewing promotional ideas and plans
- • Doing product or service demonstrations
- • Getting reports and feedback from the field
- • Providing a general update
- • Finding out about needs
- • Planning, Coordinating, and Organizing
  - • Doing long-range and short-range planning
  - • Coordinating day-to-day logistics
  - • Organizing group activities and events
- • Developing Sales Strategies and Training
  - • Discussing sales strategies
  - • Providing sales training
- • Providing Motivation and Inspiration
- • Offering Recognition
- • Planning the Next Meeting

The following section discusses each of these functions.

Social Networking. Your meeting may be called for other purposes (i.e., giving information, planning, sales training, etc.), but an important part of every meeting is the social interaction between the members of your sales group and with sales management. This networking helps to create social ties that bind people together, and, through these connections, to your organization. Also, this networking helps to make working on your team enjoyable, so people feel more motivated to be productive and committed to company goals. It's important to control this balance between socializing and work, since too much socializing can make people inefficient and distracted from work. But barring that, getting people socially involved can further your success.

Thus, allow some time at the beginning or end of meetings for people to get together. Perhaps offer some coffee or snacks, or combine the meeting with a meal to encourage this socializing. Then, after the time for social networking is over, get down to business—and make it clear it's time to focus on this, the central purpose of the meeting, now. Then, people will buckle down and focus on the job at hand.

Providing New Company and Product Information. The meeting is an ideal time to make new product announcements, hand out new product materials, or provide updates on company news. In making new product announcements, point up product highlights and benefits, and comment on what's important about any materials you hand out. Otherwise, these often may go unread.

Reviewing Any Promotional Ideas and Plans. If you are planning to send out publicity or advertising, these meetings can be used to describe what you have in mind and get feedback. The people in your group may have some good suggestions, and the meetings help to assure their support for any promotion you are planning. Also, if they know of pending PR or advertising, they can plan for it, and perhaps use it to back up their presentations. By the same token, as articles or ads about your product or company appear, let your sales group know. These are a great boost for everyone's spirits, for if the mass media says something about you, it suggests you are doing something right.

Doing Product or Service Demonstrations. These demos are ideal when you add new products or services, or use them for showing good sales techniques for selling more effectively. Some demo possibilities might be hands-on demos of equipment, taste tests of food products, and videotape presentations of people enthusiastically using your product.

Getting Reports and Feedback from the Field. Meetings are an excellent time for you—and for everyone else—to find out what everyone else is doing. In some organizations, only the person at the top really knows what is going on, because his key people report to him individually, and he guides them individually on what to do. However, people commonly work better together if everyone has a sense of what is happening throughout the organization. They feel more connected, and this sense of connection gives them a baseline for comparing themselves to others and helps them stay motivated through the team spirit and common goal that develops in the group. Then, too, open feedback helps to create a generally open, supportive context, in which people feel more attuned to helping and supporting one another; people can then use the information from others to improve their own sales efforts in the field. Also, if someone has encountered a problem, he or she can get ideas from others who have had a similar experience, as well as still other good ideas from others without this experience. Additionally, feedback can be used to find out not only what works, but what doesn't, so your group can do some collective problem solving.

Providing a General Update. Besides providing closer-to-home news on your company and product, the meeting can also be a place to share information on your field generally and consider how recent world events may affect your business. For instance, maybe a change in the law will affect your packaging. Maybe some competitors have a few new competing products people should know about. Maybe some upcoming consumer or trade shows in your industry might be of interest to your salespeople. Or maybe your people have some information to offer themselves, such as reporting on a similar product or reading an article about a relevant trend. To get others to share, encourage them to contribute actively—not just respond passively and wait for you.

Finding Out about Needs. Another key use for meetings is asking if anybody wants anything from you. Do they need more product sales materials? More samples? More masters to make flyers? More scripts or guidelines for phone calls? Find out what people want, so you can provide it—either by the next meeting or before, if people want to get it individually from you.

Doing Long-Range and Short-Range Planning. You can also use meetings to plan where you are going—both for the long-term and over the next few weeks. Such meetings also have the value of involving members of your group in the planning process, so they feel more involved and supportive. Moreover, their input on what is happening in the field and their report on their needs can help you in planning, in that you consider what's doable and best for everyone in your group.

When you open the meeting up for general discussion, listen to others' ideas and encourage input, yet at the same time stay in charge of the planning process, so if the discussion veers off into unproductive channels, griping, or internecine battles, you can rein it in and put it back on track. Also, make it clear that ultimately, you will make the decision, though you want to take into consideration what others want and need when you do.

Coordinating Day-to-Day Logistics. Another important function of meetings is working out the details, as needed, of what everyone will be doing over the next few days. For example, if people need to arrange to use the office or phones at certain times, schedule this. If you need to learn who is contacting what people to avoid overlapping contacts, ask people for this information—perhaps obtain this on a list of contacts or on an outline card to enable you to coordinate this. You can also use meetings for distributing leads, or you can do this on a one-on-one basis.

Organizing Group Activities and Events. Besides overall planning and coordination of individual activities, meetings are ideal for planning and coordinating group activities and events. Some typical examples are working out arrangements to be in a trade show; do a mass leafletting at an event; put on a cold calling campaign in a series of downtown buildings, in which each person covers a different floor or building; attend an industry conference or exhibit together; or create a social occasion such as a picnic or potluck supper. The possibilities are endless. At the meetings, decide what you want to do, determine who will carry out what role, and plan a schedule of tasks to make the event happen successfully.

Discussing Sales Strategies. If you have recommendations on how to sell certain products or contact a certain target market, these meetings are a good time to give suggestions. Alternatively, your salespeople might have their own ideas, so everyone can learn from one another. With experienced salespeople, you can spend less time on this. But with new people, this discussion of strategies is more important to help them learn what to do, such as how to find one's own leads. Or, if you come up with a list of suggested places to go and people to contact, perhaps pass it out at your meeting.

Providing Sales Training. Such training might be made a regular part of every meeting, or it could be made optional at the beginning or end of a meeting for those who are interested. Use such training to discuss or demonstrate different sales techniques to help participants expand their repertoire of sales skills. If you feel a session or two on general skills would be useful, also point out how these skills might be applied to selling your particular product. You can make these suggestions yourself, or invite group members to share how they would do it.

If you're good in sales training, lead this part of the meeting yourself, or perhaps use some tapes or videos by experienced sales trainers. For example, in our meetings, we listened to the tapes of nationally known trainers for about twenty minutes, and then discussed how to use the technique just discussed to increase our own sales.

Providing Motivation and Inspiration. Just having the meeting can be a source of motivation and inspiration to participants who attend, since it gives people a shot of energy to get together with others with similar positive goals. However, you can also incorporate specific activities into your meeting to motivate and inspire. For example, set aside a few minutes for people to share their accomplishments—a great way to get people fired up because they enjoy being recognized for their achievement, or because they see what someone else has done, and this triggers a competitive spark. Another possibility, which some group leaders do, is occasionally having a guest speaker who has a motivational message to share. Or perhaps spend a brief time listening to a motivational tape or reading an inspirational message about success, as some groups do.

Offering Recognition. Besides having people share accomplishments, use other methods at meetings to recognize and reward people, and thereby encourage everybody to greater efforts. For instance, perhaps take some time at a monthly meeting to give out certificates of achievement, ribbons, trophies, or plaques. Maybe use special gifts, such as pendants, rings, or motivational books. Perhaps offer an extra monetary bonus. You might also consider having special titles for your awards, such as: "Best Salesperson of the Month," "Highest Volume Producer," or "Most New Accounts of the Month." In fact, some sales leaders turn these recognition meetings into gala occasions, and combine them with a picnic, party, rally, or other special event. Obviously, the larger your sales group, the more you can do to make a big thing about recognition. But even with a few people, you can express your appreciation—and you can help to reinforce your words with a small token, gift, or monetary payment.

Planning the Next Meeting. At the end of the meeting, it can help you to plan the next one if you talk briefly about your ideas for the next meeting and find out if anyone wants to cover anything else. That way, by planning ahead, you can make your next meeting more productive, since you'll have a better idea of what's important to cover, and you'll involve your people in the process, which not only provides good ideas but inspires more motivation and commitment to your organization.

Also, if you are working with part-timers, check that the planned meeting date is still convenient, since part-timers' schedules may change frequently. You want to make sure that at least most of the group plans to attend the meeting. If not, depending on circumstances, perhaps reschedule that meeting or discuss and select another mutually convenient time for regular meetings.

If you are deciding on dates, a hand vote might work if most people agree. But if not, to sort through the confusion, send around a sign-up list indicating different meeting days and times so people can express their preference. Then, at a break during the meeting or while people are socializing afterwards, you can review the suggestions, see what the most preferred day and time is, and announce it before people leave. Alternatively, call everyone later with your decision as to the time which seems best to the most people. If necessary, perhaps have two meetings, which is better than not meeting with some of your people at all if they can't make the original date.

Preparing an Agenda

To have a more effective meeting, regardless of your purposes, use an agenda. This indicates what you want to cover and in what sequence, and you need to plan this out in advance. When you do, write it down so you have a clear outline. The advantage of having a prepared agenda is that you are sure to cover everything you have planned, and, if need be, you can adapt your planned agenda to spend more or less time on particular topics, or even skip the less important items.

With a small group, a written agenda for yourself alone is fine. However, as your group gets larger, consider making copies of your agenda for everyone and giving them out at the meeting or in advance. This helps to keep everyone together and lets people know what you are going to cover, so if they have suggestions for additions, they can let you know before or at the meeting in a timely way.

Exhibits 20 and 21 give some examples of my own agendas over a four-week period to give you an idea of how I organized these. You'll notice some of the following highlights:

1. I started out with a general update and passed out any new materials. As part of this update, I included:

    *   New flyers and masters;

    *   Press releases and copies of ads or articles that appeared;

    *   New lead lists;

    *   Copies of sample letters, scripts, price comparisons, and suggested marketing approaches.

2. I got feedback from people at some point in the meeting. In particular, I wanted to learn what was working, and what problems, if any, people were having. Then, we worked on resolving the problem collectively.

3. I asked people to tell me what they needed from me in terms of handouts, promotional materials, lead lists, and marketing approaches.

4. I went over sales strategies in some meetings. This discussion included things like:

   • Going over a suggested telephone script for initial calls;

   • Discussing where people should go to find their own leads in their own community;

   • Ways to approach different types of people in different settings (i.e., in shops, churches, local civic and service clubs, bookstores, restaurants, friends, associates, neighbors, etc.).

5. I reviewed some of the experiences we had together to consider what we could learn from them (such as when our group went to a trade show together).

6. I coordinated some day-to-day office operations, by going over things like using folders and files, recording messages in the telephone book, and record-keeping on various forms. I also passed around a sign-up form for using the office or meeting room at designated times.

7. I worked out plans for the group's participation in an upcoming trade show, and set up the times for people to be in the booth.

8. I demonstrated some new products by showing clips from new videotapes on our destinations; those who wanted to could then return to view these films at their leisure.

9. I concluded the formal meeting with a discussion of the upcoming meeting and rechecked whether the time was good for everyone.

10. I put on some sales training tapes for those who wanted to stay for this part of the meeting. Then, those who stayed for this joined me in a general discussion about how to apply these principles to selling our own program.

In short, as you'll see from my agendas (Exhibits 20 and 21), I didn't cover every possible function for a sales meeting in each meeting. But then, the goal is not to do everything. Rather, drawing from the possibilities, you can use your agenda to decide what to do at that meeting and in what order to deal with each topic. During the meeting, you may want to do some shifting around, due to the conversation and issues that come up. So be flexible. But having a structure in advance is important to help guide you in getting where you're going. Otherwise, it's too easy to get disorganized and ramble, so that a directed and productive sales meeting can soon turn into a social chat or a gossip-swapping session.

One good way to organize an agenda is to plan it out the day or night before a meeting. In doing so, consider what you might want to say on various topics, perhaps using the list of items included in this chapter. For instance, in planning my own agenda, I go over what's new that I want to talk about, consider any sales ideas I have had, and write down any problems I have noticed, and so forth. Essentially, I go down the list of areas previously mentioned in this chapter and see if I have anything to say on any topic.

Exhibit 20.   Sample Agenda

TRAVEL AGENDA - February 2, 1986

1. New handouts
      SF State
      Sample Price Comparisons
      Approaching Gay/Environmental Communities

2. Comments, reactions on Travel Show

3. New Files
      Travel Folders
      For Travel Associates/For Contacts
      Telephone Book for Messages/Message File
      Group Contacts Form

4. New Sources for Leads
      Better Business Bureau Book
      Singles Directory—new one in March

5. Additional places to suggest
      Laundromats—bulletin boards
      Supermarket—bulletin boards
      Bookstores/magazine shops
      Hotels

6. Reports by group members
      Ellen on Office/leads follow-up
      Mike/Bill on Gay Community
      Other?

7. New Films
      China—Time to See them
      On Kenya—Feathered Swarm; Rhino on the Run

8. Use of office/meeting room?

9. Needs from me
      Flyers? China article?
      Press materials?
      Follow-Up

10. Recent press listings/ads
      Livermore Herald
      Gentry Magazine

11. Other
      Status of Tuesday meeting for next week

12. Sales training—Tom Hopkins

Exhibit 21.   Sample Agenda

TRAVEL AGENDA - February 10, 1986

1. New handouts
        Stationery
        For non-profits
        For hotels, restaurants, retailers, theaters
        Letter to theater manager
        Ad for Trellis

2. New sources of leads
        SF Chamber of Commerce Book
        From Newspaper
        Bay Guardian

3. Posters—how many need these

4. Reports by group members

5. New films
        Video update
        Upcoming videos

6. Use of office/meeting room

7. Needs from me
        Flyers?
        Press materials
        Follow-up

8. BAEWF Trade Show—who wants to be in booth?

9. Retail programs on Africa—new book

10. Preference for future meetings
        Monday
        Tuesday

11. Sales training

Then, as I think of things I want to cover, I quickly write them down in no particular order. So I use a form of the brainstorming process, getting as many ideas as I can on a particular topic. Next, after noting down all these ideas, I rearrange and decide which ones are the most important. Typically, these then become the topics to cover first. Then, I go on to less important matters. That way, if the discussion goes longer than expected, I can cut short the discussion on the less important issues to be covered later, or perhaps drop them from the agenda entirely.

Finally, I write up my agenda in a more final form, so I'm ready to present it the next day. In addition, the agenda indicates the materials I need to have at the meeting, such as copies of brochures, flyers, and a videotape to play. That way I can get everything I need together very easily, so it's all ready when I begin the meeting. You can similarly plot out what you want to include in your own agenda.

Facilitating the Discussion

Having a preprepared agenda makes it much easier to facilitate the discussion once you start. You have a guidebook to follow, so you're in control and everyone knows it. Since you know what you want to talk about, it becomes easy to get everyone to follow along.

Begin by giving everyone a few minutes for some social networking before the meeting begins. Let everyone know in advance that the beginning of the meeting is for this purpose, so they can come to chat, have coffee, or whatever they like, if they come at this time. Then, have a clear starting time—and start then, or no more than five to ten minutes late if people are straggling in. Should lateness become a recurring problem, talk about it, and if necessary change the time of the meeting. Stress that you want people to be on time, whatever that time is, since it's very disruptive to a productive, cohesive meeting if people come at different times. Emphasize the importance of promptness from the beginning in order to instill this as a habit and expectation for everyone.

Of course, fill people in if they come late on occasion, especially for a good reason. But stress that you don't expect this to become a common practice.

If you make coming on time a priority, you'll find that others will respect this, too. And one of the keys to a successful meeting is having people there when it begins.

Also, if you have had some refreshments, for efficiency's sake encourage people to finish before the meeting. Coffee or soda at the meeting itself is fine, but otherwise, people should understand that this is a business meeting, when their full attention should be on the subject at hand. This shouldn't be a time for breakfast or lunch, which, next to lateness, is a prime distractor.

Then, when ready to start the meeting, announce this in a firm, clear way, and wait until you have everyone's attention to begin. With a small group of up to four or five people, you can be very informal and lead the meeting much like you would an ordinary conversation, with you guiding and directing from time to time. But as your group grows beyond four or five, shift to a more formal style of leadership to maintain direction and control. For example, announce each item as you come to it, rather than more casually moving from topic to topic, as in the small group.

Often at these meetings, everyone will know each other, so once you call the meeting to order, you can go right to the first agenda item. But if some people are new or haven't seen each other at meetings before, take a few minutes to start off with brief introductions—much as you might at an orientation, though briefer, perhaps just a few words about who the person is, what he does, and the areas where he will be working for your company.

As you mention each agenda item, encourage comments from others as appropriate, besides anything you might say. This way you get others involved and participating, and don't just give a one-sided report on the state of your company and your marketing plans. You want people to feel committed and be creative, and for that, you have to help draw them out. Yet, at the same time, you still need to maintain control; so if people start getting off the track, gently bring them back or thank them for their comments and move on.

Another key to successful meeting facilitation is to be open and receptive when you encourage people to come up with ideas or solve problems for others. The advantage of this approach is it creates a supportive atmosphere that helps to bring out ideas and solutions. This approach operates very much like the brainstorming method, which is designed to invite ideas without initially criticizing them, since being critical only slows up the expression of ideas or may discourage them entirely. Then, after people are finished coming up with ideas, you can winnow out those that are really good.

Also, try to even out the conversation as people participate to get everyone involved. Thus, if one person tends to talk a lot and dominate, find a diplomatic way to quiet him down by saying something supportive that draws out other comments, such as: "Well, that's a good idea. Now let's see what _____ has to say about that." Then, invite contributions from someone who hasn't said very much.

Be aware, too, of timing, so you don't spend too much time on one topic or give undue consideration to a less important topic, or let the meeting run too long, so interest flags and you go over the expected time for the meeting. It's important to keep on time, because often people will have other commitments, and they won't want to spend too much time at meetings anyway, because they make their money when they are out selling, not at meetings. So keep things flowing and compact. If people seem to get too bogged down on one point, mention this and urge them to go on. You want to plan the meeting to last a certain specified time, give or take a few minutes, so organize your agenda and plan on how much time to allot to each topic accordingly. Then, when people leave, they will feel a sense of satisfaction at having been at a tight, well organized, productive meeting. As the old saying goes—"Keep it simple"—or alternatively, "Keep it short and sweet."

Getting Feedback

The feedback process is important to learn what people are thinking, and to help in making decisions and plans. When you seek feedback, stay in control of the process by specifying the type of feedback you want and how long the feedback process will go. Then, don't let the process get out of hand, so that people start making all sorts of comments, some of which might be negative or distracting. You want to keep the feedback discussion focused and on track.

The first rule for getting feedback is to make sure that it is positive. Let people know this. Explain that it is fine to raise individual problems with a view to having the group as a whole solve them. But make it clear that off-limits, unproductive feedback consists of general criticisms about other people in the group or criticisms of you. If people have those kinds of gripes, they should take them up privately with you and with any other people who might be involved. You might possibly have a special meeting with these people to go over this, but you don't want any of this to come up in a general meeting.

Why? If necessary, explain that you aren't trying to avoid dealing with such issues, but you want to handle them in an appropriate and productive way. Thus, you want to avoid such feedback at a general sales meeting, because such griping can cast a negative tone on the meeting and kill people's enthusiasm and feelings of motivation, which is very destructive—the key to successful selling is staying positive. If people start airing gripes, this can be death to a productive meeting. As a result, if you notice such griping happening, quickly cut it off and invite people to talk personally with you later. Then, keep going and keep the meeting upbeat and light.

Second, when you're getting feedback, encourage everyone's opinion. Some people may be especially vocal, and it's fine for them to contribute and kick things off. But if they seem to be dominating or are especially intense about something, diplomatically rein them in by suggesting you'd like to see how others feel about that point. Then, invite others to give their opinions as well.

Finally, try to bring a feedback session to a close so that people feel some resolution has been reached, or that you will consider the various points of view and make some decision. For example, if there seems to be a general consensus, tie things together by pointing this out. Or if you are uncertain of what the general opinion is or what to do now, indicate that you plan to review everyone's comment and will decide something soon. The value of providing such closure is that people feel their ideas have or will lead to some action, and therefore will feel more satisfied that this has been a useful, productive meeting.

Brainstorming Sales Approaches

You can use regular sales meetings to come up with new sales ideas through brainstorming, or you can set up special brainstorming sessions for this purpose.

In either case, the process is divided into two separate stages. In the first, you come up with as many ideas as you can, without trying to evaluate or critique them. In the second phase, you review that list and decide which ideas you want to eliminate and which are viable possibilities. Then, depending on circumstances, make up a list of all the viable options and ask each person to choose from that to create his own list of what to do. Or, discuss the pros and cons of the viable options as a group, and make some group decisions about what approaches to use.

Generating Ideas

To start the brainstorming process, first explain the process you will be using. Let people know you want them to throw out as many ideas as possible in the first stage without being critical, so they will know what to do. Point out that you will evaluate these ideas in the second stage to determine which ones should be turned into a blueprint for action.

Then, after your explanation is over, throw out an open-ended question that deals with what you want to find out about. For example, ask something like: "What types of groups should we approach?" or "How many ways can we let people know about our product?"

Encourage people to express their ideas very quickly, so they don't have a chance to judge them. Whatever they think of, they should say aloud. As each idea is presented, write it down—or have someone else keep a record. Here, too, the recorder shouldn't make any judgments as to what's good or not—the recorder should just write everything down.

Keep the process going until everyone seems to be out of ideas, and then ask if anyone has any last thoughts. If so, keep going, or if not, bring phase one to an end, and explain you are now going into phase two.

Evaluating and Critiquing Your Ideas

Next, review the list. The recorder should read off each item. Ask people to raise their hands if they think it is a good, useful idea. If all or most people agree, double-star it. If about half or a substantial number respond yes, give it a single star. If only one person or just a few support it, indicate this with a question mark. Finally, if no one seems to like the idea, cross it off.

Now, review the highest priorities on this list (the ones with the most stars), and discuss the sales ideas everyone would most like to work with. Or, if people will be working independently, perhaps simply type up the list with these suggestions. Each person can then do his own selecting of what he would like to do most.

For example, Exhibit 22 illustrates how this process can be used to produce all sorts of ideas. It's a list of ideas that came from a meeting where someone wanted to promote a trip to environmental and nature groups. He was relatively new in sales and wanted some suggestions on how to approach such groups. So the group as a whole brainstormed on the topics. What could he do? Then, after the brainstorming session concluded, I listed the most promising ideas, and I made them available to everyone in the sales group, so other people who wanted to

---

Exhibit 22.   Marketing Ideas—Nature, Environmental Groups

Focus on wildlife in Kenya.

Use of special programs and presentations with films

Marketing Approaches
  Nature-oriented stores:
    i.e., REI
        Mountaineering Stores
        Camping/Ski/Sports Stores
    Distribute flyers through them; gain their sponsorship; perhaps arrange a
        video program/slide show there.
  Other shops to emphasize:
    Camera Stores
    Travel/Luggage Stores
    Safari Clothing Stores (i.e., Banana Republic)
    Restaurants with a community/student atmosphere
        i.e., Vegetarian restaurants, restaurants near campus
  Teachers in elementary schools, high schools, colleges
  Theaters playing nature oriented films
  Environmental organizations—flyers, involve leaders and members
  Special nature-oriented events
    i.e., Wildlife Rehabilitation Conference
    Make arrangements with leaders in advance about fund-raising possibili-
    ties.
    Go yourself and put out flyers; or hand out to members.
    Attempt to be included as a speaker or have videotapes included
    Find out about the possibility of being an exhibitor—and try to trade free
        space for the matching commissions-trips credits arrangement
    Stand outside as people leave or enter and give them flyers
  Churches/religious groups with nature-oriented groups
  Some nature groups to include:
    Sierra Club
    Friends of the Earth
    Outdoor Adventuring (Berkeley Group)
  Museums/collections emphasizing nature
    i.e., Academy of Sciences, Oakland Museum, San Francisco Zoo Safari
        Schools in Los Gatos
  Wearing Button—such as: Ask me about an African Safari; Want to Go
    Wild? Ask Me.
  Wearing T-Shirt—African Safari Adventures
  Maybe involve well known local naturalists, environmentalists. Maybe
    they'd like to be a leader or their name would be enough of a draw to
    plan in a free trip for them as part of a much larger group.

contact environmental and nature groups could benefit from the brainstorming session as well.

Creating Action Plans

Sales meetings are also good for working out action plans for the group and getting people to agree to carry out certain actions.

This action plan process can work well in implementing the results of brainstorming sales approaches, since it involves working out the specific activities you need to do to make a general sales approach actually happen. It's like breaking down any goal into the steps to follow to realize that goal.

For instance, say you've decided on using the general approach of cold calling downtown. The next step—on your own, or with the group as a whole—is to decide what exactly you want to do, when, where, and who will do what. Thus, you would need to decide things like:

- What part of the downtown should be used?
- What streets or buildings should be included?
- When shall we do this? What day and time?
- What kind of presentation should we make? What should we say? What should we bring with us to make this presentation most effectively?
- Who will coordinate where we meet?
- And so on . . .

When you're using this process in a group, start by developing a list of the questions about what to do that you want answered. Then throw out these questions for discussion. As in the usual brainstorming process, encourage people to express their ideas, but stay in control, so after you get the flavor of what the group is thinking, seek to achieve a consensus, bring the issue to a vote, or announce what seems the best decision yourself, based on what others have said. Your aim in this process should be to help the group consider possibilities. But then when one seems to be the strongest or most popular, quickly narrow down to that, so you can resolve each question with a decisive conclusion about how to act. Finally, when you have answers to all your questions, each one representing a part of your plan, you have created a comprehensive plan of action.

Once an action is planned, you can also use these meetings to get a commitment to action. One way to do this after creating an action plan is to get each person who will be involved to agree to a certain role (such as: "I'll reproduce the flyers so we can hand them out downtown.") Or, if each person is acting independently, perhaps get each person to make a commitment to a specific goal and to their specific plans for making that goal happen. For instance, you might ask a person to commit to making ten calls a day and spending two hours making presentations.

For reinforcement, when you do ask for such commitments, ask the person to make this agreement out loud in front of the group. This way, everyone else has heard him make it, and this will help to further his commitment to carry through, because he wants to live up to this group promise. Otherwise, if he doesn't try, he will lose face in front of the group. Such a group commitment isn't foolproof, because the person can always reappear the following week with an excuse about why he couldn't do what he said. But with everyone else listening in, a person is less likely to make a commitment and renege, just as he is less likely to make a commitment he feels in truth he can't fulfill.

Another way to get commitments is to use a sheet of paper with a statement of agreement or a certificate, in which the person pledges to do a certain thing. In this case, stress that the person is making the commitment to himself; if he doesn't keep it, the only person he is harming is himself. Then, once he understands the nature of this self-commitment, hand out the statement of agreement or certificate, and ask him to sign. If you are doing this in the group situation, you can ask several people each to make a personal commitment and sign an agreement. In this case, everyone is doing just what you asked the individual person to do. But again, the group-made commitment may be much firmer than the one made alone, simply because the person is influenced by the power of the group, which serves as a more formal reminder of the fact that "Yes, I'm making this commitment," and "I see others seeing me make this commitment, and so we all know that I'm seriously and sincerely making this commitment now."

Setting Up Incentives

The sales meeting can also be used to recognize what people have done and to develop incentives to encourage them to do even more. As such, it can supplement the more special recognition and incentive programs you might use to recognize ongoing achievements on a continuing basis. Also, at these meetings you can note if there are areas where people are slacking off, and create new incentives to get people to do more.

For example, when people give their weekly reports of what they are doing, you might give out small awards or gifts from time to time to recognize someone who has achieved or surpassed certain goals. Say a person has set a goal the previous week of making ten calls a day, resulting in five presentations a week and one big sale. The sale itself will certainly be a reward. But under certain circumstances, such as if this is the person's first big hit, it might be appropriate to reward him with a little bit more recognition, so he feels even better, which will in turn help to motivate him to do even more.

Another possibility might be using the sales meeting to find out what accomplishments are likely to occur when, so you can develop them into an organized incentive plan. For example, when people talk about their goals, perhaps use these to set up markers of achievement. Then, when people later reach these goals, you can have a special award for them already planned.

Alternatively, if people aren't doing as well as expected, and you feel they can do better, perhaps announce a new reward for anybody who achieves a certain goal. For instance, say people aren't putting enough emphasis into selling a certain product in the line, though it sells well when people do. Perhaps sweeten the pie by offering a larger commission for a certain period, or provide an extra bonus for anyone who moves a minimum volume by a certain time. Obviously, any such incentives have to be realistic; the goal they are linked to has to have a reasonable chance of being reached. But assuming the goal is achievable, such incentives will help people stay on track by keeping them fired up and eager to sell.

Incorporating Sales Training into the Meeting

Finally, the sales meeting can be a good context for some general sales training. However, in many companies, depending on circumstances, it may be best to make this training optional when working with part-time independent salespeople. The reason for doing this is that people will come from a variety of backgrounds, and some may be very experienced, others not at all. Also, people may show differing levels of interest as to whether they want to participate in a training program.

While such a program can be very valuable, be guided by the results of your salespeople. If they are doing well, they may not need this, and if they don't think they do, it's probably best to go along with their choice of what they think is right for them. On the other hand, if people aren't doing well, maybe this training can give them the help they need to improve, although in this case it may be they are not right for your company. In any case, where practical, leave it up to your salespeople to decide how much training is right for them. Certainly make the training available and encourage participation, but then be flexible in working with your people to decide what level of participation is best.

A key reason for remaining open and flexible is the wide differences you may find in people's skills and their attitudes toward training. You'll find that some people, especially those new to sales, will be extremely interested in a good training program; in fact, it may contribute to their decision to work with you. On the other hand, some people, generally those with more experience, may feel they have heard it all, and they would rather spend their time out in the field so they can sell. Then, too, there are some people with a great deal of experience, who feel they can always learn more from additional training, since everyone has a slightly different approach. So they will be eager to attend and learn—a person like that is ideal.

In sum, since people vary so much in how they feel about training, it's best to let people know that you're willing to train them and encourage them to participate, but then leave the decision up to them. In turn, to make participation easy but optional, provide the training before or after the regular meeting, allowing about one-half to one hour for training. As for what to include, see Chapter 5 on training techniques.

Index

About the Author

Gini Graham Scott is founder and president of Creative Communications & Research and has written numerous books on direct sales and business, including the bestselling *Effective Selling and Sales Management*. Scott has also hosted two radio shows: *Make Money* and *All in the Game*. She received her doctorate in sociology from the University of California at Berkeley and her ¯.D. degree from law school at the University of San Francisco.

978-0-595-46772-3
0-595-46772-5

Printed in Great Britain
by Amazon

40457923R00121